Yahweh
Is a
Warrior

Yahweh Is a Warrior

The Theology of Warfare in Ancient Israel

Millard C. Lind

Foreword by David Noel Freedman
Introduction by John H. Yoder

A Christian Peace Shelf Selection

HERALD PRESS
Scottdale, Pennsylvania
Kitchener, Ontario

Library of Congress Cataloging in Publication Data

Lind, Millard, 1918-
  Yahweh is a warrior.

  (A Christian peace shelf selection)
  Includes bibliographical references and indexes.
  1. War—Biblical teaching. 2. God—Biblical
teaching. 3. Bible. O.T.—Criticism, interpretation,
etc. I. Title.
BS1199.W2L56   296.3'87873   80-16038
  ISBN 0-8361-1233-4 (pbk.)

YAHWEH IS A WARRIOR
Copyright © 1980 by Herald Press, Scottdale, Pa. 15683
  Published simultaneously in Canada by Herald Press,
  Kitchener, Ont. N2G 4M5
Library of Congress Catalog Card Number: 80-16038
International Standard Book Number: 0-8361-1233-4
Printed in the United States of America
Design: Alice B. Shetler

15 14 13 12 11 10 9 8 7 6

To *Miriam*

Contents

Author's Preface

Acknowledgments are due:

To David Noel Freedman, who suggested that I take up this subject in the first place, who led me through my dissertation, who encouraged me to rewrite this statement for publication, and who carefully read and criticized the manuscript;

To my colleagues at Associated Mennonite Biblical Seminaries: Ross T. Bender and John Howard Yoder, who included a seminar on this subject in our Peace Studies program; Jacob Enz, whose emphatic action started this publication on the way; C. J. Dyck, who helped me get the manuscript into acceptable form as a project of the Institute of Mennonite Studies and who promoted its publication, and others of the administration who encouraged me in many ways;

To my students, who both challenged and affirmed my ideas and who were patient with me;

To my committee, John Lapp, Marlin Miller, David Schroeder, and Jacob Enz, who gave me general direction and read the manuscript; to Waldemar Janzen, who read the manuscript;

To Tim Lind, who edited the manuscript carefully to make it more readable;

To Dorothy Jean Weaver and Sandra Hess, who carefully checked all quotations and references, to the typists, Sue Yoder and Jean Kelly, who typed the manuscript several times;

To the Peace Shelf Committee of the Mennonite Central Committee and the administration of the Mennonite Publishing House, who have taken on the risks of publication;

To J. R. Burkholder, whose patient editing and suggestions were invaluable in readying the manuscript for publication. Special thanks are due to the École Biblique, Jerusalem, for the generous use of their library, and to the Ecumenical Institute, Tantur, Jerusalem, where most of these pages were written.

To all these and many others, I am indebted. Responsibility for what is said, whatever may be its inadequacy, I accept as my own.

Millard C. Lind, 1979

Foreword

"Holy war," an expression derived ultimately from the Bible as descriptive of the Israelite conquest of Canaan, enjoyed a spectacular revival in the Middle Ages in the bloody conflicts of Christians and Muslims; its terminology echoed through the so-called religious wars in Europe in the wake of the Reformation, but with the Age of Enlightenment and the triumph of Reason, it was thought that this terrifying slogan could finally be laid to rest. In recent years it has come back into use, and religious leaders in different parts of the world have summoned their followers to raise the ancient banner, and march into the fray as soldiers of their God. While timely, "holy war" does not appear to be a very promising topic for a professor of Bible in one of the traditional "peace" churches. The Old Testament itself, with its interminable litany of battles and bloodshed, punctuated by a rare vision of war's cessation and the reign of peace, has been seen as the archive of primitive violence, a record of man's crude and violent beginnings, which the species happily has outgrown, its finer sensibilities and pacific objectives being expressed and articulated in the words of the classic prophets and reaching a pinnacle of universal harmony in the teaching of Jesus of Nazareth.

Nevertheless, Millard Lind, in an original and courageous essay has challenged conventional wisdom about biblical warfare, and from a systematic reexamination of the biblical materials has presented a new and important thesis. He begins with the common recognition that for the biblical writers the ultimate (and often the only) military hero is Yahweh, the God of Israel. In contrast with the martial traditions and records of other nations, those of Israel emphasize the power and achievement of God, while minimizing those of men.

In Lind's view, this phenomenon is distinctive of Israel's experience, is not comparable to that of other nations, and hence is not to be explained by appeal to the superficially similar assertions and testimonies of the inscriptions. Broadly speaking, there are two such approaches to the biblical data. The attribution of victory to Yahweh is: (1) the expression of conventional piety, especially of a later date; (2) drawn from mythic descriptions of the struggle between Yahweh and primordial sea monsters such as Rahab and Leviathan, and the language is to be understood metaphorically or analogically in relation to Israel's battles.

According to Lind, Israel's distinctive view of warfare derives from its historical experience. The initial decisive encounters were all decided by miracle, direct divine intervention. The pivotal event is the destruction of the Egyptian chariot army in the Reed Sea. The overwhelming victory is recorded in several strands or sources of the Pentateuch: Exodus 14 is a prose account which combines several sources: J, P, and possibly E; in addition there is the poem in Exodus 15:1-18 and 21. While there is considerable variation in detail, all sources, to the extent that their views can be determined, agree that in the conventional sense there was no battle at all, that is, Israel did not participate. The defeat of the Egyptians was achieved single-handedly by Yahweh, through a violent manifestation of his power. This agreement among the sources is significant, but the critical question concerns the date of such an understanding of the respective roles of Yahweh and his people. The answer depends to a large extent on the interpretation and evaluation of the poem, Exodus 15: what is its relationship to the prose accounts, and what is its date of composition? There is no consensus but Lind adopts the position advocated essentially by the Baltimore-Harvard schools, and a growing number of scholars in the field, namely that the poem is independent of any of the prose sources, and older than all of them. It is roughly contemporary with the event, and therefore expresses Israel's original understanding of this formative event in its history.

What emerges from this reconstruction is the judgment that the unanimous conviction of the later sources that the early warfare of Israel was dominated by the personal intervention and wondrous deeds of Yahweh was rooted in the authentic memory and tradition of the community, and remained throughout the standard by which Israel's policies and behavior were to be evaluated. Thus a consistent framework is provided for the whole range of procedure and practice in the narrative of Israel's military experience. As shown by the dramatic confrontation between the prophet Isaiah and the king Ahaz, the principle and norm propounded by the prophet, of absolute reliance on Yahweh to the exclusion of military alliances (or even preparations—cf. the "defense" of Jerusalem in the days of Sennacherib's "second" attack on the city) was too much for the king, who had already sought more tangible assistance from Assyria. The point of interest and importance is that the prophet did not create a new theory of theo-politics or logistics, but as in other matters appealed to the oldest traditions of Israel, against the innovations and departures of the monarchy. The failure of the monarchy in this regard is part of the larger pattern of persistent violation of the terms of the covenant and rebellion against its Lord. Throughout it is assumed that the standards were laid down at the beginning and that, in matters of warfare as in statecraft, in religious observance and civil justice, Israel has abondoned them and adopted the manners and morals of its neighbors.

Lind makes the point, more strongly and sharply, that the ancient principle of warfare in Israel is inseparable from a specific theory of government. As Yahweh is the warrior par excellence in behalf of his people, so he is their sole Lord. While the emergence of the monarchy required various forms of accommodation, it was recognized in the central tradition that Yahweh was the original and legitimate king of Israel, and that there was no need or place for a human king to exercise divine authority (as in other countries) or to serve as agent and means of victory in battle (precisely as expected by the people who are condemned for this view).

The author has carried his thesis through the Primary History (Torah and Former Prophets), the great narrative of Israel's experience. It remains to perform the equally important task of examining the rest of the Hebrew Bible: in particular the Latter Prophets, by whom the major principle is articulated in unforgettable language, and the Writings, which reflect the thought of Israel over its whole history.

David Noel Freedman
Professor of Biblical Studies
The University of Michigan

Introduction

Ever since Marcion, the idea has been widely circulated that the God of the Hebrews, in contrast to the Father of Jesus, was angry or belligerent in such a way that Jesus, although confessed as the expected Anointed One, must be seen as rather rejecting than fulfilling the main thrust of Hebrew and Jewish hopes. Yet that Marcion was rejected by other Christians did not ward off the danger. Majority Christianity, increasingly anti-Judaic as the centuries passed, appropriated the wars against Amalek, Sihon, Og, and the Canaanites as a model for just wars and crusades, while at the same time it felt no incongruity in interpreting Jesus' rejection by "the Jews" as due to his message's being too spiritual to live up to their chauvinistic hopes.

Thus the warlike Old Testament could at the same time be used to scold the Jews for blessing violence (as if it were "their" book which "they" continue to be identified with) and taken away from them to claim the same message in favor of the righteous belligerence of Constantine, Charlemagne, and the other Tsars and Kaisers in their train; so that Christians may properly continue to follow Joshua Ben Nun rather than his new covenant namesake.

Dissent is often the captive of the language of the majority culture against which it rebels. Thus at least by the time of the fifteenth-century Czech Reformation, if not already in the age of Francis of Assisi and Peter Waldo, believers authentically drawn to and changed by the message of Jesus assumed that, as that message was novel and world-upsetting in their time, the newness of the message of Jesus in his time as well must have taken the shape of a near-Marcionite contrast between gospel love and old covenant nationalism. The sixfold "But I say to you" of the Jesus of the

Mount could be taken that way. Huldrych Zwingli, heir to the political vision of Joshua, said of two imprisoned Anabaptists that they "negate the whole Old Testament." In the history of Christian pacifism, this strand has been present ever since, heightened in recent generations by borrowings from dispensational Protestantism, which makes it easier to think that the same sovereign God may and does properly decree now this, now that. Outside the perfection of Christ, war was a fitting part of "the law"; with no surprise or apology, we confess in Christ a new moral possibility and demand. Without him the old is adequate.

The total interpretive *Gestalt* just sketched needs revision from every angle: the underlying anti-Judaism, the imperial establishment mood, the failure to perceive in the Hebrew scriptures the evolution from Joshua to Jeremiah, and in postcanonical Judaism the further evolution through Jochanan ben Zakkai to Judah "the Prince."

One core part of the task, the most strategic in some ways, is the revision that Millard Lind is undertaking. What was actually the shape of the war story in the formative experience of ancient Israel? When properly understood, does that meaning point toward or away from Jesus?

The New Testament witness seems clear. That Jesus was named Joshua is not reported as an accident. Even the "But I say to you" paragraphs on the Mount are introduced as examples of fulfilling, not abolishing the law. Jesus claims Abraham, Moses, and "all the prophets" as his precursors. It should therefore not be surprising from the gospel perspective if Lind's revision were right; but the reader must judge.

Christian interpretations of the meaning of the Old Testament are generally warped when the effort is to derive direct moral guidance from the ancient stories. This is nowhere more clear than in the reverse legalism with which majority Christianity has argued that killing must not be wrong for Christians since it was once proper for Hebrews, and God must not change.

Millard Lind has wisely avoided that modern argument as not germane to his text's concerns. He has not encountered the reverse legalism in its own terms, as well he might have:

(a) by noting in how many other ethical realms ancient Hebrew morality is not applied by Christians;

(b) by showing the profound structural difference between the wars of Yahweh and those of our own time;

(c) by doubting that God's faithfulness over time should best be described as imparting timelessness to certain specific cultural forms that obedience once took.

He has stayed by the task of reading the text for what it is about, asking what are its own questions and concerns.

The book is an exercise in ecumenically open conversation. Any point it can make must share the language of the interlocutors, who must in our age first of all be the other historically aware interpreters of the Hebrew canon. For this reason, Lind takes account of documentary hypotheses and the various historical reconstructions current in the field since the age of Wellhausen. There are other precritical or noncritical ways of reading the Old Testament—Jewish, Catholic, and conservative Protestant ways—but by the nature of the issue, his choice in favor of the encounter with critical alternatives on their own terms, was the only right one.

Because the book thus needs to be in large part addressed to other scholars in the field, its essential message may be partially overshadowed for some by the necessary attention to issues of criticism, comparison, and conflicting interpretations of the texts. Certainly the nonprofessional reader should not be put off by the apparatus of scholarship; his or her interests may be well served simply for the thread of the argument with minimal attention to the numerous footnotes. And in the first chapter, for example, the survey of representative holy war interpretations (sections A. 1 and A. 2), while essential for framing the distinctive viewpoint that Lind argues for, need not delay the reader who is more interested in finding out just what the events of Israel's warfare tell us about the will and character of Yahweh.

The book enables us to study both the events themselves and the various levels of confession, interpretation, memory, and writing through which the praise of Yahweh as warrior passed from the first "magnificat" of Miriam at the sea to the other victory chant of the other Mary. Is or is not the Son of Mary also validly to be praised as Moses' successor? If Millard Lind is right, then Jesus brings neither mid-course correction nor divine disavowal of what went before, but fulfillment of Yahweh's shalom-bringing power that was an alternative to "nationhood-as-usual" or to "kingship-properly-so-called" — from the very birth of Israel, *even* in the young nation's wars.

John H. Yoder
University of Notre Dame

Yahweh
Is a
Warrior

Chapter I

Yahweh as Warrior

The study of warfare in the Old Testament reveals that Yahweh is a God of war. Yahweh is depicted as warrior both at the beginnings of Israel's history, as early poetry and prose testify, and also at the end of the Old Testament period, as stated in prophetic and apocalyptic writings.[1] Violent political power is thus a central issue in Israel's experience of Yahweh, as this experience is set forth in the Old Testament.

But what does it mean for biblical theology that Yahweh is a warrior? My purpose in this work is to identify and discuss the main aspects of ancient Israel's theology of violent political power. The three themes to be developed in these chapters are: (1) that Yahweh as God of war fought for his people by miracle, not by sword and spear; (2) that this method of Yahweh's fighting affected Israel's theo-political structure in a fundamental way[2]; and (3) that Yahweh's warfare was directed not only against Israel's enemies but at times against Israel herself, in such cases not by means of miracle but by the armies of Israel's enemies.

Basic to all that follows is the first point, that is, the testimony that Yahweh the warrior fought by means of miracle, not through the armies of his people; "it was not by your sword or by your bow" (Josh. 24:12). By miracle we mean an act of deliverance that was outside of Israel's control, beyond the manipulation of any human agency. This conviction was so emphatic that Israel's fighting, while at times a sequel to the act of Yahweh, was regarded as ineffective; faith meant that Israel should rely upon Yahweh's miracle for her defense, rather than upon soldiers and weapons. The human agent in the work of Yahweh was not so much the warrior as the prophet.

A. *Holy War and Miracle in Old Testament Scholarship*

Twentieth-century biblical scholarship has identified and described the phenomenon of holy war in the life of ancient Israel. While earlier studies tended to emphasize the distinctiveness of the concept in Israel, and endeavored to delineate the normative traits of holy war, more recent efforts have called these findings into question.[3] The present work represents a challenge to certain key aspects of both earlier and later interpretations. My position will be best understood if it is located in relation to the major critical studies of war in the Old Testament.

Therefore we will begin by reviewing the work of eight scholars, all of whom agree that the present Old Testament documents emphasize the miraculous character of Yahweh's warfare, but among whom there are significant divergences regarding the basis for this understanding and its relationship to the actual history of Israel. In order to identify the various positions, we will group these scholars in two classes. The first four, whom we will designate as "Type A," argue that the miraculous nature of holy war is not derived from the historical event, but is rather a product of later theological reflection. The last four, designated as "Type B," question this interpretation, although each argues from a distinctive perspective.

1. *Type A Interpretations.* The earliest extensive treatment of Yahweh's involvement in Israel's battles is a work by Friedrich Schwally in 1901.[4] Through his comparative method Schwally discovered an important difference between Israel's battle reports and those of other peoples. He observed that all ancient peoples claimed the gods' participation in their battles. Outside of Israel, this meant that because the gods fought, the warriors were to fight all the harder. Within Israel, however, the claim was that divine help made it unnecessary for the warriors to fight. Schwally ascribed this difference in Israel to late Judaic historical writing which, because of its interest in edification, exaggerated the importance of faith in divine help and depreciated human action. It was an expression of pietistic thoughts, he maintained, that the warrior might bear the sword but not use it, that shouting and trumpet blowing are better than shield and spear.[5]

A later writer, Johannes Pedersen, included a section on "War" in his work entitled *Israel.*[6] Pedersen like Schwally recognized the difference between Israel's battle reports and those of other peoples, but again like Schwally he ascribed this difference to later interpretation. Among all ancient peoples, Pedersen observed, weapons alone did not decide the issue in warfare. While sword, spear, and lance were important, "it was of infinitely greater importance that those who were to use them possessed the proper psychic force" and the "efficiency of the weapons themselves in the battle depended on their consecration and consequent pervasion by holiness." Pedersen maintained that both armies, that of Israel and that of the enemy, were subject to this same law of psychic strength: "When Israel increased its psychic strength through its god, the enemy fortified himself through his own god."[7]

Pedersen proceeded to show that in the Israelite narratives a slight change was effected by the writers so that such actions as shouting and trumpet blowing did the work and the events therefore seemed like arbitrary miracles. In the battle for Jericho (Josh. 6), for example, the psychic action and noise were not organically related to the conquest of the enemy but acted independently as magical agencies. The hostile army was of no importance; Israel merely put forth her hands to receive the gift bestowed upon her. Pedersen concluded:

> By a very slight change the narrator has created quite a new picture of war out of the old elements. It corresponds to a change in the whole conception of divine action, which was to become of such significance for Israel's view of God and man. We meet with this conception of Yahweh's activity in war in the whole history of Israel's campaigns from the exodus from Egypt to the conquest of Canaan (Ex. 14:24; 17:8 ff.; 23:27; Deut. 2:15; Josh. 10:10 f.; 24:12, etc.).[8]

One of the most important recent studies on holy war is Gerhard von Rad's *Der heilige Krieg im alten Israel* (1952).[9] Like Schwally and Pedersen before him, von Rad maintained that the history behind the biblical narratives was quite different from that literally depicted by the narratives themselves, which tend to equate holy war with absolute miracle. While in the ancient period the most important feature of holy war was indeed the demand for faith in Yahweh's saving action, this assumed the synergistic action of the warriors as well; because Yahweh fought, they fought all the harder. According to von Rad, the emphasis on miracle in those narratives that exclude or downgrade the value of human fighting is not historical but theological in origin. Von Rad maintained that this emphasis arose from the changed situation during the time of Solomon (due primarily to the "enlightenment," the impact of the international wisdom literature upon Israel).[10] To demonstrate that only after Solomon's time were the concepts of holy war and absolute miracle inseparably united, von Rad selected four battle narratives as typical of many others: Joshua at Jericho (Josh. 6), Gideon and the Midianites (Judg. 7), the miracle at the Reed Sea (Ex. 14), and David's conflict with Goliath (1 Sam. 17.)[11] In all of these he viewed the emphasis on the exclusive war-like action of Yahweh as a post-Solomonic reinterpretation of the ancient reality; in the last narrative he saw even the miracle as having been demythologized.[12]

The first attempt to apply the theory of holy war as absolute miracle to a historical situation, according to von Rad, was made in the eighth century by the prophet Isaiah, when this great prophet counseled both Ahaz and Hezekiah in times of political difficulty to quit their frenzied activity and to rely upon Yahweh's miracle, the ancient way of holy war. Isaiah's proclamation that Judah was not to rely upon Egypt for armaments was based upon the prophet's naive assumption that the post-Solomonic reinterpretation of holy war was indeed a historical picture of holy war itself.[13]

Von Rad suggested that the prophets generally spiritualized the worn-out institution of holy war, seeing prophecy itself as the legal successor to that ancient institution, and themselves as the executors of the tradition.[14] Holy war, he maintained, was a major cause of the prophets' conflict with the kings, because they had secularized the institution and misused it for self-aggrandizement.[15]

Von Rad went on to state that Israel's holy war which began as an institution in the period of the Judges, was again institutionalized in the time of Josiah as an answer to the calamitous destruction of Judah's armed forces. This attempt at reinstitutionalization came to an end with the death of Josiah. After the catastrophes of 608, 598, and 587, a great new spiritualization took place with Deuteronomic rewriting of history and the Book of Chronicles.[16]

In a more recent book (1973), Patrick D. Miller, Jr., has concluded—much like Schwally, Pedersen, and von Rad before him—that ancient holy warfare was a "synergism," that is, a fusion of human and divine activity.[17] Like earlier scholars he argued that while from the beginning the emphasis was upon the action of Yahweh and while victory was understood as primarily due to a divine and cosmic action beyond any effort on Israel's part, this did not exclude Israel's fighting. He wrote:

> As the centuries passed and the traditions grew, there came a tendency to ascribe the victory solely to the miraculous intervention of Yahweh apart from any participation of the people, but in the early period of Israel's history there was no such abdication on the part of the people.[18]

It is striking that these four scholars, who wrote with such varied presuppositions regarding Israel's early history, should find such close agreement on this central point of holy war, even though they all argue that the emphasis was due to reinterpretation by the later sources.[19]

2. *Type B Interpretations.* We turn now to four scholars who agree

that the Old Testament writings set forth holy war as a product of Yahweh's miraculous action, downgrading or excluding human fighting, but they claim that this is based on factors other than late theological reflection.

The first of these challengers is Rudolf Smend.[20] In his 1963 work, Smend agreed with the "Type A" scholars that the emphasis on Yahweh's miraculous activity in the holy war narratives was the result of a relatively late rewriting. He held, however, that this revision was grounded in an early event in Israel, the event of covenant which was central to the pre-kingship confederation of tribes.[21] This covenant formed the antithesis of Israel's ancient holy war, an antithesis reflected in the chapter headings of his book.

In the chapter "Military Event and Cultic Institution," Smend proposed that war was the dynamic element in Israel's history, while the periods of peace between conflicts were evidence of a static element represented by the covenant structure.[22] His chapter on the Judges linked the major judges with war and the minor judges with peace.[23] The "Rachel Tribes" he viewed as bearers of the Yahweh war tradition, the Leah tribes (Judah, etc.) as bearers of the covenant tradition.[24] He identified the war theme as beginning with the exodus from Egypt in which only the Rachel tribes participated, and the convenantal (or peace) theme as beginning with the covenant at Sinai which was accepted soon after the event by all twelve tribes.[25] Smend considered Moses the first of the major judges, a prophetic and charismatic war leader, who had nothing to do with the Sinai event.[26]

Let us observe just how Smend differed from the "Type A" scholars. Like them, he interpreted the spiritualization of the war narratives as a later rewriting, but he argued that this revision was not a case of theologizing in a vacuum, but rather of theologizing based upon a foundational covenant event (Sinai) in tension with the foundational war event (the exodus) that had occurred at the very beginning of Israel's history as individual clans. For example, he interpreted the account of the victory of Jehoshaphat over Moab and Ammon (2 Chron. 20) as the end product of the triumph of the ancient covenant tradition over the war tradition, "when the [war] event no longer occurred and the theory enjoyed a free hand."[27] One must ask, however, whether Smend has not forced some of the evidence in order to set forth his dialectical theory of Israel's history of warfare.

A second response to "Type A" conclusions is A. Glock's 1968 comparative work on warfare in Mari and ancient Israel.[28] This study made a methodological advance upon most of the above studies in that it compared the war practices of Israel with those of a closely related northwest Semitic people, and was solidly based upon ancient primary materials, chiefly from the Mari archives.

Glock discovered minor parallels between Mari and Israel in weapons and in organization, such as the fact that diviners accompanied the army.[29] He found major parallels in such items as enlistment and compensation.[30] An important difference, however, was Israel's emphasis on surprise attacks, and the fact that there was no siege of a city before the time of David.[31]

Since Mari existed six hundred years before Israel, and since the intervening period was one in which there was important progress in armament, as symbolized by the horse and chariot, Glock claimed that Israel's failure to employ these contemporary weapons was not merely a result of political necessity, but represented a deliberate, conscious choice, a form of resistance to a caste system and to monarchy.[32] "Yahweh alone was the king and his chariot was the clouds," Glock noted.[33]

> The clouds are the war chariot of the storm god entering into battle. As with the "spear" and "shield" so the "chariot" is in the arsenal of Yahweh, not Israel.[34]

Glock maintained that Israel's early practice of warfare was closely related to her self-understanding as embodying the kingdom of Yahweh; thus holy war was an expression of Yahweh's rule.[35]

Our third "Type B" scholar is Fritz Stolz, whose 1972 work began with the assumption that there was no Israelite confederation prior to kingship, and thus there was no unified tradition of holy war.[36] He viewed the wars before the time of Saul as simply those of individual tribes.[37] He did, however, acknowledge that Yahweh was accepted as God both in North and South in the time of David, and that therefore elements of tribes from both sections may have had a common experience of Yahweh on the southern desert. Thus the Yahweh wars of the individual tribes and the gradual dissemination of Yahwism led toward a unity which was achieved only in the time of Saul, the high point of Yahweh war.[38] The characteristic Yahweh war as a political reality ended with David, when a new concept, that of the unified state, entered the picture.[39] After kingship the prophets became the theological bearers of the holy war theme in the North. Following the Northern collapse their tradition was joined with the tradition in the South (borne by the state cult) to produce finally the later writings known as the Deuteronomic and Deuteronomistic sources.[40] In these sources, according to Stolz, the action of Yahweh had nothing to do with actual political events, and holy war was thus translated into a theory independent of reality.[41]

In the light of this historical scheme, we must look at Stolz's distinctive

concept of holy war—divine power as contrasted with human powerlessness—a theme that recurs throughout his book and is developed quite differently in two separate discussions.[42] The first passage is an excursus on
holy war in connection with a discussion of Gideon.[43] He found the concept
of divine power versus human powerlessness in Deuteronomy as well as in
the pre- and postexilic psalms, and thus located its sources in the preexilic
Jerusalem temple. But he also found it outside the worship setting, especially in Hosea and Isaiah, with Isaiah clearly applying it in an actual
political situation. Since the idea occurred in both North and South, it
perhaps originated in the common experience of the individual tribes
against the superior power of the Canaanite enemy. The Gideon narrative,
however, had little to do with history; rather it originated from the pre-Da-
vidic Jerusalem mythology, which according to Stolz entered Israel's worship at the time of David. The Isaiah miracle of the defeat of Sennacherib
(Is. 37:21-38), Stolz asserted, also had doubtful historical credibility.[44]

Stolz again dealt with this holy war concept ("The Exclusive Divine
Efficacy [Wirksamkeit]") in a section devoted to the origin, development,
and life situation of the various holy war traditions.[45] Here he claimed that
the idea of divine power as contrasted with human powerlessness originated
not in Israel's political experience with the superior power of the
Canaanites, but rather in the pre-Israelite cult of Jerusalem inherited by
David. In this cult at the celebration of the New Year's festival the god
overpowers the enemy forces of chaos, and the human king partakes in this
through victory over his enemies. Stolz cited the *Enuma Elish* and Near
Eastern hymnic literature which celebrates the king as representing deity,
who alone wins the victory. Thus Stolz in this latter discussion suggested
that the idea of human powerlessness in Israelite literature was a common
feature that Israel shared with her Near Eastern neighbors. Just how this
point of origin for the concept of human powerlessness, i.e., its derivation
from Near Eastern mythology, is to be reconciled with his earlier findings
that the concept was derived from political reality, i.e., Israel's encounter
with the Canaanite superior power, Stolz does not say.

The fourth and most decisive challenge to the "Type A" treatment of
holy war is an article by Manfred Weippert that compares the experiences
of holy war in Israel and Assyria.[46] Following the methodology of von Rad's
work on Israel, Weippert analyzed the practice and ideology of holy war in
other ancient Near Eastern states, using primarily the literature of the first
millennium BC.[47] He discovered that of the thirteen features of holy war
identified by von Rad, all but two were practiced by the Eastern and Medi-
terranean states. These two features were the call-up by means of the ram's

horn (šôpār) and the consecration of weapons.[48]

More important for our present study, Weippert noted that outside of Israel as well as within, victory was often expressed not as an action of the army but as an action of the gods alone.[49] He cited the example of Assurbanipal who in a nearly biblical tone acknowledged that he owed his victories not to his own abilities but to his gods:

> Not by my own power,
>   not by the strength of my bow—
> by the power of my gods,
>   by the strength of my goddesses
>   I subjected the lands . . . to the yoke of Assur.[50]

Weippert maintained that the essential difference in Israel's concept of warfare had to do with kingship. Because of the late development of kingship in Israel, the king did not occupy the same exalted place as did the Assyrian ruler, although like him he was *vicarius dei* and vassal of the divinity. Yahweh in an incomparable measure was the god of the people, the "God of Israel." His warfare on behalf of his people was an expression of his care for all his people, not merely for the privileged individual. This motif is expressed with particular frequency in texts which treat the occupation and cultivation of the land.[51]

While Weippert recognized this difference relating to kingship in Israel, he denied that there was a fundamental difference between Israel's early charismatic political offices and those of other states. The charismatic war hero of early Israel who arose to meet the challenge of external threats was a part of the culture of the pre-kingship Israelite tribal states, a phenomenon comparable to the Arabian bedouin culture of a later day.[52] Thus Weippert asserted that there was no late reinterpretation of holy war narratives which differed appreciably from the ancient interpretation, but that both the practice and the ideology of holy war in Israel were common to other ancient Near Eastern states.[53]

3. *Summary of Scholarship.* All the studies of holy war surveyed agree that the present biblical narratives for the most part credit Yahweh with fighting the battle and discredit human fighting. The disagreements have to do with, first, whether this interpretation was late or early, and second, what is its relationship to historical events.

The "Type A" spokesmen—Schwally, Pedersen, von Rad, and Miller—all held that the exclusive emphasis on Yahweh's fighting found in these narratives is the result of *a relatively late theological reinterpretation.*

The "Type B" scholars postulated earlier historical or mythological considerations to help account for this theological reinterpretation. Thus Smend, while holding to the late theologizing, insisted that *the revision was the result of an early experience of covenant,* and that this experience was originally in a dialectical relationship to Israel's early experience of warfare, a dialectic resolved only after warfare no longer occurred in Israel. Glock was even more positive, holding that early Israel's relative powerlessness was due not merely to political necessity but also to *a deliberate, conscious choice motivated by her theo-political self-understanding.* Stolz saw *two ancient sources* for Israel's interpretation of Yahweh's wars, one the experience of pre-kingship tribes with *the superior power of the Canaanite city-states,* and the other *Near Eastern mythology.* Weippert considered Israel's emphasis upon Yahweh's miracle as *an early interpretation basically similar to the mythological expression of Israel's Near Eastern neighbors.* He thus maintained that there was no essential difference between Israel's holy wars and the holy wars of her neighbors.

Of these writers, only Glock holds that *early Israel's refusal to use contemporary weapons was a deliberate conscious choice,* a form of resistance to a caste system and to monarchy, closely related to Israel's self-understanding as the kingdom of Yahweh. He does not enlarge upon what caused Israel to make this deliberate and conscious choice.

By way of anticipation, the argument of this book agrees with all eight writers that the present Old Testament narratives for the most part emphasize Yahweh's miracle of holy war and downgrade human fighting. I reject, however, the "Type A" assumption that this emphasis is only a product of late theological reflection, and I differ from the various "Type B" writers in that I argue that the ground for this view of holy war is found in Israel's testimony to a crucial event in early warfare itself—the exodus.

B. *Holy War and Political Structure*

A second aspect of Israel's warfare—its relationship to her theo-political structure—is given only limited consideration in these chapters. Patrick Miller states the issue in these words: "Finally and most important is the fact that the establishment of Yahweh's kingship and sanctuary . . . grew out of this cosmic, historical, sacral war. . . ."[54] The question, however, is when and how Yahweh's kingship grew out of this sacral war. As we have noted, Miller holds that the texts which state that Yahweh fought alone, without the help of man, are the result of late theological reflection, a consequence of man abdicating his responsibility. This position is difficult to reconcile with the fact that Miller accepts Exodus 15 as an early hymn.[55] Our view here is that, in this earliest time, Yahweh delivered Israel without human aid (Exodus 15), and that this deliverance had a profound effect upon Israel's theo-political structure as set forth at Sinai. Yahweh, Israel's only war hero, became Yahweh, Israel's only king. Thus the principle of reliance upon Yahweh alone for military succor became imbedded in Israel's political structure.

What then was the fundamental tension of Israel's existence? Building on Miller's "Divine Warrior" theme, Paul D. Hanson postulates a dialectic at work in Israel between Yahweh the divine warrior who acts in the cosmos (myth) and Yahweh the divine warrior who acts on the plane of human history.[56] Hanson sees this dialectic in the full range of history, from ancient Sumerian times through the times of the New Testament. He regards the early mythologizing of Egypt and Sumer as a negation of history, while in classical Mesopotamia history was the mere reflection of the cosmic realm. In the early Israelite confederacy, myth and history were held in tension, but later, in the royal court of Jerusalem, history again became a reflection of cosmic events. In contrast to the royal court, however, prophetic Yahwism affirmed history as the context of divine acts. Then the Apocalyptic eschatology of the post-prophetic period became indifferent to the restraints of history. And finally, gnosticism negated history—a return to pre-Israelite conceptions.

While Hanson regarded the dialectic as a tension between myth and history, Smend, as noted above, saw the dialectic as a tension between what Israel regarded as two historical experiences, the ancient covenant tradition and war tradition, the former winning out over the latter after warfare was (presumably) no longer an issue in Israel.[57]

The thesis of the following chapters is that the issue of Israel's history did not lie in the tension between "myth" and "history" (Hanson) but in the question of *how* "myth" related to "history." In Israel's foundational event, the exodus, Yahweh the divine warrior overcame Egypt, not by means of human warfare, but by means of a prophetic personality who heralded a message brought to pass by miracle. There was, indeed, human activity, but it was the action of a prophet, not a warrior.

Nor did the tension lie between two ancient institutions of Israel, the Sinai covenant and warfare (Smend); rather it was caused by an event that had happened within warfare itself, the escape from Egypt by prophetic agitation and miracle. This event, occurring within the institution of warfare, provided the basis for the new structure of the Sinai covenant, the rule of Yahweh founded upon Torah and prophetic word. *The central issue of Israel's self-understanding therefore was Yahweh's relation to history through Torah and prophetic word, as brought into tension with Near*

Eastern myth where the gods were related to history through the coercive structures of kingship law and military power. This tension between the "prophetic structure" of Israel and the "kingship structures" of her neighbors is not only intrinsically evident in much of Israel's literature, but is specifically stated by that literature, as we shall see.

C. Yahweh Wars Against Israel

A third aspect of holy war which we will discuss in this work is Yahweh's warfare against his own people Israel. This theme is a minor one in the early period of Israel's history, but becomes central in the interpretation of the events of 722 and 587, the collapse of Samaria and Jerusalem. While such a theme is found only occasionally in Mesopotamian literature, in Israel it becomes the key to her demise as set forth by the Deuteronomic historian and by the preexilic prophets. When Israel became like Egypt, Yahweh turned against his own people just as he had been against Egypt. This emphasis shows that the concern of the biblical writers with regard to warfare was not merely another nationalism, but a profound moral conviction.

D. Method and Scope: The Primary History

The method of this study is exegetical and descriptive; I simply work my way through the biblical texts, beginning with the patriarchal narratives and ending with the theology of the Deuteronomic historian.[58]

The material from Genesis through 2 Kings (minus the Book of Ruth which in the Hebrew Bible is classified among the Writings) is known as the Primary History.[59] This great work begins with the narratives of creation and primeval man and continues through the history of Israel to the time of the exile. It has a measure of unity and a point of view of its own quite distinct from that of the later Chronicler (1 and 2 Chronicles, Ezra-Nehemiah) which in the main is a secondary history. The unity of its first segment (Genesis through Numbers) with the Deuteronomic history (Deuteronomy—Kings) was probably the work of the first redactor who followed the Deuteronomic historian, a redactor responsible for the epilogue from the death of Josiah to the exile (2 Kings 23:26—25:26). His fingerprint is found in the anachronism that Abraham had been called from Ur of Chaldea (Gen. 11:31), and that the history of Israel had come full circle in the exile by Israel's returning there (2 Kings 25:24, 26).

I have confined my study to the Primary History because it forms perhaps the most important segment of the Old Testament. It contains the oldest traditions of warfare, and thus is essential to my purpose. Besides these older traditions, the work contains younger traditions with which the older may be compared. These traditions of warfare set forth Israel's basic theology of warfare and provide the foundation for understanding warfare in the prophets and later biblical books. In the last chapter, I will point up briefly some of the main lines of the further contribution that the prophets and apocalypticists make.

In summary, we will examine Israel's thought regarding violent political power and will argue that the theology of "Yahweh as warrior" includes three major emphases. First, according to Israel's ancient testimony Yahweh delivered his people from Egypt by a prophetic leader rather than by a warrior. Yahweh's warfare in support of this prophet took the form of a nature miracle rather than ordinary human fighting. This event provided from the beginning the fundamental paradigm for Israel's holy war. Second, the exodus event formed the basis for Israel's "prophetic" political structure, a structure that rejected ordinary concepts of kingship grounded in the exercise of violence as representative of divinity. This radical "prophetic" reorientation of Israel's politics shaped the main tension of Israel's history in her contacts with the Near Eastern kingship states. We cannot deal with this theme extensively in this book, but will simply note some of the connections with Yahweh's warfare. Third, the traditions testify that as Israel became like these Near Eastern states, Yahweh's war was also directed against Israel herself.

Chapter II

Warfare in the Patriarchal Period

Since the people of Yahweh had their beginnings in the escape from Egypt and the event at Sinai, both described in the Book of Exodus, an examination of the patriarchal narratives is only introductory to our main task. But the promise at the heart of the Genesis narrative speaks of nationhood, land, and national destiny, goals that in the usual life of nations are expressed in the realities of political power and its possible eruption in violence. With this promise at the beginning and influencing the rest of the biblical story, we must give attention to the relation of warfare to the Abrahamic covenant. In the second place, we will deal with those patriarchal narratives in which conflict is resolved peacefully. Finally, we will examine those narratives in which conflict erupts in violence.

Our discussion will be concerned both with the way of life of the patriarchal period as it is portrayed by the narratives, and with the use and meaning of these accounts as they developed through the process of transmission and redaction. The essentially peaceful character of these narratives has posed problems for scholars who argue that the narratives originated in the time of the kings. Thus Julius Wellhausen recognized the difficulty of harmonizing their peaceful nature with his assumption of a late origin:

> ...it is remarkable that the heroes of Israelite legend show so little taste for war, and in this point they seem to be scarcely a true reflection of the character of the Israelites as known from their history.[1]

This contrast of peaceful patriarchs with later warlike Israel compelled Hermann Gunkel to break with Wellhausen's concept of the late literary fiction of the patriarchal narratives and to hold that

> most of the legends of the patriarchs were known before Israel came into
> Canaan. This assumption is supported by the character of many of the le-
> gends of Genesis: the complaisance and peacefulness of the figures of the pa-
> triarchs are by no means Israelitish characteristics.[2]

While we may wish to question Gunkel's view of what is genuinely Israel-
itish, there is good reason to accept the narratives as evidence of the peaceful way of life of the patriarchs.

The pacifistic nature of the patriarchal narratives may have been conditioned by the political weakness of the clans which had no status as states.
As sojourners among the Canaanite city-states the patriarchs were hardly
prepared to challenge their superior power. This political weakness was
transcended, however, by the religious experience of the patriarchs, namely
their experience of promise in encounter with the God of the fathers,
identified as El. What was impossible to achieve in the present they were
promised for the future. They were thus given a "politics of promise" which
sustained them in their political weakness, helping them to develop an
identity and maintain a way of life independent from that of the Canaanite
city-states.

This politics of hope and the peaceful way of life that was developed in
the patriarchal period of political weakness must also have been regarded as
having relevance for Israel in its time of political strength. At any rate, these
early traditions continued to live throughout the time of empire, a time for
which it would seem that they were not particularly fitted. Or was something else involved here? What were the redactors seeking to say when at
various times and places they gathered up these traditions to preserve them
and to promote them among their own generation? This is a question that
we must ask especially of J who probably worked at a time when the empire
was at its zenith (tenth century BC), and who thus would seem to have
promoted a politics developed in a period of weakness for a time of political
strength.

A. Warfare and Promise

The patriarchal promise is theo-political in character, having to do
with nationhood, national destiny, and land (Gen. 12:1-3).[3] In each of the
literary recensions of the Pentateuch the promise of land provided legitima-
tion and motivation for the occupation of Canaan by the tribes.

> And when Yahweh brings you into the land of the Canaanites, the Hittites,
> the Amorites, the Hivites, and the Jebusites, which he swore to your fathers to
> give you, a land flowing with milk and honey, you shall keep this service in
> this month (Ex. 13:5,J).[4]

Then Yahweh said to Abram, "Know of surety that your descendants will be sojourners in a land that is not theirs, and will be slaves there, and they will be oppressed for four hundred years; but I will bring judgment on the nation which they serve, and afterward they shall come out with great possessions.... And they shall come back here in the fourth generation..." (Gen. 15:13-16, E?).[5]

And you shall do what is right and good in the sight of Yahweh, that it may go well with you, and that you may go in and take possession of the good land which Yahweh swore to give to your fathers (Deut. 6:18, D).[6]

I appeared to Abraham, to Isaac, and to Jacob, as God Almighty, but by my name Yahweh I did not make myself known to them. I also established my covenant with them, to give them the land of Canaan (Ex. 6:3-4a,P).[7]

In this need for political legitimacy the Bible compares with other Near Eastern state religions.[8] Without divine authorization, an ancient people would hardly have risked battle. Standing as it does at the head of the salvation history (Gen. 12:1-3) and in the oldest recension of the Pentateuch (J), the patriarchal promise with its theo-political aspects of nation, land and national destiny provides an orientation for the entire biblical story.

The distinctive nature of this element in biblical faith, however, is precisely its emphasis upon promise, the act of God, and not upon command and the response of man. The promise of land "appears throughout the patriarchal stories like a red thread".[9] This "red thread" of promise is likely a reflection of patriarchal religious experience, an experience that mitigated the weakness of the patriarch's political position. The classic example of promise as religious experience is the narrative of covenant oath, an oath that reinforced the promise of land (Gen. 15:7-12, 17-18), and that answered to the helplessness and unbelief of Abram (15:8).

The general authenticity of the patriarchal covenant as set forth in Genesis 15:7-12, 17-18 is quite widely accepted since A. Alt's article on the God of the patriarchs.[10] The present text of Genesis 15 unites what are obviously two traditions.[11] The first is the promise of a son and great posterity (1-6), and the second is the promise of land (7-21).[12] If the chapter is treated as a unity, the emphasis is on the promise of land.[13] The covenant (7-21) has to do only with land, though posterity is obviously presupposed (v. 18).

In the covenant ceremony described in verses 12, 17, 18 (the meaning of which is suggested in Jeremiah 34:17ff.)[14] God alone commits himself; Abram is entirely passive. David N. Freedman observes that in this ceremony Yahweh assumed the role of the inferior, or vassal, binding himself by solemn oath to the performance of certain obligations to Abraham. In this covenant, God is bound by his own oath, but Abraham is not. The divine commitment is thus unconditional, and this obligation or service is comparable in all respects with the obligation of the slave to his master. The difference is that the obligation is limited to the oath, and the obligation was self-imposed.[15]

It is important to note that while the promise involved community and national destiny, the sole point of the unconditional covenant of Genesis 15:7-21 was the promise of land. While the unconditional character of this covenant as exegeted by Paul (Romans 4) has always been recognized by the church, the content of that covenant, the promise of land, has unfortunately often been spiritualized.[16] God's promise of land and Abram's response of faith have seldom been recognized as the basis for a new political order, an alternative to violent political power. If one truly believes in the promise of grace that God will *give* the land, then one has no need to take the way of works by fighting for it. The logic of Paul's doctrine of grace—calling for a response of faith rather than works—is here prefigured in the unconditional promise of land. (It may be that Paul was also making this point with regard to possession of the land, if his writing was directed against the violent Zealot movement that gained control of Judean politics in the decade after the letter to the Romans had been written.[17])

Recent studies of Genesis 15 confirm the exegesis of the church that this covenant is unconditional. L. A. Snijders says that in Genesis 15 the covenant is quite one-sided, that Abram's role is passive.[18] Norbert Lohfink comments that the context of Genesis 15 demands that we accept the expression "to cut a covenant" (v. 18) as a statement of a one-sided oath of God made to Abraham.[19] He quotes the German commentator Jepsen who maintained that the covenant *(berit)* with Abraham in Genesis 15:18 is a "one-sided promise"—a guarantee of land for Abram's posterity.[20] M. Weinfeld attempts to find an ancient Near Eastern analogy to the one-sided character of this covenant in his comparison of the Abrahamic covenant to the "covenant of grant."[21] Gerhard von Rad states, "The ceremony proceeded completely without words and with the complete passivity of the human partner!"[22] I know of no commentator who challenges the one-sided character of this covenant, the very point by which it is differentiated from the later covenant of Moses.

Because commentators have paid almost exclusive attention to the formal structures of the covenants and have disregarded content, this Abrahamic covenant is sometimes seen as contradicting the two-sided commitment of the Mosaic covenant, and as similar to the one-sided covenant between Yahweh and David (2 Sam. 7).[23] Thus George Mendenhall took the Mosaic covenant, with its dual responsibility, as the foundation for Israel's radical break with the power-oriented kingship covenants of the ancient Near East, but questioned the intent of the Abrahamic covenant on this matter, because its formal structure paralleled the one-sided character of the covenant of the Davidic dynasty that legitimated the violent political power of the kingship.[24]

If, however, one takes into account both the formal structure and the content of the Abrahamic covenant, another view is more persuasive. The covenant with Abraham, by making land the gift of God, surely rejects the violent power principle, and is thus in continuity with the power orientation of the Sinai covenant, even though the form is different. But on this point both the Abrahamic and Mosaic covenants are in sharp contrast with the Davidic covenant. We will, however, need to reserve judgment concerning the total intent of the Davidic covenant at this point, for it can be claimed that continuity of the Abrahamic covenant with the Davidic covenant is to be found in the limitations on kingship in the Davidic covenant rather than in those "legitimizing" features of that covenant which tended to make Israel similar to any other Near Eastern state. According to Freedman, the Davidic covenant "represents an attempt to amalgamate features of both the Abrahamic and the Mosaic covenants, emphasizing both the divine commitment and the human obligations; at least as we now have them, the Abrahamic covenant is purely promissory, and the Mosaic covenant is purely obligatory. The royal covenant is an attempt to blend the two, and mix responsibility with privilege."[25]

What did J mean when he communicated this unconditional covenant, formed in a time of political powerlessness, to a nation that had arrived at the zenith of its power? The unconditional character of this covenant, whether cited by Paul in the time of the Zealots (Rom. 4) or by orthodox Judaism as represented by the Neturei Karta, has left its indelible impress upon the community that professes the faith of Abraham.[26]

B. The Promise of Land and Patriarchal Conflict

The striking fact that in the patriarchal narratives, except for one slight reference (Gen. 48:22), the possession of land never becomes the occasion for warfare strongly supports our view that the unconditional character of the promise of land was a foundational political principle. The patriarchs are sojourners in the land, who keep going simply by relying on Yahweh's promise.

In his redaction of the ancient traditions, J set forth Israel's history as a counter-history to that of the nations. The call of Abram (Gen. 12:1-3) is contrasted with a "democratic" Sumerian city-state (11:1-9).[27] Both the city-state and Israel were originally migrating societies (11:2; 12:1). The citizens of the city-state "found a plain in the land of Shinar and settled there" (11:2). Abram, on the other hand, was to go to the land that Yahweh would show him (12:1). While this immediate relation between divinity and people was a characteristic type of patriarchal religion, J's use of this ancient concept to set forth Yahweh's relationship to Israel, even in the tenth century BC when Israel had settled down and had become a kingship state, is an example of the writer's self-conscious archaizing tendency, rooted in religious conviction.

J refused to "modernize" his thinking.[28] He did not accept the mythological thought of other settled peoples who saw their land as the center of the earth, the place where the cosmic mountain or primeval hill jutted forth from the underwaters, and thus the place where divine powers were available to the world.[29] Though the Old Testament writers at times moved in this direction (Ezek. 28:12), they were held back by historical memory. In biblical religion the immediacy of the relationship between people and land ("blood and soil") was thus broken. Not land, but the relationship between Abram and Yahweh who had called him, the relationship between a people and their God, gave to the community of faith its identity. Land, while important, was Yahweh's gift, and that perspective governed its possession, use, and defense.

Oriented toward the promise (Gen. 13:14 ff.), Abram was quite ready to give the circle of the Jordan to Lot. He said to Lot, "Let there be no strife between you and me, and between your herdsmen and my herdsmen; for we are kinsmen" (13:8). Isaac surrendered his water rights to Abimelech, the "Philistine" king of Gerar, without a struggle (Gen. 26:1-33, J). What would such narratives mean centuries later to an empire that had killed two thirds of the Moabites (in biblical thought the descendants of Lot, Gen. 19:37f.), and had subjugated the Philistines (2 Sam. 8:1 f.)?

The Jacob narratives deal with a similar theme of sacrifice for the sake of peace. Jacob left his homeland after his brother Esau threatened to murder him because Jacob had stolen the blessing and thus became heir to the promise (Gen. 27—28). After his sojourn in the land of Laban, Jacob returned to face his competitor for the promise, but with a new strategy for dealing with the conflict—a voluntary acceptance of subjection related to an encounter with a divine messenger (Gen. 32).

The play on the names Jacob-Israel (32:3—33:17, J) with the new character that the name "Israel" implied is connected with Jacob's subjection to Esau (identified with Edom).[30] Throughout the narratives in Genesis 32 and 33, Jacob put himself in the position of a vassal (*'ebed*) to his lord (*'adôn*) Esau (Gen. 32:4, 5, 18; 33:8, 13 ff.). This is treaty terminology, used by a vassal in relation to his suzerain, as is evident from the Ugaritic texts.[31] It may well be that Jacob's "presents" (*minhâ*)[32] should be translated "tribute" (Gen. 32:13, 18, 20, 21; 33:10) in light of the fact that 32:14-15 is a tribute list that might be compared with tribute lists of a later period of the Assyrian king, Shalmanezer III (858-824 BC).[33]

The argument for a treaty context is strengthened by the fact that Jacob bowed down to his brother seven times (Gen. 33:3), a number used in the Amarna letters to decribe the obeisance of Canaanite kings to Pharaoh.[34] The biblical text places a great emphasis on this obeisance in that not only Jacob but the various eponymous representatives of the Israelite tribes also bowed down, both North and South: the maids with their children (33:6), Leah and her children, and last, Joseph and Rachel (33:7).

Jacob's new approach to the problem was successful, as suggested by his settlement in the land (Gen. 33:15 ff.). By making himself a vassal to Esau, Israel gained the land and was able to live at peace.

What would this narrative mean to an empire that in the time of David had slain "every male in Edom" (1 Kings 11:15 f.), and was unable to pacify this southern enemy? Later Talmudic commentators understood very well the political import of this passage in Genesis. They reproved Jacob for the words which he had spoken to his archenemy Esau:

> When Jacob called Esau "my lord," the Holy one, blessed be He, said to him: "Thou hast abased thyself and called Esau 'my lord' eight times. I will raise up eight kings of his descendants before thy descendants. . . ."[35]

There can be little doubt that these materials in Genesis ran counter to the spirit of nationalism. These narratives have little resemblance to the ancient hero stories of non-Israelite traditions.[36]

C. Joseph and Intertribal Conflict

If the above narratives treat mainly the patriarchal and Israelite relationships with surrounding peoples, the Joseph narratives deal with relationships between the eponymous ancestors of the twelve tribes. Here again we do not concern ourselves so much with what may have been the historical roots of these materials as with the use to which they were put by the various redactors, especially J.

Let us assume that J directed his narrative to the situation existing between David-Solomon and the tribes, a situation that occasioned the revolt of Absalom and then of Sheba ben Bichri, and later the revolt against Rehoboam.[37] The latter revolt resulted in the division of the kingdom, the North led by the Joseph tribes, especially Ephraim, against the dynasty of David in whom they had no portion (1 Kings 12:16). The revolt was probably based on two complaints: that David and Solomon had introduced the institutions of a highly developed officialdom and specialized troops, institutions foreign to the political tradition of Israel, and that Judah had been granted preferred status in the kingdom, exempting her from the corvée and heavy taxations.[38] If the king tended to be identified by the Davidic covenant with the patriarch Jacob-Israel, it was not without meaning that in Joseph's dream the patriarch himself bowed down to Joseph (Gen. 37:9-11, J).[39] Judah's involvement with his brothers in selling Joseph into slavery in Egypt (37:25-27, J) may have had some relevance to the hated corvée in the time of Solomon; what did it say to Judah's political leadership that J emphasized Judah's role as Joseph's protector?[40] May the redactor have been speaking to the problem of the contemporary style of leadership when he tells how Judah, pleading the case of Benjamin, reconciled Joseph to his brothers by offering himself as Joseph's slave in place of Benjamin (44:18-45:15)?[41] Was J recommending a political strategy when he told how Joseph relieved his brothers of their burden of guilt by forgiveness, a forgiveness based upon the theology that it was not his brothers but God who had sent Joseph to Egypt in order that Joseph might be an instrument of survival (45:4-8, 14 f., J)?[42]

D. Patriarchal Narratives of Violence

Violence, to be sure, is not absent from the patriarchal accounts. The first example to appear in the main sources is the story of revenge for Shechem's rape of Dinah, a revenge perpetrated by the clans Simeon and Levi (Gen. 34, J).[43] This narrative has to do not so much with individuals as with the interrelations of ethnic groups, and thus it has a political dimension. It is "history novelistically interpreted."[44] The clans' act of violence is probably referred to in the "Testament of Jacob" (49:5-7) where as judgment the tribes would be "driven from Jacob/ scattered from Israel."[45] Simeon became a rudimentary tribe in the South, ultimately to be absorbed by Judah, while Levi went down into Egypt and lost all territorial rights.

Thus, the judgment of the editor is that, far from establishing the promise by fighting, the two tribes who had once been vigorous lost their territorial claims in central Palestine by fighting for their honor.[46] The alternative to their violence would have been a peaceful way of penetrating the land (34:8-10). But instead, the Jacob clans proposed deceitfully that the Shechemites were to convert to the way of the clans and to become like them (Gen. 34:14-17).

The issue of the chapter is how to deal with "folly in Israel," a sex violation which "ought not to be done" (Gen. 34:7). Such "folly" later caused a war between the tribes resulting in the near extinction of Benjamin, as recorded in Judges 19 and 20.[47] This "folly" is also expressed in the violation of Tamar by her brother Ammon, an incident that touched off violence in the family of David when Absalom avenged his sister by murdering Ammon (2 Sam. 13).[48] May J have had this incident in mind when he included this narrative in his work? According to Deuteronomic law, such "folly" was to be punished by stoning (Deut. 22:13-21).

In Genesis 34, the two generations, while agreeing that the offense was serious, differed on how to deal with the problem. The patriarch Jacob was peace-loving and conciliatory, while the younger generation was deceitful, vengeful, and heedless of the consequences of its violent action.[49] This represented a definite break between the generations on how to respond to such matters, since Jacob's conciliatory attitude is not isolated but is a reflection of similar attitudes on the part of Abraham and Isaac as shown in the three narratives that tell of the violations of Sarah and Rebecca (Gen. 12:10-20, J; 20:1-18, E; 26:6-11, J). The author of *The Testaments of the Twelve Patriarchs* saw already in the second century BC that these three narratives dealt essentially with the same problem as that of Dinah's violation.[50] In astonishing contrast with ancient legends dealing with national honor, these three narratives portray the patriarch as quite ready to give the matriarch away.[51] As each narrative makes clear, the matriarch was saved by divine intervention. Evidently the patriarch, caught in the web of political weakness, was committed to trust in such intervention, and perhaps in the ingenuity of the matriarch herself. All four of these narratives not only ran against the grain of ancient concepts of ethics and honor, as is evident from Genesis 34:7, but also have proved troublesome for modern commentators, who contrive ingenious explanations to mitigate their offensiveness.[52]

That the editor J sided with the older generation and opposed the concept of ethics and national honor of the younger generation is evident in his editorial opinion that the act of the clans was one of deceit (34:13). This is all the more impressive since J in the patriarchal narratives seldom makes editorial judgments of a moral nature.[53] Throughout the story, J presents Hamor and Shechem in a good light and the sons of Jacob in a poor light.

Later Jewish interpreters reversed the judgment of J to side with the sons of Jacob against the older patriarchs. The *Book of Jubilees* (second

century BC) extols the sons of Jacob for executing "righteousness and up-
rightness and vengeance on the sinners."[54] Instead of considering Levi
punished as does the "Testament of Jacob" (Gen. 49:5-7), it sees Levi as
rewarded by being chosen for the priesthood.[55] In *The Testaments of the
Twelve Patriarchs*, Levi tells how he was commanded by an angel: "Execute vengeance on Shechem because of Dinah, thy sister, and I will be with
thee because the Lord hath sent me."[56] In this writing Levi defends his violent behavior in his break with his father. He sees himself as the executor of
"the sentence of God" against Shechem.[57]

Von Rad has noted an example of holy war language in Genesis 35:5:
"And as they journeyed, a terror from God *(hittat 'ĕlōhîm)* fell upon the
cities that were round about them, so that they did not pursue the sons of
Jacob."[58] He linked this verse with the event of chapter 34.[59] If such a rela-
tionship was intended, Genesis 35:5 explains why the surrounding area did
not take vengeance upon the clans of Jacob for their destruction of
Shechem. This motif of the "divine terror" is a common one not only in the
Bible but also in other ancient Near Eastern literature.[60]

Another allusion to violence is found in Genesis 48:22. In this statement Jacob says that he took with his sword and bow "one mountain slope"
(RSV) or "Shechem" (Speiser).[61] This allusion to "*šĕkem*" is enigmatic, but
may refer to the event of chapter 34.[62] If so, the evaluation of the event
would seem to be positive, agreeing with the judgment of the younger
generation in regard to the conflict. This is the only allusion in the narratives to a pre-Mosaic conquest by an Israelite tribe or clan.[63]

We have left the discussion of Abraham's battle with the kings of the
East (Gen. 14) until last because the chapter is an isolated source which differs considerably in its portrayal of Abraham from the other sources.[64] In
light of the texts from Ebla, this source will need to be taken with historical
seriousness, and may date Abraham (and Lot) to the latter part of the third
millennium BC.[65] Here Abram is involved in the world of international relations, and is portrayed as a warrior prince who defeats a coalition of Eastern
kings that raids Canaan. May Abram as sojourner *(gēr)* or "Hebrew" (*'ibrî*,
Gen. 14:13) have been in the employ of the coalition headed by the king of
Jerusalem?[66] The fighting in the chapter is a rescue operation of a related
clan, and is connected neither with covenant nor land. May it have entered
the tradition in the time of David to tie that city to the patriarch Abram, as
well as to give a precedent to David's wars?

The blessing of Melchizedek: "And blessed be' Ēl 'Elyôn, who has delivered your enemies into your hand!" appears to relate the event to the language of holy war.[67] This clause, "who has delivered your enemies into your

hand," occurs scores of times in the war narratives of the Old Testament, though usually with a different verb.[68] The phrase is not unique to Israel. For example, it is found in the Assyrian annals from the time of Sargon: "Bel has given your enemy into your hand."[69] The phrase has special meaning to Israel only as it is qualified by the God of election and covenant. Abram's attack of the invading kings at night may indicate his inferior military position in relation to the enemy. But a discussion of just how election and covenant may qualify the motifs of holy war will have to wait for the next chapter.

E. Conclusion

Although this chapter is prefatory to our study of holy war, that does not negate its importance. Here are some of the earliest traditions of Israel, rooted in the pre-Mosaic experience. Most of these traditions are pacifistic; they delineate a particular self-identity and a way of relating to the Canaanite city-states by a people who had no political standing. This way of life was grounded upon a religious experience, a "politics of promise." Developed in a period of weakness, this "politics of promise" with its concomitant way of life in relation to the eponymous ancestors of Moab, Ammon, and Edom, to the Philistines, and to intertribal strife, was promoted by J in a time of Israel's political strength.

It should be no surprise that a few traditions of violence are found in these ancient materials. The question is, why have so few traditions of patriarchal violence been handed down to us? Were there no more such traditions that might have been selected by the redactors? That would hardly seem credible, but if no more, why no more? And if there were more, why did the redactors make this selection, a selection that scholars long since have noted as in tension with the later warlike narratives of ancient Israel?

Chapter III

Warfare and the Exodus

In contrast to the peaceful narratives of Genesis, Exodus 1—15 is a story of conflict, the conflict of an enslaved people with the most powerful empire of the day.[1] The resolution of this conflict, through nature plagues climaxed with the victory at the sea, was seen by Israel as Yahweh's central act of salvation for his people.

The exodus is referred to in every stratum of the Pentateuch, in the prophetic books, and in the writings.[2] The victory was foundational for the Israelite community as the people of Yahweh.[3] It was the sign of Yahweh's steadfast love (Ps. 136:10-15) and was the basis for confidence in his future saving acts when Israel encountered political difficulties (Is. 63:11-19). It was the ground for Yahweh's demand for faithfulness to him and to his law.[4] Finally, the exodus was united by the prophets with the concept of the chosen people.[5]

It is important that we acknowledge the total message of the various Exodus 1—15 traditions. The relatively few minor disagreements among these traditions should not blind us to the unified witness of the whole.[6] Johannes Pedersen's assertion that Exodus 1—15 as a unified entity was used in preliterary times to celebrate the passover festival serves as a corrective to the splintering of this tradition by literary and form criticism.[7]

Reading this account as a unified whole makes it obvious that the exodus and wilderness period is the time of holy war "par excellence," more significant than either the period of the judges (following von Rad) or the conquest (Miller).[8] The Exodus 1—15 material is somewhat more extensive than the twelve chapters of the conquest in the Book of Joshua. In addition, the place of the exodus in the rest of the Old Testament tradition as well as in the post-Old Testament tradition through the New Testament and Talmud is a central one.[9] Thus the exodus rather than the conquest or judges provides the fundamental paradigm of holy war in the Old Testament.[10]

While this holistic view is essential, to understand more precisely what is said and even to add to the impact of the whole we should examine the various traditions of Exodus 1—15 individually.[11]

We begin with the Reed Sea accounts, the best authenticated of the traditions of the exodus and follow with a discussion of the vocation of Moses and the plagues.[12]

A. The Reed Sea Traditions

1. *The Song of the Sea (Ex. 15:1-21).* On the basis of Ugaritic comparative studies, an important segment of biblical scholarship has recognized the ancientness of certain poetry found in the Pentateuch and elsewhere in the Old Testament.[13] David Noel Freedman designates and dates five lengthy pre-kingship poems as follows:[14]

Poem	Date of Event	Composition of Poem
Genesis 49	14-13th Century BC	11th Century BC
Exodus 15	13-12th	12th
Numbers 23—24	12th	11th
Deuteronomy 33	12th	11th
Judges 5	12th	12th

The importance of this dating is that it qualifies the classic literary hypothesis by recognizing a literary witness of ancient Israel that is approximately contemporary with the events of which the documents speak. Furthermore, these poems predate kingship and thus provide us with an alternative to a reordering of priorities in the direction of empire that may have been made in the kingship period, when most of the ancient tradition was put into written form.[15] The Song of the Sea may thus be dated as early as the first half of the twelfth century BC.[16] It is a victory hymn of the same literary type as the Song of Deborah (Judg. 5) and other Near Eastern nonbiblical war poetry, such as the hymn to Ramesses II and the epic of Tukulti-Ninurta.[17]

The song was no doubt used in worship; verse 21 may have been an antiphonal refrain of the dancing women as they responded at appropriate places to the longer song.[18]

THE SONG OF THE SEA
(Exodus 15:1-21)

(1) Then Moses and the people of Israel sang this song to Yahweh, saying,
"I will sing to Yahweh, for he has triumphed gloriously;
    the horse and his rider he has thrown into the sea.
(2) Yahweh is my strength and my song,
    and he has become my salvation;
this is my God, and I will praise him,
    my father's God, and I will exalt him.
(3) Yahweh is a man of war;
    Yahweh is his name.

(4) "Pharaoh's chariots and his host he cast into the sea;
    and his picked officers are sunk in the Red Sea.
(5) The floods cover them;
    they went down into the depths like a stone.
(6) Thy right hand, O Yahweh, glorious in power,
    thy right hand, O Yahweh, shatters the enemy.
(7) In the greatness of thy majesty thou overthrowest thy adversaries;
    thou sendest forth thy fury, it consumes them like stubble.
(8) At the blast of thy nostrils the waters piled up,
    the floods stood up in a heap;
    the deeps congealed in the heart of the sea.
(9) The enemy said, 'I will pursue, I will overtake,
    I will divide the spoil, my desire shall have its fill of them.
    I will draw my sword, my hand shall destroy them.'
(10) Thou didst blow with thy wind, the sea covered them;
    they sank as lead in the mighty waters.

(11) "Who is like thee, O Yahweh, among the gods?
    Who is like thee, majestic in holiness,
    terrible in glorious deeds, doing wonders?

(12) Thou didst stretch out thy right hand,
    the earth swallowed them.

(13) "Thou hast led in thy steadfast love the people whom thou hast
      redeemed,
    thou hast guided them by thy strength to thy holy abode.
(14) The peoples have heard, they tremble;
    pangs have seized on the inhabitants of Philistia.
(15) Now are the chiefs of Edom dismayed;
    the leaders of Moab, trembling seizes them;
    all the inhabitants of Canaan have melted away.
(16) Terror and dread fall upon them;
    because of the greatness of thy arm, they are as still as a stone,

till thy people, O Yahweh, pass by,
  till the people pass by whom thou hast purchased.
(17) Thou wilt bring them in, and plant them on thy own mountain,
  the place, O Yahweh, which thou hast made for thy abode,
  the sanctuary, O Yahweh, which thy hands have established.
(18) Yahweh will reign for ever and ever."
(19) For when the horses of Pharaoh with his chariots and his horsemen went into the sea, Yahweh brought back the waters of the sea upon them; but the people of Israel walked on dry ground in the midst of the sea.(20) Then Miriam, the prophetess, the sister of Aaron, took a timbrel in her hand; and all the women went out after her with timbrels and dancing.
(21) And Miriam sang to them:
  "Sing to Yahweh, for he has triumphed gloriously;
  the horse and his rider he has thrown into the sea."

a. *Celebration of Yahweh's Military Victory.* There is no question but that the exercise of military power is the theme of this poem. As a victory hymn, the poem celebrates Yahweh's victory over Pharaoh and his chariotry at the sea. The theme is set forth in verse 3: Yahweh, the warrior. His act of war is succinctly stated in verse 4: he has cast Pharaoh's chariots, his army, and picked officers into the sea. He has symbolically sent forth his two messengers, his majesty *(gā'ôn)* and his fury *(ḥārôn)*, who have overthrown the enemy and consumed them like chaff (v. 7).[19] The warlike, destructive purpose of the enemy is described in verse 9. Typical Near Eastern language of holy war is used in verses 14-16.

b. *The Character of Yahweh's Victory.* This military power, however, is exercised neither by Israel nor through Israel. While the event is described as a battle, it is not a battle in the conventional sense. Freedman states well the point of view of the biblical writer:

> The victory was total—and totally Yahweh's. Israel contributed nothing then or later, except to march under divine guidance. While the poet's view is essentially the same as that of the bulk of biblical writers, historians and prophets, it is radically stated, and suggests a certain background or orientation on the part of the poet, to which the views of Isaiah or Hosea may be compared. But perhaps we should not press a poet too far in any particular direction.[20]

We note that Yahweh is first called warrior *(YHWH' 'iš milḥāmā, v. 3)* in a situation where he exercises his judgment by a nature miracle, where Israel does not fight at all. This is especially decisive since the Reed Sea deliverance forms the paradigm for Israel's future salvation.[21] If one does not take seriously Israel's own understanding of the foundation character of the exodus event, the meaning of holy war in Israel would be little different from that of Israel's neighbors.[22] Patrick Miller in his otherwise excellent treatment of Yahweh as warrior overlooks this testimony of Israel's earliest poem, and so considers the absence of Israel's military participation in the event as a late interpretation reflecting an assumption of human irresponsibility.[23]

c. *The Effect of Yahweh's Victory on the Concept of Holy War.* Yahweh's victory over the Egyptian forces had its effect upon subsequent relations of the people of Yahweh with her neighbors. After the description of Yahweh's victory, the second part of the poem (13-18) describes the march of the people under Yahweh's leadership to Sinai.[24] For our purposes, it makes little difference whether the march is to Sinai or Canaan, for the point is the same. The sea event has a causal effect upon relations with other Near Eastern peoples. The Egyptians went down "like a stone" (v. 5); the nations whom Yahweh's people subsequently contacted were "as still as a stone" (v. 16). Thus the effect of the exodus as a paradigm for Yahweh's saving action in Israel's difficult experiences of the future is found within the poem itself. The passage of Israel through the Reed Sea was the archetype for Israel's passage through the paralyzed sea of nations. Later Old Testament writers follow the lead of the writer of this poem in viewing the sea and exodus as an archetypal event.[25]

Also important is the fact that the exodus event qualified Israel's perception of holy war language. Such language as "tremble" *(yirgāzûn)*, "pangs" *(hîl)*, "dismayed" *(nibhălû)*, "melted away" *(nāmōgû)*, "terror and dread" *('ēmātâ wāpahad)* is holy war language that Israel had in common with the Near East.[26] However, for Israel these words and phrases gain new meaning by their use in connection with the exclusive act of Yahweh at the sea. It is likely that hereafter these clichés had for Israel not simply a meaning common to the mythological frame of reference of the Near East, but rather they incited a memory linked to the exodus event. It will not do merely to compare language across cultures without noticing particularities in a given culture that polarize words toward a different meaning.

d. *Yahweh's War; Yahweh's Kingship.* The exodus event left its mark not only upon Israel's holy war institution, but also upon the institution of kingship. The Song of the Sea climaxes with the kingship of Yahweh. Enthroned in his sanctuary on Mount Sinai, "Yahweh will reign for ever and ever" (v. 18). Yahweh the warrior becomes Yahweh the king. The close relationship of these two institutions is suggested by the form of the poem. Following the introduction the main body of the poem begins with the first thematic statement, Yahweh the warrior (v. 3), and ends with the thematic statement of Yahweh's kingship (verse 18 forms an *inclusio* with verse 3).[27]

The movement of the entire song is similar to the Baal epic, wherein Baal the warrior defeats Yam, then builds a palace and is declared king.[28]

While recognizing the historical basis of the Song, in contrast to the Baal epic, it is important to note other significant differences between this poem and its Near Eastern background. It is not sufficient simply to say that the main difference between Yahwism and its Near Eastern background is that Yahweh is the God of history, for other gods also were involved in battles, and thus entered into their people's history.[29] It is the *way* in which Yahweh entered into history that makes the difference.

The Mesopotamian conception of gods acting in history is well illustrated by the reliefs of Assur-nasir-pal II. These, reliefs from the ninth century BC, show the king attacking the enemy, standing on his war chariot with drawn bow. Above him flies the image of the god Assur, also with bow drawn against the enemy.[30] In a victory relief of the same king, both king and the god above him parade with slung bow.[31] George E. Mendenhall says of this:

> The art expresses even more graphically than the language the fact that there *can* be no conceivable difference of opinion between the policies and operations of the divine state and its ultimate supernatural authority—its "god," which is nothing but the symbol of the state itself: Assur the god *is* Assur the state.[32]

The contrast to the Assyrian conception is not that Yahweh has no people, or that his people do not rely upon power, but that they rely solely upon Yahweh's miraculous power. In the thought of the Song of the Sea Yahweh is involved in Israel's history by the fact that he *alone* is warrior. This experience was institutionalized in that Yahweh *alone* is king.[33] The experience of Yahweh as the sole warrior at the sea results in the experience of Yahweh as the sole king at Sinai.

Other ancient peoples of the Near East testify to the miraculous intervention of their gods, and it is probable that at least some of these testimonies were grounded in fact. Perhaps the best examples are found in the annals of the Hittites. Mursilis II reported in the annals of the first ten years of his reign that his army camp saw an object (*kalmišanaš*) and that this object destroyed the land of the cities of Arzawwa and Apšaš.[34] In the same account this king tells how the gods seized his enemies, who had broken the oath of the covenant, and that brother cast down brother.[35] Later annals relate that the people of Kalašma broke their oath, were seized by the gods, and that brother betrayed brother, friend betrayed friend, and the one killed the other.[36] Mursilis also tells of a miracle that occurred while his army pursued the Sunapaššäer. The proud weather god stood beside the king, and it rained all night so that the enemy could not see the king's troops. In the early morning another storm came up and went before Mursilis' troops, making them invisible to the enemy; the storm suddenly lifted so as to make possible an attack.[37]

In these statements of "miracle," however, it is obvious that the warrior-god does not displace the warrior-man; the king-god does not displace the king-man. Outside of Israel the experience of divinity in history was god *and* king. Within Israel the experience of divinity in history was Yahweh *versus* king. This contrast was expressly stated by Gideon who as a successful warrior was invited by the Shechemites to take the logical step of institutionalizing his status by beginning a dynastic kingship. He replied in terms of the tradition: "I will not rule over you, and my son will not rule over you; Yahweh will rule over you" (Judg. 8:23).[38]

This same radical departure from ancient Near Eastern tradition is demonstrated in the narratives of Samuel by his opposition to ancient Near Eastern tradition as expressed by the demand of the people: "No! but we will have a king over us, that we also may be like all the nations, and that our king may govern us and go out before us and fight our battles" (1 Sam. 8:19b, 20). This demand for human kingship was recognized by the tradition as a rejection of the kingship of Yahweh and was connected with the people's choice of other gods: "They have not rejected you, but they have rejected me from being king over them. According to all the deeds which they have done to me, from the day I brought them up out of Egypt even to this day, forsaking me and serving other gods, so they are also doing to you" (1 Sam. 8:7, 8). This self-conscious contrast to the nations accurately reflects the situation in early Israel as shown in the earliest poetry (see also Num. 23:21; Deut. 33:5). Through her experience of Yahweh's miraculous power at the sea, Israel knew the kingship of Yahweh long before she adopted human kingship.

"The Legend of King Keret" (14th century BC) reveals that the place of the king in the Canaanite city state was approximately that of the king in Mesopotamia.[39] In the legend King Keret leads a military campaign against King PBL in an attempt to secure a bride. Royalty is an attribute of the god El and the text stresses the personal father-son relation of El and King Keret.[40] The concern of the legend is with the preservation of the social order, with appropriate rites of the king "[who performs] on behalf of the community the rites proper to the transition from one phase of nature to the next."[41]

In Egypt, art from the beginning of Egypt's history through the New

Kingdom portrays that Pharaoh was the one element necessary to assure victory over the enemy. King Narmer, perhaps the first king of Egypt, is portrayed on a palette from Hierakonpolis as a towering, godlike figure wearing the white crown of Egypt. A battle mace is in his hand; his left hand is seizing the hair of an Asiatic who is on his knees before him.[42] This palette is dominated by the figure of Narmer who has complete victory over the enemy. Though the Pharaoh himself was a great god, he was not alone, however, but was aided by other gods of the pantheon depicted in the palette by a falcon representing the god Horus.

There are many representations of this artistic theme from every period in ancient Egyptian history, suggesting that the Pharaoh exercised an even greater monopoly of power than did the Mesopotamian and Canaanite king. In Egypt Pharaoh was the state, and in principle no one was free.[43] Thus the portrayal of our poem, ascribing both victory and kingship to Yahweh alone, stands in even greater contrast to the political thought of Egypt where the human king was deified and given responsibility for military and kingship functions.

Israel's radical rejection of human kingship for the sole kingship of Yahweh influenced the literary character of the Song of the Sea. For example, in the Egyptian victory hymn to Ramesses II the king is the central figure. He fights for his army and gives the victory, while the action of the gods supports him.[44] Again, in the Assyrian triumphal hymn of Tukulti-Ninurta I, while the gods and army are more active than in the case of Egypt, the king is nevertheless central.[45] The centrality of human kingship in these hymns is reflected by an emphasis on the first person singular pronoun in the Egyptian, Assyrian, and other ancient Near Eastern war annals.[46] In contrast to this, Yahweh is the chief subject of the Song of the Sea. Pharaoh, on the other hand (along with the "enthroned" of Philistia, the chiefs of Edom, the leaders of Moab, and "the enthroned" of Canaan, all human political leaders), is the antagonist of Yahweh.[47] This antagonism of Yahweh toward political rulers is emphasized by the exodus narratives, as we shall see, and is exemplary of Yahweh's opposition to what is commonly designated as kingship both within and without Israel.[48] Not kingship but his people are the object of Yahweh's concern throughout the poem and narratives.

e. Yahweh's War and Worship. Bertil Albrektson, in a study of the theme of history in Israel's traditions, discovered that Israel differed significantly from her Near Eastern contemporaries in the emphasis upon history in her worship.[49] Though other Near Eastern peoples included a minimal amount of history in their liturgies, Israel's use of this theme was far more extensive. If the Song of the Sea is early as we have assumed, it is the first witness of this phenomenon. The body of the song addresses Yahweh and must originally have had some cultic purpose. The liturgical introduction to the song (vv. 1-2) as well as the liturgical explanation at the end (vv. 19-21) were probably written somewhat later than the poem, demonstrating that the poem continued to be used in the cult.[50]

This early orientation of the cult toward history was essential to the very structure of Israel's life. If Yahweh alone is ruler of his people, that rule must be mediated to Israel's existence as a people, and how else but through the liturgy? The worship of Israel therefore broke out of the usual cultic matters and was oriented toward the celebration and expression of the rule of Yahweh in Israel. Yahweh's foundational act on behalf of his people was celebrated and mediated anew in the act of worship. Holy war as experienced in Israel thus affected the actual structure of Israel's corporate existence.

One song cannot sustain or develop by itself the weight of all this meaning. It can be only an early and fragile witness to a larger stream of conviction, the strength and meaning of which can be understood only by studying other documents, and ultimately by an assessment of the total legacy of the community. Thus we will broaden our research by examining the prose narratives of the sea episode as found in the Book of Exodus.

2. *Narrative Sources.* The narratives of the sea in the Book of Exodus (Ex. 13, 14) are attributed by critical scholarship to the three traditional Pentateuchal sources, J, E, and P. There is substantial agreement on the de-lineation of these sources. We follow here the analysis of Martin Noth who sees in J evidences of the intertwining of two oral traditions.[51]

a. The Sea Event Depicted as Battle. These narratives resemble the Song of the Sea in that they depict the event at the sea as a battle. For example, Israel went up from Egypt "equipped for battle" (13:18). The verb "to encamp" and its cognate "camp" are used both of Israel and Egyptians (13:20; 14:2, 9, 19, 20). While these terms are not necessarily military, Exodus 14:20 speaks of the "camp of Egypt" which is balanced by the "camp of Israel." Since the first refers to a military encampment, it would seem that the second should also have such a reference. The word "fight" is used in 14:14. "Discomfited" (14:24) is a holy war term (see Josh. 10:10; Judg. 4:15; etc.), and "clogging" (14:25), used in reference to chariot wheels, may also refer to such "discomfiture."[52] The Egyptian call for a retreat is in terms of a battle where again the word "fight" is used. The summary statement is the language of military defeat: "Yahweh routed the Egyptians in the midst of the sea"(14:27).

b. *The Nature of the Battle.* As we have seen, the narratives use the conventional language of warfare, but like the Song of the Sea they do not describe a battle between two armies in the usual sense of the word.

A straightforward reading of the several traditions (see note 51) yields the following result: According to J, Yahweh divided the sea by a strong east wind which dried it up so that Israel was able to reach the other bank. The Egyptian army that followed was thrown into confusion, and at the break of day was drowned when the sea returned to its place. While the report is somewhat naturalistic in that the immediate agency was the wind, the narrator interprets the event theocentrically. It is Yahweh who saves Israel from the power of Egypt. E gives a fragmentary witness to only a few insignificant details. P, usually regarded as the youngest source, recounts that Pharaoh set out after the people, and that Moses stretched out his hand and parted the waters so that a corridor was formed with walls of water on either side. Israel passed through this corridor on dry ground. After their passage, Moses again stretched out his hand over the sea and the waters flowed back to drown the Egyptian army. It is evident that while P heightens the point of the miraculous, his account does not differ essentially from that of J. The action was that of Yahweh alone who by an act of nature delivered his people from the Egyptian army. On this central point, the two narratives agree with the song; indeed on this point all witnesses to the sea event, young and old, are in agreement.[53]

What are the implications of this unanimous witness? The two interpreters who on this point best demonstrate the watershed between scholars are Martin Noth and Gerhard von Rad. As a historian Martin Noth simply observes and reports what all the accounts say. He writes:

> The different variants of the story of the miracle at the sea wrought by Yahweh which are in part certain, in part only demonstrable with probability clearly disagree in their representation of the details of the event. But the essential elements of the contents are the same in all forms of the story; and this similarity shows itself all the more clearly against the background of the differences in the individual narratives. All agree in speaking of an act of God in which it was God alone who acted . . . .[54]

He points out that the oldest source, J, is most emphatic on this point:

> According to J, Moses meets the fear of the people with that cry of 'Fear not' which used to introduce the powerful attack of Yahweh to protect his people. Yahweh himself will lead the war, and Israel need only stand there and witness the victory of Yahweh over the enemy (vv. 13 f.). This then is what Moses dares to say. Just as in J Moses is only the messenger sent to the Israelites in

Egypt to announce to them the acts of Yahweh (3:16 f. J), so also now Yahweh himself will do everything.[55]

In contrast to Martin Noth, von Rad argues for "the omnicompetence of analogy" in order to test a historical event, and sees this testing as the basic task of biblical criticism.[56] This means that to understand the rise of Israel the critic must assume that the "real history" of Israel's beginnings was more or less the same as that of other nations, and that in the case of the sea event Israel fought hard just like other peoples had done. In von Rad's view, any uniqueness in Israel's religion was not caused by the juncture of word and deed in actual historical event, but by a later theological reflection that reconstructed past history. Von Rad held the Reed Sea episode was reconstructed by J as a result of fundamental changes that took place in Israel at the time of kingship, especially the development of the Solomonic "enlightenment" which reflected the influence of international wisdom literature on the Israelite tradition.[57]

Most theologians who challenge the exodus tradition of nature miracle either follow von Rad's interpretation or some variant of it to reconstruct "what really happened." For example, Hyatt cites the various elements noted above that suggest a battle, and concludes that these support the probability of a military encounter between the Israelites and the Egyptians, though he admits this is never stated in the narrative. His appeal is to "common sense" which is presumably based on the way things usually happen, in other words, von Rad's "omnicompetence of analogy."[58] Lewis S. Hay sets forth a similar argument in his essay, "What Really Happened at the Sea of Reeds."[59] He admits that his presuppositions are those of von Rad's "holy war," though he gives a different explanation of how the tradition changed to its present statement.[60]

A third interpretation is represented by Manfred Weippert.[61] He notes that in the Near Eastern war annals victory is often expressed as the action of the gods alone, although it is obvious that the armies fought. He maintains that the Old Testament narratives are to be interpreted in the same way, that is, that ascribing victory to Yahweh alone was a Near Eastern way of saying that the troops won. Thus Weippert takes issue with Schwally, Pedersen, von Rad, Miller, and all others who interpreted the Reed Sea event as a pious rethinking or re-theologizing at a time far removed from the realities of the event. On the contrary, Weippert believes that the writers were simply using a conventional formula for describing an army's victory in battle.

A fourth interpretation of the miracle is that of Loewenstamm who holds that in the beginning there was only a myth of Yahweh battling another god, as in the case of the Baal myth. Only later in Israel's history was myth "historicized," and the enemy became Egypt.[62]

We will deal with these interpretations only briefly since an expanded treatment would be outside the scope of our topic.

(1) Let us take Loewenstamm's argument first. As Frank Cross points out, a study of the documents shows that the course of development *within Israel* was not a gradual movement from myth to historicization of myth. On the contrary there was an early break from myth, though as we saw in the Song of the Sea a residue of mythical elements remained. Only with Davidic kingship was there a remythologizing. (For an example, see Psalm 18, especially verses 7-15.) After kingship a renewed emphasis on history occurred, though myth still maintained a greater place in the period of the apocalyptic literature than in early Israel. The movement from dominantly mythical to dominantly historical patterns is not a natural tendency, as evidenced by the perennial resurgence of mythic forms and language in biblical religion, for example, in royal theology, apocalypticism, gnosticism, and the Qabbalah.[63]

(2) To a certain extent Weippert's thesis is obviously tenable. The Near Eastern king ascribed his victories to divinity, and his purpose in recording his annals was to report to the god how he had discharged his obligation as the god's servant. However, an examination of the examples cited for comparison by Weippert reveals that it is after all obvious that the troops fought, or in some cases simply made an appearance as a result of which their "epiphany" frightened the enemy into surrender. In the very few cases where this is not obvious there may well have been a "miracle."[64] At the sea, on the other hand, it was Pharaoh who had the chariotry and who thus terrified Israel. Yahweh had no well-armed troops to make an epiphany; his epiphany must therefore be something else—the storm according to the oldest sources. Infantry had no chance against chariotry unless some unexpected event occurred to give them the advantage.

(3) As for the argument of Hyatt and Hay, there was of course the possibility of a stratagem as is indicated in the Song of Deborah, which in cooperation with a storm might give the infantry the advantage. But while ruses or tricks are clearly indicated on other occasions such as in the Song of Deborah, there is no indication of such a scheme here, nor in any of the exodus traditions. Exodus traditions are often listed side by side with conquest traditions in which the former are stated only as an act of Yahweh while in the latter human fighting is freely acknowledged.[65] This would seem to indicate that the biblical writers were not adverse to reporting that Israel had fought where indeed that had happened.

(4) Most of the above arguments apply to von Rad's interpretation as well. An additional argument is the early date of Exodus 15. If the Song is early, von Rad cannot be right in suggesting that the Reed Sea event was the result of theological reflection in kingship times. Furthermore, J wrote in the monarchic period, when the standing army was a necessary ingredient of empire. It is not likely that a pietistic tradition that Israel need not fight would develop then. In J's view of Israel's paradigmatic event, faith demanded not that Israel fight but that she stand still and wait for Yahweh's act (Ex. 14:13-14) It is more likely that such a statement could be made by J, in a time of empire, only on the basis of a firm tradition of such thought.

Israel's fundamental difference from Near Eastern societies must have a sufficient explanation. This difference is well stated by Martin Noth:

> Yet in spite of all these historical connections and possibilities for comparison, "Israel" still appears a stranger in the world of its own time, a stranger wearing the garments and behaving in the manner of its age, yet separate from the world it lived in, not merely in the sense that every historical reality has its own individual character, and therefore an element of uniqueness, but rather that at the very centre of the history of "Israel" we encounter phenomena for which there is no parallel at all elsewhere, not because the material for comparison has not yet come to light but because, so far as we know, such things have simply never happened elsewhere.[66]

Some of these differences were noted in the song where we saw the relationship between the absence of human warrior and the absence of human kingship.

Our understanding of the Reed Sea event should not center primarily on the physics of the miracle, described somewhat differently in the various sources, but upon the reversal experienced by the people. The community that despaired and expected destruction from the Egyptian army was suddenly saved through an act other than their own (presumably by a violent storm as it is stated in the oldest sources) and this act of grace became the foundation for the community's future life.

c. *Yahweh as Actor: The Key to Israel's Writing of History.* The unique emphasis in Israel's historiography is that Yahweh, rather than any human leader, is the primary subject. This contrasts with the common focus on the king as prime mover of history in Near Eastern annals. Thus, in the J narratives of the exodus event, Yahweh is the central leader. His name appears about a dozen times; he is directly responsible for Israel's salvation. Moses is his servant (14:31) who acts as prophetic mediator of Yahweh's word (14:11-14) and is in the background to the extent that his name is mentioned only three times. Fragmented E gives a similar picture with God mentioned four times (13:17-19), angel of God (14:19) once, and Moses once (13:19). In P, Moses comes somewhat more to the foreground as he is named five times (14:1, 21, 26, 27) and Yahweh is named seven times (14:1, 4, 8, 15, 18, 21, 26).

These figures are somewhat deceiving, however, since Moses acts as prophetic mediator who receives Yahweh's oracles (14:2-4, 15-18, 26) and acts throughout upon them. Thus P is not essentially different from J in setting forth Yahweh as leader of the event.

It is obvious in all recensions that Pharaoh and his host are the antagonists of Yahweh while Israel is the object of Yahweh's concern. While the prose narratives do not call Yahweh warrior nor celebrate him as king, he clearly has the place of political leadership which in Near Eastern annals is assigned to kingship. Yahweh's deliverance of Israel at the sea obviously affected the way history was written, as well as portrayed a new form of political power.

3. *Summary of the Sea Traditions.* The literary history of the sea traditions in the Book of Exodus represent a scope of time of about six centuries. The Song of the Sea, composed in the twelfth century, is the oldest while J, E, and P achieved their present form in approximately the tenth, ninth, and sixth centuries. These traditions thus portray the width and depth of conviction concerning the exodus in Israel, with very little change from the earliest to the latest Old Testament times. The biblical traditions outside the Book of Exodus extend even farther this general picture.

As we have seen all of these traditions (a) portray the event as a battle, the exercise of military power; (b) but they agree that it is not a battle in the usual sense, for Yahweh is the sole warrior who gives political salvation to his people by an act of nature; (c) and they reflect a close relation between historiography and the sea miracle. It is by means of Yahweh's immediate action that the song and prose recensions portray Yahweh's leadership in history. (d) J draws out an implication for faith. At this foundational event Israel was not to fight but to "Fear not, stand firm, and see the salvation of Yahweh, which he will work for you today. . . . Yahweh will fight for you, and you have only to be still" (Ex. 14:13 f.).

(e) The song goes beyond the prose narratives in seeing a causal connection between the miracle and relations with other nations, a connection which may well qualify holy war language of the ancient Near East as it is used in Israel. (f) Also, the song parallels Yahweh the warrior and Yahweh the king: Yahweh alone is warrior and Yahweh alone is king. Yahweh's kingship may also be reflected in the prose narratives by his place as leader of Israel. (g) Finally, the song clearly marks a reorientation of Israel's worship to the leadership and rule of Yahweh in history. The cultic use of material in the Book of Exodus became the chief institutional means for celebrating and perpetuating Yahweh's victory for Israel and his rule over the whole of Israel's life.

B. *Vocation of Moses and Flight from Egypt*

"By a prophet Yahweh brought Israel up from Egypt, and by a prophet he was preserved" (Hos. 12:13). This statement by the eighth-century prophet is an excellent summary of all the traditions in the Book of Exodus that concern the flight from Egypt. Even the Song of the Sea, the only tradition in which Moses is not mentioned, is ascribed to Moses by its liturgical setting.[67] There is no objective ground for doubting the tradition that Moses was associated with the exodus.[68]

1. *Flight from Egypt: A Freedom Movement.* The tradition of the plagues in the Book of Exodus is recounted by J, E, and P.[69] This means that the plague account was also a part of G, the foundational tradition in the pre-kingship period. In addition Psalm 78, a tenth-century psalm, is a variation of the Exodus plague accounts, a fact that again points to the ancientness of the tradition.[70] The narrative of the plagues is thus rooted in the early formative period of Israelite history.[71] Beginning with Exodus 5, it reaches a climax in the Reed Sea accounts (Ex. 14), to which the passover tradition was attached, probably at an early date.[72]

The story of the plagues is one of a conflict between two peoples, although the conflict is not described in terms of a battle as is the crossing of the sea. However, the language of "despoiling" *(niṣṣēl)* the Egyptians mentioned in two summary statements in Exodus 3:22 (J) and 12:36 (J) finds a close parallel in 2 Chronicles 20:25, which tells of despoiling a defeated army. This may suggest that in the view of the writer the people leave Egypt as victors of a battle.[73]

The flight of Israel from Egypt should be set within the context of a larger freedom movement in the ancient Near East. The word "Hebrew" *('ibrî)* appears thirteen times in Exodus 1-10; this is nearly half of all the occurrences of the word in the Old Testament, and represents by far the word's densest usage in any one passage.[74] Its occurrence is always in the oldest recensions of the Pentateuch.[75] This term "Hebrew" is usually regarded as a cognate of the term *"ḥabiru"* (Akkadian), referred to also in Egyptian records in the period between the fifteenth and twelfth centuries. It is generally accepted as referring not to a nationality but to "outsiders" of an inferior social position, a class to which the biblical Hebrews presumably belonged.[76] An example of the freedom propaganda of this movement is communicated in a letter of Rib-Haddi, king of Byblos, to Pharaoh which shows that the *habiru* called on the citizens of an enemy town to depose their leaders by violence.[77] The *habiru* might also attack a town in order to drive out its leaders. The objective of their propaganda was to win the population of "all the lands" to the *habiru,* and to form an alliance so that they "may have peace forever."

It is not my purpose to show that Moses and the Hebrews in Egypt fit the above movement exactly, but only to show that there were freedom movements besides that described in the Exodus, and among the very social class of which the Hebrews were a part.

In contrast to the violence of the *habiru,* however, the conflict of the plagues, like the Reed Sea encounter, was not a battle in the usual sense of the word. Yahweh was the deliverer of Israel and the chief actor in the drama. Pharaoh of Egypt was his antagonist. The historiography of the various recensions in respect to the leadership of Yahweh corresponds to what we have discovered above in the traditions of the sea.[78] One can understand this strange drama between the God Yahweh and Pharaoh only as one understands the role of Moses, the human leader on the side of the slaves.[79]

2. *Birth Story of Moses and His Slaying of the Egyptian.* The birth story of Moses is to some extent similar to a common Near Eastern motif, as illustrated by the birth story of Sargon of Akkad.[80] However, in the Hebrew setting the story is not one of "rags to riches," but moves in the opposite direction. A member of the ruling class, Moses forsakes his status to identify with the slaves.[81]

The two questions that the Hebrew asked Moses in the account of the slaying of the Egyptian raise the fundamental question of political legitimacy, the basis for political authority: "Who made you a prince and a judge over us? Do you mean to kill me as you killed the Egyptian?" (Ex. 2:14). This initial question is central to the entire story and comes again to the surface in the call narrative (3:11, 13; 14:1) and in the narrative of the plagues (5:4, 22-23). This question of power and political legitimacy is not merely a biblical one but was stated rather cynically a century before Moses in a letter of the Prince of Byblos to Pharaoh: "Do you not know the land of Canaan, that it follows behind the one who has power?"[82] Moses on this occasion took the way of the *habiru* freedom fighters. He did not engage in a frontal attack against Pharaoh, but used stealth and a single incident of violence to alleviate the immediate situation. The question asked by the Hebrew, however, made it apparent that a demonstration of power or at least a threat of such a demonstration, was essential to establish political legitimacy not only with Pharaoh but internally with the Hebrews as well.

It may not be insignificant that according to the tradition Moses was of the house of Levi (Ex. 2:1), a house already associated with violence in the Book of Genesis.[83] The story of Moses may well represent the conversion of that house from its "secular" to a "religious" vocation.[84] Only when Moses met Yahweh at Horeb (Ex. 3—4), as Jacob had met the angel at Peniel, was Moses like Jacob converted to a new way in human relations.[85] Before his call, Moses tried to gain freedom by violence; after the call, he became Yahweh's messenger of freedom.

3. *The Call of Moses.* The call of Moses presented a new foundation for political authority. The issue is not only implicit in this material but, as noted above, is explicitly dealt with in the call itself as well as in the conflict between Yahweh and Pharaoh. It is not a question of "powerlessness" against power, for Yahweh specifically states in the call that power will be used:

> I know that the king of Egypt will not let you go unless compelled by a mighty hand.[86] So I will stretch out my hand and smite Egypt with all the wonders which I will do in it; after that he will let you go (3:19, 20).

The point of difference, however, has to do with the application of political power in the situation. In Egyptian political thought the king himself was divine and, as one of the gods, wielded military power to subdue the recalcitrant will. Similarly, the Mesopotamian king, though less than divine, was the representative of the gods to exercise this power in the life of the community.[87] In the call narrative, however, and in the conflict that follows, Moses did not represent the exercise of this power, nor did any other officer of Yahweh's people. Yahweh alone by his wonder exercised this power, and Moses was but his messenger who spoke Yahweh's command and gave his warning.

The call of Moses and the call of Gideon (Judg. 6:11 ff.) are two comparable pre-kingship call narratives in the Old Testament. The call of Moses is represented by both J and E, which probably means that it was found in G before the defeat at Shiloh, thus representing an early testimony to the prophetic character of the call.[88]

It may be significant that the extant Near Eastern calls are accounts of calls to kings or other administrative persons.[89] For example, the Egyptian emperor Thutmosis III recounts how he received his call to be ruler of Egypt,[90] and Hammurabi tells how he was named by Anum and Enlil (Mesopotamian sky and storm gods)

> to promote the welfare of the people . . .
> to cause justice to prevail in the land,
> to destroy the wicked and the evil . . . .

He was "called by Enlil" (associated with coercive political power) to "[make] affluence and plenty abound."[91]

In contrast to these kings, Moses was not to execute Yahweh's deeds but to be his messenger.[92] Kingship was reserved to Yahweh alone. Yet his will needed to be made known. In the case of Moses, the conflict was between Yahweh and Pharaoh. A major purpose of the conflict was that the Egyptians might know Yahweh: "And the Egyptians shall know that I am Yahweh, when I stretch forth my hand upon Egypt and bring out the people of Israel from among them" (7:5; cf. 7;17; 8:10, 22; 9:14-16; 10:1-2). To know Yahweh was to discover a whole new reality of political power: that the God who has no human representative to exercise the coercive "Enlil" power is nevertheless the Lord of history, a God who exercises his power on behalf of the weak against the strong, and who announces his will through his prophet. It was only to his call that the prophet could appeal as validation for his political authority when challenged by the king (cf. Amos 7:14 f.).

The unique relationship of the Israelite prophet to Yahweh's holy war is not found in those passages that present the prophets as like the prophets of Mari, who only gave an oracle to the warrior-king concerning whether or how the battle was to be fought (2 Kings 3). It is rather to be found in the prophet-leader who as God's messenger dared to engage the enemy political leader with Yahweh's word alone. That Moses established a pattern of prophetic leadership in relation to holy war is suggested by the resemblance of the call of Gideon, in which the Egyptian experience is explicitly mentioned, to the call of Moses.[93] Thus the prophetic figure of Moses is important for an understanding not only of the religion but also of the politics of ancient Israel.

4. *Summary of Moses' Vocation and the Flight from Egypt.* The narratives of the conflict of the plague tradition are ancient. The conflict however, is not specifically described in terms of holy war, and thus differs in this respect from the traditions of the sea. Nevertheless, the event was for Israel a freedom movement, and the divine plagues obviously took the place of the human strategy and warfare of conventional battles. The role of the prophetic figure of Moses is essential to the story, and the question of his political legitimacy surfaces in the narrative of his slaying of the Egyptian, his call, and the plagues. To know Yahweh was to experience a

new foundation for political legitimacy. The new foundation was not a human office which represented the divine "Enlil" power, but a prophetic office in which Yahweh's messenger spoke Yahweh's word of promise to the enslaved people and his word of threat to Pharaoh. Yahweh reserved the "Enlil" power to himself, a power which thus could not be manipulated by the human community, but the message could be believed and acted upon by Moses and his followers.

C. *Conclusion*

What conclusion can be drawn regarding these exodus traditions in relation to the questions raised in chapter one? In the first place it is obvious that all traditions emphasize the exclusiveness of Yahweh's miracle. This is true not only of the younger traditions (see the "Type A" scholars), but also of the very oldest, even of the poetical tradition which is assumed to be contemporary with the event. In the second place, the recognition of Yahweh as warrior issues in the recognition of Yahweh as king. Thus the Sinai tradition of Yahweh as ruler is not a "peaceful" tradition held in tension with the war tradition (Smend), but is complementary to the war tradition; in fact, the war tradition is the foundation of the Sinai tradition. In the third place, the tension of history is not "myth" versus Yahweh's act in history (Hanson) but the recognition that Yahweh acts in history by means of a prophetic figure who announces Yahweh's will to save, rather than by means of a representative of the "Enlil" or warrior function.

It is beyond the scope of this work to examine the Sinai narrative to determine whether its testimony agrees with the exodus traditions.[94] We only note here that Exodus 19:3-6 and 20:1-17, those materials within the Sinai tradition conforming most closely to the ancient Near Eastern international treaties, begin with an acknowledgment of Yahweh's deliverance from Egypt, followed by specification, threat, and promise.[95] In other words they include the two main interests of Near Eastern kingship, protection from the outside and provision for internal rule. Furthermore, the covenant law collection (as well as all other law codes of the Pentateuch) is oriented directly to Yahweh and covenant rather than to human kingship, to which all ancient law collections outside of Israel are oriented.[96] The Sinai covenant is indeed a "kingly covenant," as Martin Buber long ago defined it, albeit a covenant that sets forth the kingship of Yahweh rather than the kingship of man.[97]

Chapter IV

The Conquest as Yahweh's War

Like the exodus, the story of the conquest is that of a military operation. Yet the conquest narratives are of a spirit different from those of the exodus. In the exodus Israel is saved from slavery by Yahweh who alone does the fighting, aided by an aggressive, prophetic personality. The conquest involves aggressive warfare in which Israel also fights, led by the warrior, Joshua. While the exodus presents the theological problem of the righteousness of Yahweh's judgment, the conquest poses in addition an ethical problem as Yahweh commands Israel to fight. The problem is well summarized in Joshua 10:40:

> So Joshua defeated the whole land, the hill country and the Negeb and the lowland and the slopes, and all their kings; he left none remaining, but utterly destroyed all that breathed, as Yahweh God of Israel commanded. (Cf. Josh. 10:28-43; 6:21; 8:24 ff.; Judg. 1:17)

The conquest, described differently in Joshua 1—12; 13:1-6; and Judges 1, has elicited three differing interpretive approaches from biblical scholars. Some interpreters have regarded the Joshua narratives as etiological tales that reflect little if any history, and regard the conquest as a primarily peaceful settlement as suggested by Judges 1.[1] Others see the conquest as involving a great deal of violence, based not only on the simplified account of the Book of Joshua, but on the archaeological evidence as well.[2] This violence, some commentators believe, may have been mitigated somewhat by a "peasant revolution" touched off by the invasion of the Yahwists, in which the lower strata of society rejected the oppressive rule of their feudal overlords.[3]

In the biblical texts, the conquest is limited to the lifetime of Joshua, and is clearly set off from the period of the Judges. This is perhaps a simplification, as the Song of Deborah (Judg. 5) suggests. In this song the story of the conquest is continued by telling of the concerted action of a number of tribes that overpowered the Canaanite forces of Sisera. Because of the ancient character of the Song of Deborah, we will examine this source first. Afterward we will examine the conquest narratives, and finally the Shechem covenant of Joshua 24.

A. *The Song of Deborah*

The Song of Deborah (Judg. 5) is one of the two substantial poems in the Bible probably composed in the twelfth century BC.[4] The other is the Song of the Sea, undoubtedly the older, which we have discussed in the previous chapter. The form of these songs resembles the Canaanitic models (which immediately preceded them) more closely than it does the later Hebrew poetry.[5]

Again it should be noted that these ancient poems antedate kingship, and therefore give us a view of Israel's pre-kingship thought regarding history and Yahweh's participation in it. As this is not "primitive" but sophisticated poetry, this means that there was of necessity an educated group in pre-kingship Israel that was capable of leading Israel in the verbalization of her faith.[6]

The Song of Deborah, like the Song of the Sea, is a unified victory hymn. This type of literature is not unique to Israel; it is found both in Egypt and Mesopotamia.[7] These contemporary literary types are important to students of Judges 5 because (a) the life situation for which they were written is beyond dispute, and (b) they present no textual uncertainties due to oral composition and transmission.[8] They contain a mixture of what critical scholars have called "secular epic" and "religious hymnody," as does the Song of Deborah. This invalidates earlier biblical form criticism which separated these two elements in the text, and held that the hymnic elements were a later literary feature.[9] But the unity of hymnic and epic features in Near Eastern victory odes is the rule, not the exception.[10] The Song of Deborah from the perspective of its literary type presents a harmonious whole.[11]

The Song of Deborah is thus a victory hymn that celebrated Israel's military defeat of the northern Canaanite cities. This victory gave to the tribal confederation hegemony over the Esdraelon valley and positions farther north.[12]

THE SONG OF DEBORAH
(Judges 5:1-31)

(1) Then sang Deborah and Barak the son of Abinoam on that day:
(2) "That the leaders took the lead in Israel,
    that the people offered themselves willingly,
    bless Yahweh!

(3) "Hear, O kings; give ear, O princes;
    to Yahweh I will sing,
    I will make melody to Yahweh, the God of Israel.

(4) "Yahweh, when thou didst go forth from Seir,
    when thou didst march from the region of Edom,
the earth trembled,
    and the heavens dropped,
    yea, the clouds dropped water.
(5) The mountains quaked before Yahweh,
    yon Sinai before Yahweh, the God of Israel.

(6) "In the days of Shamgar, son of Anath,
    in the days of Jael, caravans ceased
    and travelers kept to the byways.
(7) The peasantry ceased in Israel, they ceased
    until you arose, Deborah,
    arose as a mother in Israel.

(8) When new gods were chosen,
    then war was in the gates.
Was shield or spear to be seen
    among forty thousand in Israel?
(9) My heart goes out to the commanders of Israel
    who offered themselves willingly among the people.
    Bless Yahweh.

(10) "Tell of it, you who ride on tawny asses,
    you who sit on rich carpets
    and you who walk by the way.
(11) To the sound of musicians at the watering places,
    there they repeat the triumphs of Yahweh,
    the triumphs of his peasantry in Israel.

    "Then down to the gates marched the people of Yahweh.

(12) "Awake, awake, Deborah!
    Awake, awake, utter a song!
Arise, Barak, lead away your captives,
    O son of Abinoam.

(13) Then down marched the remnant of the noble;
        the people of Yahweh marched down for him against the mighty.
(14) From Ephraim they set out thither into the valley,
        following you, Benjamin, with your kinsmen;
    from Machir marched down the commanders,
        and from Zebulun those who bear the marshal's staff;
(15) the princes of Issachar came with Deborah,
        and Issachar faithful to Barak;
        into the valley they rushed forth at his heels.
    Among the clans of Reuben
        there were great searchings of heart.
(16) Why did you tarry among the sheepfolds,
        to hear the piping for the flocks?
    Among the clans of Reuben
        there were great searchings of heart.
(17) Gilead stayed beyond the Jordan;
        and Dan, why did he abide with the ships?
    Asher sat still at the coast of the sea,
        settling down by his landings.
(18) Zebulun is a people that jeoparded their lives to the death;
        Naphtali too, on the heights of the field.

(19) "The kings came, they fought;
        then fought the kings of Canaan,
    at Taanach, by the waters of Megiddo;
        they got no spoils of silver.
(20) From heaven fought the stars,
        from their courses they fought against Sisera.
(21) The torrent Kishon swept them away,
        the onrushing torrent, the torrent Kishon.
    March on, my soul, with might!

(22) "Then loud beat the horses' hoofs
        with the galloping, galloping of his steeds.
(23) "Curse Meroz, says the angel of Yahweh,
        curse bitterly its inhabitants,
    because they came not to the help of Yahweh,
        to the help of Yahweh against the mighty.

(24) "Most blessed of women be Jael,
        the wife of Heber the Kenite,
        of tent-dwelling women most blessed.
(25) He asked water and she gave him milk,
        she brought him curds in a lordly bowl.
(26) She put her hand to the tent peg
        and her right hand to the workmen's mallet;
    she struck Sisera a blow,
        she crushed his head,
        she shattered and pierced his temple.

(27) He sank, he fell,
>> he lay still at her feet;
> at her feet he sank, he fell;
>> where he sank, there he fell dead.

(28) "Out of the window she peered,
>> the mother of Sisera gazed through the lattice:
> 'Why is his chariot so long in coming?
>> Why tarry the hoofbeats of his chariots?'
(29) Her wisest ladies make answer,
>> nay, she gives answer to herself,
(30) 'Are they not finding and dividing the spoil?—
>> A maiden or two for every man;
> spoil of dyed stuffs for Sisera,
>> spoil of dyed stuffs embroidered,
> two pieces of dyed work embroidered for my neck as spoil?'

(31) "So perish all thine enemies, O Yahweh!
>> But thy friends be like the sun as he rises in his might."

1. *A Celebration of Israel's Participation.* In contrast to the Song of the Sea in which there was no human fighting, this song celebrates the fact that the people and commanders "offered themselves willingly" (v. 2, *běhitnaddēb 'ām;* see v. 9). This human effort occupies most of the poem, indeed all of it except verses 3-5, 19-21, 28, 31. The militia of the six participating tribes was led into battle by the prophetess Deborah and the military commander Barak.

While this song is comparable to the victory hymns of Egypt and Assyria, it differs from those literatures at the essential points where Israel's institutions differed. The king was central to victory in the Egyptian and Assyrian examples. He received help from the gods, perhaps even ascribed victory to the gods, but as one of the gods (Egypt) or as a servant of the gods (Mesopotamia) he was centrally involved in the victory.[13] In early Israel, though there was a culture developed enough to produce this outstanding poem, there was no kingship.

In the absence of human kingship, the poem names many different persons and groups, a unique phenomenon in ancient Near Eastern war literature. The name "Israel" makes its earliest appearance in biblical literature in this song, eight times in all, seven times in the first eleven verses.[14] In addition to Israel, the people, Shamgar, travelers, peasantry, Deborah, commanders of Israel, people of Yahweh, Barak, remnant of the noble, Ephraim, Benjamin, Machir, Zebulon, Issachar, Reuben, Gilead, Dan, Asher, Naphtali, Meroz, Jael, Sisera's mother, and the chief of her maid servants

are all mentioned in the song. Four of these persons are women. (Women
are also involved in other war literature, especially as singers and dancers.)

2. *The Confederation of Tribes.* Although Israel had no kingship, she
nevertheless had a structure, a confederation of tribes. The existence of this
pre-kingship tribal federation is strongly contested by some scholars today.[15]
However, this early war hymn clearly acknowledges a reality called "Israel," and even enumerates ten tribes, unlike the Song of the Sea which
does not hint of a confederation. This may suggest that there was a pre-
Mosaic, patriarchal confederation called "Israel" and that this confederation was converted to Yahwism by the Yahweh-worshipers from the
Southern desert.[16]

Israel in the Song of Deborah becomes "the people of Yahweh" (*'am
YHWH,* Judg. 5:11), the only term used of the people in the Song of the
Sea. That this Israel was a confederation of tribes is further suggested by the
fact that ten tribes are named, while only six participated in the battle
(Judg. 5:14-18). The naming of ten tribes indicates that there was an expec-
tation based upon some political reality other than the fact of common participation (of only six tribes) in the battle.[17] That there were ten rather than
twelve tribes would appear to agree with the evidence that the two tribes of
Levi and Simeon were lost to the North,[18] and with that of the later division
between North and South in the time of Rehoboam (1 Kings 11:26 ff.).[19]

3. *Celebration of Yahweh's Victory.* While one partner in the Song is
Israel, the other partner, mentioned even more frequently, is Yahweh.[20] Although the participation of the tribes is the stated subject of the song,
Yahweh is their leader throughout. He is even responsible for the participation of the tribes, and is therefore praised for it (vv. 2, 9). The human leader
most often mentioned is Deborah; she is named only three times (vv. 7, 12,
15).

Even though the involvement of the tribes is the subject of the song,
there is no mention of the tribes' actual participation in the battle (vv. 19-
22). The key word of verses 19-22 is "fought." The subject of this verb is first
the enemy, "the kings" (v. 19), then the stars (v. 20) who fight against the
kings. This mention of the stars is not merely mythological, for the two
references to the torrent Kishon (v. 21) indicate that this is an actual nature
event that changed history.

> The reason for the Israelite military success in the Kishon valley was primarily
> due to the opportune rainstorm (v. 21), which made the plain waterlogged
> and thus hopeless terrain for the Canaanite chariot force....[21]

The naming of the Kishon, the situation of the battle, and the fact that Israel as in the experience at the sea is hopelessly pitted against chariots, all imply that this is fundamentally a historical reference.

The absence of human kingship in Israel means that Yahweh was king of the federation. He was the one who gave unity, direction, and victory to the tribes. Yahweh fought, not through his people, but through a miracle of nature. As noted in the discussion of the Song of the Sea, it is this experience of Yahweh as "man of war" that gives specific and unique character to Israel's experience of holy war. Thus from the beginning of Israel's history as depicted by the Song of Deborah, the poet downgrades Israel's fighting to the point of not even mentioning it. The decisive action in the battle was seen as that of Yahweh, who as political leader of Israel again came to the aid of his people. This basic conviction in Israel's thought—that human fighting was not efficacious in the winning of the battle—is therefore not a late theological development, but dates from the beginning of Israel's history.[22] If we are to take the early poetry at all seriously, it follows that this theologizing was based upon historical events.

4. *The Nature of Israel's Participation.* In the light of the emphasis upon Yahweh's nature miracle, we should look closely at the human participation in the Song of Deborah. There are two types of participation involved: the participation (and nonparticipation) of the tribes which is the subject of the song, and the participation (and nonparticipation) of Jael and Meroz (vv. 23-27). Considering the latter first, Meroz is cursed for not coming "to the help of Yahweh" (v. 23). This phrase, so significant to von Rad for his understanding of Israel's ancient warfare, occurs only once in the Old Testament, while the opposite statement of Yahweh coming to the help of man occurs many times.[23] Seldom if ever is it said in the Assyrian or Hittite Annals that the king helps the gods, but repeatedly the god comes to the help of the king.[24] In the Song of Deborah the phrase in verse 23 is not used of the tribes, but only of Meroz, an entity (town or tribe) which unfortunately is unknown to us.

While Meroz is unknown to us, it is parallel in the song to Jael, "the wife of Heber the Kenite," a "tent-dwelling woman" (v. 24). In the introduction to the hymn, she is mentioned together with "Shamgar, son of Anath" (v. 6), and probably had the same relation to him that Deborah had to Barak.[25] She was a Kenite, a descendant of the father-in-law of Moses, a priestly family as indicated by the fact that her husband had pitched his tent at "the oak in Zaanannim, which is near Kedesh" (4:11). Shamgar is not an Israelite name, but Hurrian. In the El Amarna age many persons with Hurrian and Indo-European names were among the aristocratic, ruling class of Canaan. That he was among this class is suggested by the fact that he was "the son of Anath" (v. 6), a thoroughly Canaanite name used in the Ugaritic tablets of the warrior goddess, consort of Baal.[26] "Anath" indicates that Shamgar was part of the Canaanite military class, perhaps a leader of a mercenary troop or of a Canaanite city, who became a "savior" of Israel (3:31).[27] Though Jael was closely related to the Yahwists, her house had a covenant with "Jabin the king of Hazor" (4:17), the enemy of Israel, as well as a relation of some kind with Shamgar, the Canaanite friend of Israel. Perhaps as a holy woman her prophetic gifts were recognized both by Israel and by the Canaanite city states, though it is obvious that Sisera trusted her liaison relationship with Hazor.[28]

Unlike Jael who surprised Sisera by casting her lot with Israel, Meroz did not come "to the help of Yahweh." This juxtaposition would suggest that Meroz, like Jael, may have been somewhat neutral and friendly with both sides of the struggle but did not cast its lot with Israel, perhaps for fear of reprisals if Israel were defeated.[29] Thus the phrase, to come "to the help of Yahweh," is not used of the Israelite tribes but only of non-Israelites who lived among and were friendly with the tribes, and who in times of crisis came to the help of Israel and Yahweh. Another case in point is the non-Israelite Shamgar (Judg. 3:31). If we thus assume that both Meroz and Jael were outsiders, then the curse and blessing of verses 23-24 correspond to the curse and blessing of the patriarchal promise in its dealing with the outsider (Gen. 12:3), rather than to the promise and threat of the Mosaic covenant, which deals with the insider.[30] The Song of Deborah thus unifies the patriarchal traditions with the Yahwistic ones.[31]

Concerning the other type of participation, that of the tribes, we have seen above that the decisive victory was won by Yahweh through a nature miracle, not by means of the tribes but apart from them. Their cooperation was no doubt important to draw the enemy into the trap of the Kishon and to take political advantage of the event, but in the thought of the poet the trap itself was created and sprung by a force beyond the control of the human community. Israel, through the word of Yahweh given by Deborah, could only cooperate with that power; there was no way by which she could manipulate that power for her own ends. This is not to argue that the tribes did no fighting. It is at this point that the Song of Deborah differs from the Song of the Sea. That difference is not fundamental, however, since in both cases Israel must rely on Yahweh's action for victory. The tribes were involved in what amounts to mop-up exercises after the victory had essentially been won. There is no concept of synergism here, i.e., that Yahweh fought the battle through his people.[32]

This leads us to a discussion of the alleged relationship of the curse in this song (v. 23) and the curse of the Mosaic covenant. Some commentators have argued that while the covenant forms of the Old Testament do not include a demand that the tribes come to the military aid of Yahweh, this is nevertheless to be assumed on the basis of analogy with the Hittite international treaty, where the demand that the vassal come to the help of the suzerain is an important part of the specifications.[33] The Song of Deborah is seen as major supporting evidence that the Mosaic covenant assumed that which the Hittite treaty made explicit.[34]

What may be said in reply to this argument? First, while the analogy of the Hittite international treaty has made an important contribution to Old Testament studies, we must resist the temptation to do our exegesis on the basis of analogy with extra-biblical literature. Rather, we must take seriously those differences which are evident in the biblical literature itself. For example, the Hittite treaty upholds a form of feudalism, but the Mosaic covenant has taken a feudalistic institution and transformed it so that it rejects feudalism by making Yahweh the sole ruler. The Hittite treaty demands that the vassal come to the military aid of the suzerain; the Mosaic covenant includes only nonmartial demands.

Second, in two respects the Song of Deborah does not lend itself as evidence in support of the claim that the Mosaic covenant assumed what the Hittite treaty made explicit. One is the emphasis on voluntarism stated twice in the poem ("the people offered themselves willingly," vv. 2, 9). The other is that the nonparticipating tribes, though derided, are not cursed.[35] The derision of verses 15b-17 should not be confused with the curse of verse 23. Nor should the praise of verses 14-15a and 18 be confused with the blessing of verses 24-27. The tribes are both praised and derided, but in this song they are neither blessed nor cursed.

5. *Leadership in the Song of Deborah.* We have already noted the central place of Yahweh in the Song of Deborah. This is all the more remarkable since the subject of the poem is the voluntary involvement of the people and commanders. The song affirms the leadership of Yahweh by praising him even for the people's response, and particularly by recognizing the decisive nature of the storm.

Besides Yahweh, however, there are other leaders. The first of these is Deborah, named three times in the song (vv 7, 12, 15). A closer look at the place of Deborah in the song will be included in our discussion below of the prose account of the battle of Deborah. The second is Barak who is named once (v. 12). Besides these were the "commanders of Israel" (v. 9). As in the Song of the Sea, Yahweh is here opposed not to the gods but to kings and princes who dare to fight against him (vv. 3, 19). It is surely significant that

Israel has no specialized troops, "the mighty" of verses 13 and 23 (*baggib-bôrîm*). The two times that such troops are mentioned they are on the side of the enemy whom Yahweh opposes.

      6. *The Life Situation in Which the Song Was Used.* Since the Song of Deborah is a victory hymn, it was obviously used in worship. The introduction (v. 1) suggests that the song was composed immediately on the occasion to celebrate the victory. This is quite possible.[36] Certainly it must have been used in subsequent, perhaps yearly, celebrations of worship, and would thus exert a continuing influence in the life of Israel.

      7. *Comparison of the Song of Deborah and the Song of the Sea.* The Song of Deborah is of the same genre as the Song of the Sea; both are victory hymns. While the subject of the Song of the Sea is exclusively the victory of Yahweh by his miracle, the subject of the Song of Deborah is the human participation in the victory. Israel and many involved groups and persons are mentioned. Nevertheless the Song of Deborah resembles the Song of the Sea in that the decisive act was in both cases that of Yahweh. While the respective acts are different enough to give credence to each as an individual event, they are enough alike that the Song of Deborah must have reminded its celebrants of the sea event. The two songs may signify something of a continuous march from the sea to the land of Canaan. The perspective of the first song is forward from the sea to Yahweh's abode, likely Sinai. The perspective of the second song is achieved by a flashback, Yahweh's march with his people from Sinai to the present moment in the land.[37] The Song of the Sea looked forward in anticipating that Yahweh's miracle would affect his people's relations with the nations. The Song of Deborah was a testimony that Yahweh did indeed act again for the salvation of his people from the nations. Thus while both songs are oriented toward Yahweh's miracle and while Yahweh's miracle is in both cases decisive, the Song of Deborah is an adjustment to the fact of Israel's participation in victory. Both of these ancient pre-kingship hymns were a part of Israel's worship. Is it not to be expected that the memory of the events they relate would have an effect on Israel's future wars? The Song of the Sea was a confession foundational to Israel's existence, and thus we might assume that memory to be the more prominent. The Song of Deborah, while an adjustment, is evidence that the memory of the event at the sea was a repeatable experience.

B. *The Prose Narrative of the Battle of Deborah*

      Judges 4:4-22 is a tenth-century prose narrative which relates essentially the same story as the earlier Song of Deborah.[38] Here a small militia of perhaps two hundred men from the tribes of Zebulon and Naphtali (the two most zealous tribes according to Judges 5:18) was hopelessly pitted against the chariotry of Sisera.[39] Although the prose account gives the proper setting (4:6-7) for a nature event such as that described in the song, it does not detail the event itself, but rather simply states that "at Barak's advance, Yahweh struck terror (*wayyāhām*) into Sisera, all his chariots and all his troops" (4:15).[40] The word "struck terror" (*hāmam*) is also found in Exodus 14:24. Striking similarities between the accounts in Exodus and in Judges suggest that the same writer or editor may have been responsible for both, and point again to the fact that conventional holy war language when used by Israel must usually be interpreted in the light of Israel's foundational event at the sea.[41]

1. *Comparison with the Song of Deborah.* It is of special interest that this younger prose account concentrates less on the miracle itself than does the older song, unlike a similar comparison of prose and poetic versions of the sea event. Moreover, the prose narrative has a different emphasis in regard to the leadership. The song names Deborah three times and Barak twice, while the narrative names Deborah four times and Barak nine times.[42] These statistics may be somewhat deceptive, however, since where Deborah and Barak are named together, Deborah is named first (vv. 9, 14). Throughout the narrative, Deborah is the one through whom Yahweh gives the orders which Barak carries out. Also, in the end Barak misses glorification as a war hero since Sisera is killed by a woman (vv. 9, 22).

This change from an emphasis upon the miracle in the older song to a greater emphasis upon the human actors in the younger narrative is contradictory to the claims of many scholars that the earlier thought stressed synergistic action, while the younger thought was less realistic and tended to depreciate human involvement.[43] Perhaps this change reflected in the prose account is to be expected, as the prose was written in the time of the early kings when there was an intensified interest in the army and empire.

2. *Leadership of Deborah the Prophetess.* Deborah is called a prophetess (Judg. 4:4, 5, E). As noted earlier, there is no reason to regard such a designation as a read-back from later times, as there were prophets and prophetesses in Mari as early as the first half of the second millennium, and prophets at Ebla in the mid-third millennium.[44] From her center in Ephraim, Deborah judged Israel, probably giving oracular judgments of the cases which came up to her. However, her task was not necessarily strictly judicial, for the word *šāpaṭ* may mean "to rule" as well as "to judge" and the point of Judges 4 is that she gave a judgment for war with Sisera (v. 6).[45] Her authority was recognized by "Israel," an Israel which at this point cer-

tainly included the tribes of Zebulon, Naphtali (vv. 6, 7), and Ephraim. We have already noted in our discussion of the song that Israel was made up of a federation of tribes.

The action of Deborah in this conflict differs from that of Moses in that Deborah gives a call to Barak, a military leader. This difference parallels the adaptation in holy war itself, that is, as we have noticed, the inclusion of human fighting. It is an adjustment which Moses also made after the exodus by his acceptance of the military role of Joshua (Ex. 17:8-16).[46] Martin Buber was critical of this division between the revelatory office and the military office, feeling that it had the effect of splitting the unity of the sacred and secular. But Buber failed to appreciate the real threat against which the Yahwist tradition was set—the entrenchment of a secular power that would use religion to achieve its own ends. This threat was seen with clarity by Samuel, who accepted the further adjustment of kingship only under great pressure.

While Deborah's call of Barak does represent an adaptation, when viewed from the perspective of the foundational Reed Sea experience, there was nevertheless an attempt to maintain something of the Mosaic concept of political power. The recognized human leader in Israel was a prophetess, whose task was to communicate the will of Yahweh. The call which she gave to Barak, the military leader, was only for the specific task of this one battle (vv. 6, 7). Pre-kingship Israel had no continuous military leadership. The strategy of the battle of Deborah was indicated by Yahweh who would "draw out" Sisera to meet Barak by the river Kishon, a trap that only Yahweh could spring. The glorification of the human military leader was further downgraded by the fact that Sisera fell not by the hand of Barak but by the hand of Jael, a woman.

The story of Deborah shows that the prophetic office of the kingship period had antecedents even in the period of the Judges.[47] The relationship of the prophetess Deborah to Barak had in it the seeds of the conflict which later developed between Samuel and Saul, the conflict between prophet and king.[48] The issue set forth by Hosea in regard to the exodus was also very much alive in the time of Deborah:

> And Israel served for a woman,
> And through a woman was it preserved...
> And through a prophet did Yahweh bring Israel up from Egypt,
> And through a prophet did he preserve... (Hos. 12:13).[49]

This juxtaposition of prophet and woman may not be unrelated to the main point of our discussion. The depreciation of the military hero and the normal concepts of military power was due to the new type of leadership experienced in ancient Israel.

C. The Narratives of Conquest in the Book of Joshua

The Book of Joshua depicts the conquest as three sweeping campaigns. First, the Israelites crossed the Jordan and cut through the heart of the land (Josh. 1—9). Second, they overthrew the coalition of five kings to the South (Josh. 10); and finally, they defeated the northern kings at Merom and occupied their cities (Josh. 11).[50] We must examine carefully the crossing of the river and the battle of Jericho, as these were seen in ancient Israel as paradigmatic of the entire conquest, and then look at the other battles in a more summary fashion.

The story of the crossing of the Jordan and the fall of Jericho is told in Joshua 1—6, nearly one half of the conquest material. Chapter 1 is introductory and is generally agreed to be the work of the Deuteronomic historian.[51] This is followed by the story of the two spies (chap. 2), the crossing of the Jordan (chaps. 3—5:1), the memorial of stones (chap. 4), circumcision, passover, Joshua's meeting with the commander of Yahweh's army (chap. 5), and the fall of Jericho (chap. 6). These chapters are traditionally seen as ancient recensions—J E, or contemporary with J E (tenth to ninth centuries BC)—with several additions by the Deuteronomist and the Deuteronomic historian (seventh to sixth centuries BC).[52]

1. *Crossing the Jordan*. Many scholars hold that some of the Joshua 1—6 materials were used in a cultic ceremony, just as were the two songs (and perhaps some of the other exodus materials as well).[53] The cult in Israel emphasized not conventional cultic matters, but the rule of Yahweh in historical situations, including the conquest. How much of the Joshua 1—6 material in its present form was obtained from a ritual context is open to question. Some commentators would say all of chapters 1 to 6.[54] A convincing case can be made, however, only for chapters 3 to 5. This includes the crossing of the Jordan and the ceremonies at the entry of the land, which are presently inserted between the two narratives of the conquest of Jericho (chaps. 2, 6).[55] We will examine this probable cultic ritual of chapters 3 to 5, then the narrative of the battle of Jericho itself, dealing first with the tenth-to-ninth-century sources and second with the seventh-to-sixth-century sources.

The worship festival was probably a yearly commemoration at Gilgal at the time of the passover in the month of Nisan (5:10-12).[56] It included a procession from Shittim to Gilgal (3:1; 5:10; cf. Mic. 6:5) of which the most important act was the "crossing of the border" (the Jordan River) into

Canaan.[57] This border crossing was regarded by the ancient sources as an act of war. The procession began with sanctification which was required in holy war or in approaching a sanctuary (Josh. 3:5). It was led by the ark, the palladium of battle. From Shittim to Gilgal (Mic. 6:5) was "the decisive movement of the Conquest," just as Gilgal was the battle camp of the conquest (Josh. 10:6).[58] After the river crossing twelve stones were set up in the camp to symbolize the tribal federation (suggesting that the procession was celebrated in the pre-kingship period; 4:2-5, 8-10, 19). Israel was then circumcized in preparation for the passover festival. After the passover was the feast of unleavened bread, which symbolized that the wilderness period was over and that Israel was now living on the land (5:10-12). The ceremony ended when Joshua met the "commander of the army of Yahweh" (5:13-15), probably the divine messenger who led the assembly of Yahweh in battle.[59]

Though Israel's crossing of the border represented an act of war, it was not a battle in the conventional sense of the word. As Cross observes, the "repetition of the Exodus is the transparent symbolism in the processional."[60] Here as at the Reed Sea, Yahweh opened the river and gave the land. In these ancient recensions from the tenth to ninth centuries BC, the pattern of the exodus was used to symbolize the conquest. The miraculous crossing was a "recapitulation" of the event at the Sea of Reeds. This "recapitulation" did not work against Israel's historical consciousness; it was still the Jordan that was crossed, though it was the mighty Yahweh of the exodus who brought Israel through.[61] The Egyptian experience was also referred to by the ancient recensions in Yahweh's response to the circumcision: "This day I have rolled away the reproach of Egypt from you" (5:9).[62] Even more important is the final command, "Put off your shoes from your feet; for the place where you stand is holy" (5:15). The shoe was used in land transactions as a sign of ownership.[63] The holy place of Mount Sinai is now transferred to the land of Canaan.[64] The land belongs neither to Joshua nor to the people, but to Yahweh, who will apportion it justly for the use of his people. Throughout this ancient material, it is also obvious that Joshua's leadership is legitimized by being likened to that of Moses.[65] Though unlike Moses he is a military commander, yet as Moses left Egypt without fighting so Joshua entered Canaan without fighting.

It can hardly be contested that in this ancient literary material the flight from Egypt and the crossing of the sea are used as a paradigm for the conquest. If it is indeed true that these ancient literary sources adapted a cultic ritual from Gilgal (behind which lay the historical event itself), then this paradigmatic use of the flight and sea event was a fact of Israel's pre-kingship period. This characteristic corresponds to the findings of our exegesis of the Song of the Sea in which it was suggested that already there this paradigmatic idea was expressed.[66] The concept of Yahweh fighting the battle and Israel not fighting at all was not a late theological development but was already expressed in Israel's pre-kingship literature, a concept which is there stated as grounded in a historical event.

The additions of the Deuteronomist and Deuteronomic historian of the seventh to sixth centuries BC move farther in the above emphasis.[67] For the Deuteronomic historian the miracle at the Jordan was a sign to the people that Yahweh would drive out their enemies before them (3:10). For the Deuteronomist the twelve stones serve as a teaching function and memorial of Yahweh's miracle (4:6-7). While the crossing for this redactor was due to Yahweh's miracle, he emphasizes Israel's future participation in the conquest when he states that forty thousand of the tribes East of Jordan crossed over fully armed for battle (4:12-13).[68] The Deuteronomist is explicit in showing the Reed Sea as a paradigm for the Jordan crossing, as he exhorts fathers to teach their children that "Yahweh your God dried up the waters of the Jordan for you until you passed over, as Yahweh your God did to the Red Sea, which he dried up for us until we passed over..."(4:23). Yahweh did this "so that all the peoples of the earth may know that the hand of Yahweh is mighty" and that Israel may "fear Yahweh your God for ever" (4:24). These are both political reasons. In a long explanation, the Deuteronomist connects the patriarchal oath, deliverance from Egypt, the wilderness wandering, and the occupation (5:4-7). The Deuteronomic historian goes somewhat beyond the older writers in exalting Joshua, perhaps because of his interest in giving king Josiah a model of leadership to emulate (3:7). However, regarding our central point—that the pattern of the Egyptian experience served as a model for the conquest—there is little difference between the older sources and the younger; the younger Deuteronomistic source may stress human participation somewhat more than the older sources by naming the forty thousand "ready armed for war" who cross the Jordan (4:13).

2. *The Battle of Jericho*   Our study of the battle of Jericho must begin with an attempt to identify the context of the source. One possibility is that chapters 1 to 6 formed a liturgical unity.[69] If this is the case, chapters 3 to 5 qualify the interpretation of the battle of Jericho and show that this battle was understood by ancient Israel in relation to the event at the sea. There is little evidence, though, that chapters 1 to 6 were a liturgical unity.

A second possibility is that the older materials in chapter 6 are also a liturgy of pre-kingship Gilgal. Chapters 3 to 5 would then originally have been a liturgy for a feast of seven days, celebrating the river crossing and climaxing in the passover, while chapter 6 would be a second liturgy for the second seven days, celebrating the present reality of the conquest by ritualizing the conquest of the first city.[70] This view would also imply that chapters 3 to 5 reflect ancient Israel's understanding of the battle described in chapter 6. While this solution may be more plausible than the first, there is little evidence that chapter 6 was tied in such a liturgical manner with chapters 3 to 5.

A third possibility, which we will provisionally accept, is that chapters 2 and 6 formed an ancient nonliturgical narrative unity (tenth to ninth centuries BC) of the battle of Jericho, which was only later placed in its present position.[71] In the study which follows we will distinguish between the older and younger sources where pertinent.

Joshua 2 is an account of the mission of the spies, beginning with their command from Joshua (v.1), and ending with their report to Joshua (v. 24).[72] It tells of the covenant made between Rahab the harlot and the spies, a covenant that is fulfilled as narrated in chapter 6 (6:17b, 22-27).[73] The two chapters are thus tied together by the ancient recensions.

The mission of the spies was not merely to investigate Jericho, but to search out "the land" (seven usages in chapter 2), though Jericho is specifically mentioned (2:1). This suggests that Jericho, the first city to fall, was symbolic of the entire conquest.[74] Thus the mission of the spies was evidently to get the pulse of the population and through this to discern the will of Yahweh for holy war. In the light of the Amarna materials and the spies' contact with Rahab, the spies may actually have functioned as Yahwistic propaganda agents.[75] At any rate the report they bring back is in holy war terms: "Truly the Lord has given all the land into our hands" (2:24a).[76]

The ancient narratives also tie the conquest of Jericho and the land to the event at the sea, as is shown by the statement of the harlot Rahab: "For we have heard how Yahweh dried up the water of the Red Sea before you when you came out of Egypt" (2:10a).[77] According to the older recensions, the harlot expects that Yahweh will act again for his people as he had acted at the sea. The younger recensions make the same point when they show the harlot quoting inversely from the Song of the Sea:[78]

Joshua 2:9 *nāpĕlâ ʾēmatkem ʿālēnû*	(a) *Your terror fell upon us*
nāmōgû kol-yōšĕbê hāʾ āreṣ	(b) *All the enthroned of the land melted away.*
Exodus 15:15b *nāmōgû kōl yōšĕbê kĕnāʿan*	(b) *All the enthroned of Canaan melted away*
Exodus 15:16a *tippōl ʿălêhem ʾēmātâ*	(a) *Upon them terror fell*

In this quotation it seems apparent that conventional Near Eastern holy war language is given a specific Israelite orientation by the exodus event, a fact we have already noted in our discussion of the Song of the Sea.[79]

The decisive act in the fall of Jericho is presented as a miracle (6:1-21), which is then followed by human fighting. While the miracle is connected with a ceremony, the march around the wall, and in this respect is different from either of the two songs, the main pattern of the decisive event followed by human fighting is comparable to the Song of Deborah.[80] Yahweh does not fight synergistically through Israel.

The decisive leader in the battle narrative (6:1-25) is Yahweh, whose name occurs twelve times. He occupies the position that the king occupies in the war annals of Egypt, Mesopotamia, or Canaan.[81] This leadership of Yahweh is maintained despite the leadership of the war leader Joshua, whose name occurs eight times. Yahweh's leadership is maintained by the oracle (vv. 2-5), the ark, and above all by the miracle itself. Besides Joshua, the following are mentioned: the people of Israel, the men of war, the people, the priests, armed men, rear guard, the messengers or spies, every man, Rahab the harlot with her father, mother, brothers, and all her kindred.

Joshua is the human war leader, and as such compares with Barak in the Song of Deborah. The striking difference is the absence of other pro-phetic leadership; Joshua as war leader appears to receive oracles directly (6:2). While a study of the office of Joshua would take us beyond the scope of our discussion, we should note that chapters 3 to 5 emphasize Joshua's close relationship to Moses (3:7; 4:10, 12, 14; 5:15), though all but the last reference are ascribed to the later sources.[82] As war leader in the conquest, Joshua was commissioned by Moses for a special task, just as Barak was commissioned by Deborah in the crisis with Sisera. There is also the ques-tion whether the emphasis placed upon Joshua as war leader may have been due in a certain measure to a read-back from the period of kingship.[83] Perhaps the most significant thing about Joshua in respect to our thesis is that he had no successor.[84] The office of war leader has no continuing place in Israel's early political structure.

The *hērem*, the devotion of the spoils to Yahweh and the destruction of all life (6:17-19, 21), was a holy war institution that Israel held in com-mon with other peoples of the Near East. This is evident from the Mesha tablet where the same verbal root is used (*ḥrm*).[85] It cannot be overem-phasized that all of Israel's institutions of holy war as such were held in common with Near Eastern peoples.[86] The difference between Israelite and other Near Eastern holy war is the radical reorientation of the holy war institutions in ancient Israel in terms of the issue of political power. This is graphically illustrated by the Mesha stone; "I Mesha (the king of Moab)..." stands in contrast to the concept of leadership set forth above, where the leader is Yahweh.[87]

3. *Summary of the Jordan Crossing and Battle of Jericho.* We have examined the narrative of the crossing of the river (Josh. 3—5) and the conquest of Jericho (Josh. 2, 6) independently. On the main point of our discussion their witness essentially agrees. Both the crossing of the river and the battle at Jericho were considered as acts of war and as such were symbolic of the entire conquest. Both emphasized the miracle of Yahweh and both saw the miracle of the sea as the paradigm for Yahweh's activity in the conquest. In relation to the two songs, the crossing of the Jordan resembled most closely the Song of the Sea in that there was no fighting. The conquest of Jericho resembled the Song of Deborah in that there was a decisive miracle followed by human fighting. So far as leadership is concerned there is no essential difference. Yahweh is the leader; Israel is the one whom he leads. Joshua is the military leader on both occasions. He is compared with Moses in the narratives of the crossing, and he might be seen as having a relationship to Moses similar to that of Barak to Deborah in the Song of Deborah. In both the narratives of the crossing and of the conquest of Jericho there is little difference between the older and younger recensions. The element of the *ḥērem* illustrates a main point of our thesis: that while the individual elements of the institution of holy war were common to Israel and her neighbors, the institution as a whole was reoriented in Israel toward a different concept of political power—the unilateral rule of Yahweh.

4. *Other Battles of the Book of Joshua.* The other battle narratives in the Book of Joshua do not require a lengthy discussion. We will not consider historical questions, and will be concerned with recensions only where pertinent.[88]

a. *The Battles of Ai: Joshua 7:1-8:29.* Two battles are described in this material, a defeat and a victory. In the narrative of the battle of defeat (7:1-26), once again we notice the use of spies, who brought back a report and suggested a battle plan (7:2-3).[89] Since we will discuss this account with other narratives of defeat in chapter VI, we will not deal with it further here.

In the victory narrative of chapter 8, no miracle is indicated. Victory is achieved through a stratagem instead. The ark is missing, and even that usually devoted to Yahweh was taken by Israel as booty (8:2, 27).[90] Conventional holy war motifs and language are found in the passage.[91]

The leader Joshua stretched out his javelin towards Ai (8:18, 26) which is likely a parallel with a corresponding act of Moses (Ex. 17:8-13).[92] The fact that Moses stretched forth his staff (Ex. 17:9) while Joshua stretched forth a javelin (v. 18) may reflect the difference in their vocations, the one a prophetic and the other a warrior type.

The name Yahweh is used in the chapter only five times while Joshua, on the other hand, is named seventeen times, a proportion represented mainly by the older sources.[93] Conceivably the influence of early kingship was responsible for this disproportionate emphasis on Joshua. Yahweh does maintain the leadership in the chapter through the oracles and the emphasis upon his command. The fighting men, the people, elders of Israel, rear guard, Israel, all referring more or less to the militia, are also mentioned.

b. *The Treaty of Gibeon: Joshua 9*. Although this is not a battle report, we deal with it briefly for it tells of the establishing of an alternative relationship to the people of Canaan, comparable to that established with Rahab (2:12 ff.; 9:6 ff.). The Egyptian experience (v. 9) and Moses are both mentioned, though perhaps in a younger recension.[94] The fear which the Gibeonites had of destruction shows that such destruction was not merely a later Deuteronomic idea.[95]

c. *The Jerusalem Confederacy: Joshua 10:1-15*. The Israelite Confederation with headquarters at Gilgal now turned its attention to the south. In this narrative the battle was won by a surprise attack followed by three miracles: confusion (v. 10), hailstones (v. 11), and the long day (vv. 13-14), all in the oldest recensions. These miracles and other holy war motifs (vv. 8, 14) emphasize Yahweh's leadership, though the name Yahweh occurs seven times while Joshua is named eight times.[96] Joshua's army is referred to as "people of war," "mighty men of valor," "Israel," "men of Israel," and "all Israel."

d. *The Southern Campaign: Joshua 10:28-39*. Unlike the preceding material, this is a list consisting of brief notes on the conquest of six cities in Judah.[97] Only two of the list include conventional holy war language stating that Yahweh gave the enemy into Israel's hand (vv. 30, 32). Both of the latter are from the oldest sources.[98]

e. *Hazor and the Northern Confederation: Joshua 11:1-15*. The narrative of the battle with Jabin, king of Hazor, and his confederates follows somewhat the same pattern as the battle with the Jerusalem confederacy, though no miracle is involved.[99] Rather, the defeat was achieved by a surprise attack (v.7).[100] The mention of chariots suggests the unequal nature of the contest (v.6). Conventions of holy war occur throughout.[101]

The name of Yahweh occurs six times, and that of Joshua eight times.[102] Despite this the narration maintains the leadership of Yahweh by means of oracles, holy war conventions, and emphasis upon his command. Joshua is related to Moses twice (vv. 12, 15), both times by a younger recension.

Joshua's action in hamstringing the horses and burning the chariots (vv. 6, 9), utterly denying their potential usefulness, illustrates dramatically the ideology of ancient Israel. Superior weaponry was rejected, in order to demonstrate trust in Yahweh as warrior. This stance of weakness was in the first instance no doubt due to political necessity, but was augmented by self-conscious opposition to such weapons. Not only Joshua but David as well acted on the basis of this religious conviction, though David compromised the point (2 Sam. 8:4). Ancient Israel never had a significant number of chariots before Solomon (1 Kings 9:19 ff., 10:26). Israel's criticism of chariotry was linked with her criticism of kingship, because she saw it as belonging to a feudalistic pyramid structure, a slavery as real as the slavery of Egypt (1 Sam. 8:11 ff.; cf. 1 Kings 9:22).[103]

The Song of the Sea portrays Yahweh as fighting against the chariots of Egypt. In Israel, as stated in her ancient poetry, only Yahweh has chariots, and they are the clouds (Hab. 3:8; Deut. 32:13).[104] The Syrians heard the sound of Yahweh's chariots and fled (2 Kings 7:6). Isaiah commands Israel not to rely upon the horses and chariots of Egypt but to rely upon Yahweh (Is. 31:1).[105] Yahweh's chariots are connected not with the leadership of a human king but with the leadership of his prophets (2 Kings 2:11 f.; 6:17; 13:14). This negativism toward the horse and chariot was probably extended by early Israel to other weapons as well.[106]

f. *Summary*. All of the three battle narratives discussed above (sections a, c, and e) included the elements of a ruse or surprise attack; one mentions the occurrence of other miracles. Yahweh is recognized as leader of Israel in each of the three narratives, though Joshua's role is a large one, and his name is mentioned more frequently than that of Yahweh. Joshua is paralleled with Moses by an ancient recension in one of the narratives, while he is stated as being under the command of Moses by a younger recension in another narrative. Israel and the militia are recognized in each of the narratives. Israel's religious ideology is apparent in the aftermath of the battle of Hazor when Joshua hamstrung the horses and burned the chariots.

If we compare the narratives of the Jordan crossing and conquest of Jericho (sections C.1 and C.2 above) with these battle accounts, it is evident that the former narratives view the particular action described as symbolic of the entire conquest, while the latter simply relate individual episodes. These former narratives, as well as the significant battle accounts from the rest of the book, stress the fact that ancient Israel was an inferior power in numbers, in social organization, and in weaponry. This weakness was not merely the result of political necessity, but, as we have seen, represented a self-conscious rejection of superior weaponry, grounded in reliance on the act of Yahweh.

D. The Shechem Covenant

The covenant event at Shechem (Josh. 24:1-28) is isolated from the rest of the Book of Joshua in terms of both literary and tradition history.[107] It is fundamentally made up of an ancient unified text, which may have had a few ancient supplements, followed by a Deuteronomistic editing.[108] This latter is difficult to assess since the tradition of the Book of Deuteronomy is old (a core goes back to ancient Shechem) and is rooted in worship experiences that celebrated covenant, perhaps the Horeb (or Sinai) covenant itself.[109] There should be little doubt concerning the unity of the foundational text, which has patterns parallel to the international Hittite treaty forms, though the feudalistic kingship structures served by the Hittite forms are revolutionized.[110] The historical situation of the Shechem passage may have been the celebration of the extension of the Sinai covenant to the Shechemites, or a covenant between certain Northern tribes and other groups.[111] This Shechem covenant may have formed the constitutional basis of Israel during the period of the Judges.

The patterns of this covenant (v. 25, *bĕrît*) reflect the interests of any government—external and internal order—though the emphasis is inverted as compared with the Sinai covenant.[112] The historical introduction deals with warfare. This takes the form of a prophetic oracle (v. 2) with Yahweh speaking throughout (except for v. 7a?). The oracle begins by saying that on the other side of the Euphrates the patriarchs served other gods. Then Yahweh became their leader and increased their community. In Egypt Yahweh gave them not military leaders but prophetic and priestly leaders, Moses and Aaron. Both the plagues and the sea traditions are mentioned by the ancient source. The foundational war act of the Shechem covenant, like the Sinai covenant, is the act of Yahweh's deliverance from Egypt. The historical recital differs from the Sinai covenant, however, since here the Egyptian deliverance is followed by conflict with the Amorites who fought with Israel beyond the Jordan. But Yahweh gave them into Israel's hand (v. 8). Also the king of Moab fought against Israel (v. 9), but Yahweh delivered Israel out of his hand (v. 10). After Israel crossed the Jordan, the men of Jericho fought against Israel, but Yahweh gave them into Israel's hand (v. 11).[113]

All the above is from the oldest source which states that in the foundational act of deliverance from Egypt Yahweh alone acted, while in the conquest instances Israel fought, though Yahweh was responsible for her victory. This candid recognition of the differences in the two types of action should give us some confidence in Israel's historical veracity in reporting about the Egyptian event. The two events, deliverance from Egypt and conquest, were not far apart historically and may not have been far removed in time from this celebrating community at Shechem.[114] The conventional holy war language, "I gave them into your hand" (vv. 8, 11), with its counterpart, "I delivered you out of his hand" (v. 10), may well have been given specific Israelite meaning by the paradigmatic event of the exodus that precedes it (vv. 5-7); in any event such language is closely tied to Israel's salvation history.[115]

The younger Deuteronomistic source enlarges the Balaam reference (9b, 10a) and lists the peoples who fought against Israel in West Jordan. Thus the younger source emphasizes with the older that there was human fighting. The younger source makes explicit that which is implicit in the older sources, the denial of the efficacy of all human fighting: "And I sent the hornet before you . . .; it was not by your sword or by your bow" (v. 12).[116] Yahweh did not use human weapons. It would appear that here again the statement is ruled by the exodus paradigm. Though both older and younger writers maintain their historical realism by reporting that in the later battles Israel fought, Israel's situation in these later battles corresponds with that of the exodus event in the fact that she was politically and militarily weak. The miracle of the exodus event was therefore historically relevant even when Israel fought.

It is significant that the occasions of the human fighting are set forth within the historical introduction. The oldest and youngest sources are in agreement that even when Israel fought it was not an obligation, as is the case in the international treaties. In early Israel Yahweh alone was obligated as king and warrior. Any fighting by Israel was placed in the introduction to the covenant along with his act, and the efficacy of the human fighting was denied.

Obligation as emphasized in this covenant had to do with loyalty to Yahweh and to him only. The emphasis upon choice and decision reflects the kind of political leader that Yahweh is, and the kind of institutions by which he rules. The difficulty involved in that choice is stressed in the ceremony that follows (vv. 19, 22), ascribed by Noth to the Deuteronomistic source.[117]

According to the text, the life situation in which this covenant was made was the cult: Israel presented herself before Yahweh (v. 1).[118] Israel's cult had to do primarily with the rule of Yahweh, giving form to her existence as a nation. Cult, prophetic word, and dedication to a new experience of political power were here integrally related.[119]

In this ceremony Joshua as leader fulfills a prophetic function. In the light of the absence of other prophetic leadership in the Book of Joshua, might it be that he functioned throughout the time of conquest in more of a prophetic role than the narratives imply?[120]

E. Conclusion

In this chapter we have reviewed many different types of material: a victory hymn, holy war narratives, a cultic processional ritual (Gilgal), and a covenant ritual (Shechem). In this diverse material there are remarkable points of agreement. The victory hymn, the holy war legends, and the covenant ritual mention human participation in battle. Yet all of these materials ascribe victory to Yahweh. Some testify to his victory as an act of miracle, independent of the human fighting. Two holy war legends ascribe his victory to a ruse or surprise attack.

The ritual procession of crossing the Jordan is an exception to the above in that this symbolic act of war, a transparent recapitulation of the act at the sea, was accomplished by Yahweh's miracle alone. Here is an "idealization" of the conquest. Yahweh opens the river to lead Israel across. There is no fighting, not even Yahweh's act of judgment. He gives the land to his people. This "idealization" was made in pre-kingship times and was continued in both early and late sources. It is obvious that the early sources regard the sea event as the pattern for the conquest. The late sources amplify even further the paradigm of the exodus event.

This use of the exodus and sea event as a paradigm is also found in the narrative of the conquest of Jericho, again in both the older and younger sources. It is transparent in the Song of Deborah. This emphasis qualifies conventional holy war language, as the narrative of the battle of Deborah substitutes conventional holy war language for the miracle set forth in the song. Even the holy war language in the battle narratives where the exodus event is not mentioned probably evoked in early Israel the memory of an event like that of the sea as the archetype for the present battle.

It is significant that the writer's use of the paradigm did not negate Israel's historical memory, at least insofar as we can tell. Human fighting is freely acknowledged in all the materials, except of course in the crossing of the Jordan. Yet the military situation in the conquest was similar to that at the sea in that Israel was militarily inferior to the enemy, both in terms of social organization and weaponry. Joshua's hamstringing the horses and burning the chariots suggest that that inferiority was not only forced upon Israel but was abetted by deliberate religious choice. Ascription of the victory to Yahweh had social and political meaning; it was not merely a pious phrase.

All of these materials set forth Yahweh as leader, though the Joshua war narratives name Joshua more often than Yahweh. The relation of the prophet (or prophetess) to this type of Yahweh leadership is suggested by the Song of Deborah and is emphasized even more by the prose narrative (Josh. 4). The prophet is the leading human figure representing the federation, and the military leader is called and directed by him/her to meet the individual crisis. The military leader does not hold a permanent office in the confederation. The Joshua materials may seem to contradict this, but Joshua is seen in the sources (both older and younger) as carrying out the command of Moses, and he has no successor at his death. Joshua may well have been given a call through the prophetic personality to fulfill a special task. In addition, in Joshua 24, Joshua himself fulfills a prophetic function. May this have been his original and most basic function, and may he have functioned as leader more in terms of giving oracles to the enquiring tribes (Judg. 1) than the Book of Joshua implies? At any rate the Deborah-Barak relationship suggests that the later Samuel-Saul and prophet-king relationship had deep pre-kingship roots. As we have seen in chapter III, the roots of the prophet as theo-political leader go back to Moses himself. This prophetic concept of leadership is intrinsically related to the new concept of political power.

Finally, what can be said about this material in relation to the issues raised in chapter I? (1) Again we have seen that the emphasis upon Yahweh's miracle and the downgrading of human fighting is decisive both in the most ancient materials as well as in the younger materials. If there is any difference, some of the younger materials may move slightly toward an emphasis on greater human activity. This finding contradicts the view of the "Type A" scholars that the minimizing of human fighting is a later theological development. (2) Equally important, most of the materials that emphasize miracle do not do so merely by using generalized holy war language, but set forth the event in terms of the paradigm event at the sea. This is against the conclusion of Weippert that the miraculous interpretation of holy war characteristic of Israel's ancient sources is no different from the emphasis of the Assyrian Annals. Israel emphasizes from earliest times an original event of Yahweh's intervention which becomes the paradigm for the holy wars that follow. (3) The leadership of Yahweh is maintained throughout. A voluntary commitment to his sovereignty is emphasized in the Shechem covenant. Thus while Yahweh is seldom if ever called "king" in these passages, his central position in these materials is the same as that ascribed to the king in comparable ancient Near Eastern writings.

Chapter V

From the Judges to King David

The period of the judges, extending across the twelfth and eleventh centuries, appears in the biblical narrative as a time of conflicts and battles with numerous neighboring tribes and nations. Historically, it cannot be divided neatly from the conquest, although the present text delineates the period sharply with the death of Joshua.[1] The significant conflicts included:

Enemy	Judge-leader	Century	Reference
Cushan-rishathaim of Aram Naharayim	Othniel	12th	Judg. 3:7-11
Moab	Ehud	12th	Judg. 3:12-30
Canaanite coalition	Deborah; Barak	12th	Judg. 4:1-5:31
Midianites	Gideon	12th	Judg. 6-7
Ammonites	Jephthah	11th	Judg. 10:6-12:7
	Saul	11th	1 Sam. 11:1-11
Philistines	Shamgar	12th	Judg. 3:31
	Samson	12th	Judg. 13:1-16:31
	Eli	11th	1 Sam. 4:1-7:2
	Samuel	11th	1 Sam. 7:3-11
	Jonathan	11th	1 Sam. 14:1-35
	Saul	11th	1 Sam. 28:1-29:11 31:1-7
	David	11th	1 Sam. 17:1-58 23:1-5
Amalekites	Saul	11th	1 Sam. 15:1-33
	David	11th	1 Sam. 30:1-31

There were also the battles of Abimelech (eleventh century, Judg. 9), the battle of the tribe of Dan for Laish (twelfth century, Judg. 18), and the civil war against Benjamin (eleventh century, Judg. 19-20).

Most of these battles did not involve all Israel. The redactors of this material gathered together disparate narratives featuring the exploits of local military leaders who only occasionally achieved political authority beyond their own tribe. These leaders ruled over "Israel," a term used rather loosely for a contracted or expanded entity of tribal units. Most of these military men were not religious leaders interested in a revival of Mosaism, but were motivated by a craving for personal revenge (Judg. 8:18 ff.), outbursts of national feeling (Judg. 3:16 ff.), or desire for position (Judg. 11: 7 ff.).[2]

Of these battle narratives, only four portray the battle as won by the miraculous intervention of Yahweh. These are the battles of Deborah against Sisera (Judg. 4—5), Gideon against the Midianites (Judg. 6—8), Samuel against the Philistines (1 Sam. 7), and Jonathan against the Philistine garrison (1 Sam. 14). We have already discussed the first of these, and have noted its significance due to the nature of Judges 5 as a primary source.[3] This account maintained that victory resulted from Yahweh's intervention through an act of nature, though there was human cooperation in preparing the trap and in taking advantage of Yahweh's act. The importance of prophetic leadership is obvious for this type of experience just as it was necessary for the event of the sea, where human military action was entirely lacking.

In this chapter we will concentrate especially upon the battle of Gideon against the Midianites and the battle of Samuel against the Philistines, as well as upon the changes in leadership that these events occasioned. The rest of the conflicts will be dealt with in summary fashion.

A. Gideon and the Midianites: Judges 6—8

The individual narratives of Judges are bracketed by an editorial framework which in the case of the Gideon narratives consists of 6:1-10 and 8:28.[4] The Gideon narratives, found between these passages, are much older than the framework itself.

1. *The Prophet's Indictment: Judges 6:7-10.* The editorial framework of the Gideon narrative includes the story of a prophet (6:7-10) whom Yahweh sent to the assembly of Israelites to indict them for their apostasy.[5] This story along with the ancient narrative of Deborah (Judg. 4) witnesses to the presence of the prophet in the judges period.[6]

The institutional setting in which the prophet spoke is suggested by verse 7, which says that Israel "cried to Yahweh," meaning that Israel had gathered to make a public lament because of their bondage. In this assembly Yahweh through his prophet presented his legal case (*rîb*, pronounced rîv) against his people, explaining why they were in bondage (cf. 10:6-16).[7] The prophet began his case by telling of the deliverance from Egypt in words very close to Exodus 20:2: "I led you up from Egypt, and brought you out of the house of bondage; and I delivered you from the hand of the Egyptians" (6:8, 9).[8] Here again, in material which may date to the ninth century, the Egyptian deliverance leads the list of Yahweh's acts for his people, and may well be the paradigm for the acts which follow and for the statement of the occupation: "I ... gave you their land" (6:9). This characteristic also occurs in the ancient legal case formula of the Philistine and Ammonite war: "Did I not deliver you from the Egyptians and from the ... Philistines?" (10:11)[9]

The presentation of Yahweh's legal case continues by referring to the first commandment (6:10). It is obvious that this case is based on the Sinai covenant, and in this introductory framework (perhaps placed in this position by the Deuteronomist) it is applied to the Midianite difficulty.[10] Thus in the introductory framework, at least by the seventh century BC, and probably before, the Midianite oppression is explained in terms of the events of the exodus and of Sinai.

2. *The Call of Gideon: Judges 6:11-32*.[11] This is the only ancient narrative in the Book of Judges where Yahweh calls his servant in a direct way.[12] In this respect the call of Gideon compares to the call of Samuel (1 Sam. 3:2-14) of the same general period, to the call of Moses of the exodus period, and to the later calls of the writing prophets (Is. 6; Jer. 1; Ezek. 1-3; etc.)[13]

The call of Gideon is unique among all of these calls in that while it is direct, Gideon is not designated as the bearer of Yahweh's word, but is commissioned for a military act. In this respect the call is more like that given by Yahweh through his prophetess to Barak (Judg. 4), or through his prophet to Saul (1 Sam. 9).[14] The direct nature of this call to a military leader is a fundamental distinction, making the call of Gideon unique and isolated from all other calls of the Old Testament.

This call of Gideon is obviously patterned after that of Moses, to which it compares even in some of its formulations:[15]

The Commission (cf. Is. 6:9)

Judg. 6:14 Go in this might of yours and deliver Israel from the hand of Midian; do not I send you?	Ex. 3:10 (J) Come, I will send you to Pharaoh that you may bring forth my people, the sons of Israel, out of Egypt.

The Objection (cf. Jer. 1:6)

Judg. 6:15   And he said to him, "Pray, Lord, how can I deliver Israel? Behold, my clan is the weakest in Manasseh, and I am the least in my family."

Ex. 3:11 (E)   But Moses said to God, "Who am I that I should go to Pharaoh, and bring the sons of Israel out of Egypt?"

Promise of Divine Help (cf. Jer. 1:8)

Judg. 6:16   And Yahweh said to him, "But I will be with you...."

Ex. 3:12 (E)   He said, "But I will be with you...."

Signs

Judg. 6:17   And he said to him, "If now I have found favor with thee, then show me a sign that it is thou who speakest with me...."

Ex. 3:12 (E)   He said ... "And this shall be the sign for you, that I have sent you: when you have brought forth the people out of Egypt, you shall serve God upon this mountain."

Besides this formal similarity to the call of Moses, the Egyptian deliverance is specifically mentioned as a contrast with Israel's present difficulty, and as the paradigm for Israel's deliverance:

> (Gideon speaking): "And where are all his wonderful deeds which our fathers recounted to us, saying, 'Did not Yahweh bring us up from Egypt?' But now Yahweh has cast us off, and given us into the hand of Midian." And Yahweh turned to him and said, "Go in this might of yours and deliver Israel from the hand of Midian; do not I send you?" (6:13, 14).

While the call concerns Yahweh's act and Gideon's response to it (vv. 11-24), the second part of the story (vv. 25-32) has to do with Gideon's response to the first commandment through the destruction of the altar of Baal. Thus in its general structure this call is comparable to the message of the prophet in Judges 6:7-10 in that it emphasizes the two foundation pillars, the exodus and the Sinai covenant.[16]

There are evidences of Israel's compromise with the Canaanite order in this call. For example, Gideon is addressed as a mighty man of valor (*gibbôr heḥayil*, v. 12), a term designating specialized troops and not used in earliest times of Israelite militia.[17] Adjustments to the environment such as these may account for the fact that while Moses was commissioned to deliver his people as a bearer of Yahweh's word, Gideon's call is to military action and is isolated from all other direct calls in this respect.[18]

3. *Gideon's Battle: Judges 7:1-22.*[19] The theological concept of Yahweh's fighting for his people is expressed in the oracle to Gideon (7:2-3):

"Yahweh said to Gideon, 'The people with you are too many for me to give the Midianites into their hand, lest Israel vaunt themselves against me, saying, "My own hand has delivered me." ' "[20] Gideon reduced the number of his men, first by calling for volunteers and then by a "test" of how the volunteers drank (vv. 3-8).[21] While the numbers are exaggerated, the theme of the reduction in numbers should be taken seriously.[22] Gideon fought the Midianites with a small body of men, employing some kind of ruse tactics such as those described. In the confusion that followed, the Midianite marauders mistook friend for enemy and proceeded to destroy each other. Again the fundamental action was seen as that of Yahweh:

> They stood every man in his place round about the camp, and all the army ran; they cried out and fled. When they blew the three hundred trumpets, Yahweh set every man's sword against his fellow and against all the army . . . (7:21-22).

As this narrative stands, it compares somewhat with the battle of the Song of Deborah, where the decisive battle was fought by Yahweh, and where Israel afterward pursued the enemy. If, however, Gideon's pursuit of the enemy (7:23 ff.) is a confusion of this narrative with a narrative of revenge, then the battle (7:19-22) compares to that described by the Song of the Sea where Israel did no fighting.

The call of Gideon and the description of the battle suggest that the ancient narrator viewed this confrontation as analogous to the event at the sea. Later enlargements to be found in the narrative only accentuate this point. As Robert Boling says of the victory:

> It was, at last, no contest (vv. 16-22). Gideon did no fighting, and Yahweh won. The victory was strictly analogous to the one at the Reed Sea (Exod. 14—15), and it made good the promise of Deut. 32:36.[23]

We assume in our discussion that the characteristics of Yahweh's war recounted in the narrative have roots in history. Even those who do not make this assumption and who see in the narrative the report of a successful local battle which was only later reoriented to the Israelite league must acknowledge that it is thus reoriented even in the early sources on the basis of the older exodus event.[24]

The ancient narratives and the younger framework agree on the essential point that the event of the exodus is the paradigm for the understanding of the battle of Gideon. This point (that the exodus is used as a paradigm), which relates to the battle of Jericho as well as the battle against Midian, is not considered by von Rad when he writes of the transformation of these narratives due to the Solomonic enlightenment.[25]

4. *The Office of Gideon: Judges 8:22-23.* What was the office of Gideon? Surely he was not a prophet, though his call is comparable to a prophetic call. This call, inasmuch as it is the only direct call given to a military person in the Old Testament, would seem to be a compromise move toward kingship, inasmuch as we have examples of such calls given directly to kings in Near Eastern literature.[26]

One would expect Gideon to be classified as a judge, but the verb "judged" *(šāpaṭ)* is never used of Gideon.[27] Perhaps the office of judge is nevertheless indicated by reference to the ephod (8:24 ff.).[28] The act of judging may have involved the mobilization of Israel for a Yahwistic war, or it may have referred to the interpretation and application of the law.[29]

Gideon, of course, did not become a king.[30] The request of the "men of Israel" to Gideon associates deliverance from the enemy with kingship: "Rule over us, you and your son and your grandson also; for you have delivered us out of the hand of Midian" (8:22). We have noted that this connection of military deliverance with kingship was already made in the Song of the Sea, and that it was a common connection in the literature of the ancient Near East.[31] In the Song of the Sea, Yahweh was recognized as deliverer and king in the absence of a human deliverer. A similar connection is implied in Gideon's answer to the men of Israel. The deliverance had occurred by the miracle of Yahweh, evidently with no fighting on the part of Gideon and his troops. Gideon, true to Yahwism as rooted in the Mosaic tradition, answered these "men of Israel" by saying, "I will not rule over you, and my son will not rule over you; Yahweh will rule over you" (8:23). Gideon saw the rule of Israel by a man as a contradiction to the rule of Yahweh.

There is no reason to doubt that this Mosaic Yahwism existed in the time of Gideon.[32] While this understanding of human rule and divine rule as incompatible is unique in ancient Near Eastern literature, the memory of divine rule prior to human rule is found in Akkadian literature, in a description of the first world: "Formerly kingship did not exist in the lands, and the rule was given to the gods."[33] In contrast to other Near Eastern nations, the roots of Israel's religious dogma were found in the experience of holy war itself, more precisely in the experience at the sea. This experience had its implications not only for warfare as we have seen in the battle of Gideon, but also for the very structure of Israel's political existence. Ancient Israel was free from the slavery of Egypt and from the oppressive character of government founded upon human violence.

Gideon's rejection of monarchy is followed by Abimelech's acceptance of it (Judg. 9). However, Abimelech was not king over "Israel," though some Israelites were involved in his "island of monarchy at Shechem."[34] His kingship represented a return to the pre-Israelite (Canaanite) political organization of that city.

Robert G. Boling observed of this turbulent period:

> . . . it is impossible to make sense out of the welter of traditions by thinking of Israel in this early period in geographical terms. Israel is, rather, a movement straining to remake the country through individuals who have agreed to live under one law, modeled on the international order, with Yahweh as their only king and with all the uncertainty that belongs to such a style of life.[35]

B. Samuel and the Philistine Conflicts.

A third battle narrative that sets forth Yahweh's action as decisive to victory is Samuel's battle against the Philistines (1 Sam. 7), a battle that occurred sometime after the fall of Shiloh (1 Sam. 4). Martin Noth regards this narrative as the creation of the Deuteronomic historian.[36] But this chapter, along with the so-called "anti-kingship" sources of 1 Samuel, should not be too hastily written off as a younger and thus less reliable source. Other scholars regard these materials as more ancient.[37]

1 Samuel 7 emphasizes that Yahweh in the time of Samuel established peace between Israel and the Philistines:

> So the Philistines were subdued and did not again enter the territory of Israel. And the hand of Yahweh was against the Philistines all the days of Samuel. The cities which the Philistines had taken from Israel were restored to Israel, from Ekron to Gath; and Israel rescued their territory from the hand of the Philistines. There was peace also between Israel and the Amorites (7:13-14).

This statement is expressly contradicted in 1 Samuel 9:16, 10:5, 12:2 ff., 19 ff. The very reason for the people's demand for kingship in chapters 8 to 12 is the Philistine threat. This would indicate that chapter 7 is an independent ancient tradition inserted here by the Deuteronomic historian even though it does not coincide with the tradition of chapters 8 to 12.[38] Even under David the Philistine cities were not made a part of Israel's territory but were subjected to Israelite tribute (2 Sam. 8:1). The Deuteronomic historian certainly knew this fact.

There are other indications that his chapter is not simply a creation of the Deuteronomic historian as Martin Noth has argued. In verse 2 the specific mention of time, "some twenty years," is probably Deuteronomistic, while the more indefinite statement, "a long time passed," is likely a part of the original narrative.[39] In style and content, chapter 7 is tied to chapters 5 and 6, the reestablishment of Israel after the Philistine defeat.[40] Furthermore, the ceremony of putting away the foreign gods (v. 4) is an ancient one, much older than the Deuteronomic historian (see Gen. 35:2 ff.); the water ceremony (v. 6) is also ancient, not found in Deuteronomy. Finally, the sacrifice made by Samuel at Mizpah is hardly according to Deuteronomic law, nor was the building of the holy place at Ramah (vv. 9, 17). It is therefore likely that this material is fundamentally ancient, and that it was preserved at this holy place of Mizpah. Its latest date may be as early as the time of David, as the narrative may constitute a criticism of David's warlike activity.[41]

W. F. Albright proposes a solution to the divergent traditions of Samuel, not by forcing a choice between the apparently contradictory roles posited for Samuel (judge, prophet, priest) but by arguing for the genuine complexity of the person of Samuel, whom he regards as the first great religious reformer since Moses.[42] He sees Samuel as whipping up patriotic and religious fervor to the point where he won one or more victories over the Philistines. As a result of these victories the Israelites were able to exact important concessions from the Philistines, while remaining somewhat under their subjection in a calculated truce (1 Sam. 13:19-23).[43]

1. *Return of the Ark and the Plagues: 1 Samuel 5 and 6.* First Samuel 7:2-17 deals with the two fundamental interests of any state, internal order (vv. 2-6, 15-17) and external security (vv. 7-14).[44] The section begins with a reference to the ark, which ties the material to chapter 5 and 6. The return of the ark was regarded by both the Philistines and Israel as a defeat for the Philistines, and this defeat was the foundation for the new order which Samuel afterward established.[45] The basic authenticity of the return of the ark (chaps. 5—6) is not to be doubted, as the description of the pestilence sent by Yahweh which occasioned the return strongly suggests a bubonic plague. Nearly every Near Eastern source from the Late Bronze Age indicates some type of pestilence, and Joshua 22:17 as well as this narrative reveals that bubonic plague was present in Israel in the Early Iron Age.[46] The similarity between this plague and the deliverance from Egypt was obvious to the ancient writers, and it is explicitly referred to in two places: 4:8b: "These are the gods who smote the Egyptians with every sort of plague in the wilderness"; and 6:6: "Why should you harden your hearts as the Egyptians and Pharaoh hardened their hearts?"[47] The seven months of 6:1 may be a parallel to the seven days of Exodus 7:25.[48] It would seem evident that the development of the narrative in 5:6-12 and 6:1-6 was strongly influenced by the narratives of Egyptian plagues.

The peace upon which Samuel was able to establish the new order was therefore founded on an experience of deliverance which the early narrators themselves saw as analogous to the deliverance from Egypt. The ark was delivered from the Philistines, just as Israel had been delivered from Egypt, by the power of Yahweh alone. Israel did not raise a hand. The Egyptian event thus provided the pattern for understanding the return of the ark, a fact which must have had its effect both upon the morale of Israel and upon the hesitancy of the Philistines.

2. *Reconstruction of the Internal Order: 1 Samuel 7:3-9.* That Samuel did not build the new order around the ark may have been due to his own appreciation of the corruption of the previous order. In any event, Samuel restored neither ark nor priesthood.[49] Nevertheless the new order was not a "secular" order of human kingship, but a cultic order, which had to do not merely with cultic practice but with the rule of Yahweh alone (vv. 3-5). While the language of this passage may be younger and Deuteronomistic to some degree, the idea is not.[50] It deals with the first commandment, which is fundamental to the earliest "*rîb*" poetry, in which Yahweh's case against the people is presented, and to the "*rîb*" oracles of the ancient prophets.[51] Samuel acts throughout as priest and above all as a prophet in that he intercedes for the people:[52]

> Then Samuel said, "Gather all Israel at Mizpah, and I will pray to Yahweh for you" (v. 5).
>
> And the people of Israel said to Samuel, "Do not cease to cry to the Yahweh our God for us, that he may save us from the hand of the Philistines." So Samuel took a sucking lamb and offered it as a whole burnt offering to Yahweh; and Samuel cried to Yahweh for Israel, and Yahweh answered him (vv. 8, 9).

By this intercession Samuel is linked with Moses (Ex. 32:30 ff.; cf. Jer. 15:1). Thus here again the paradigm for Israel's understanding of this crisis is the Egyptian deliverance and the wilderness experience.

Besides acting as priest and prophet, Samuel functioned as judge: "And Samuel judged the people of Israel at Mizpah" (v. 6b). It seems evident in this context that Samuel's judging concerned Israel's sin and relationship with Yahweh. Though close to the idea of intercession, the judging probably had to do with the "*rîb*," a speech in which the judge or prophet presented Yahweh's legal case against his rebellious people (cf. 1 Sam. 12:7; Deut. 32; Mic 6:1-8) concerning their sin and faithlessness to the order of Yahweh. It is in this context that Samuel's position as a judge should be understood (vv. 15-17). In the Mosaic order apodictic and casuistic law are experienced within the context of covenant relationship. The judging of Israel's relationship with her political leader Yahweh is concerned with faithfulness to his law in the relationship between covenant members.[53]

3. *The Philistine Conflict: 1 Samuel 7:7-14.* Samuel's reconstruction of Israel's internal order and the gathering at Mizpah, based upon Yahweh's victory through the return of the ark, was a threat to Philistine hegemony to which they immediately responded (v. 7). The subsequent victory over the Philistines is clearly somewhat overstated (vv. 13, 14), as we have noted above. What is the writer's intention? Can it be directed against the war policy of David or later kingship, based on his conviction that Samuel's new order was sufficient to control the Philistines? In any case, this obvious exaggeration should not detract from the probability of some kind of victory or "stand-off" achieved under Samuel with regards to the Philistines.[54] The background of the plague with its resultant terror may well have set the mood for an event such as that described here (v. 10).

The role of Samuel in the battle is not that of a military leader. Here again, it is important to see how the exodus, Israel's most fundamental experience of Yahweh's war, fits into Yahweh's new prophetic-cultic order described above, an order which is contrasted to human kingship in 1 Samuel, chapters 8 to 12. Hans Joachim Stoebe points out that verses 10 to 14 do not portray the event in the conventional manner of holy warfare.[55] Samuel does not in the power of the Spirit call up the militia for a war campaign (contrast 1 Sam. 11:6 ff.). He is not a war leader who by divine support achieves victory. Fundamentally, the Israelites appear to do nothing, but attack only after the battle is decided. Stoebe holds that this emphasis upon Yahweh's miracle betrays a considerable distance between the writer's theologizing and the event itself. He suggests that the presentation betrays a relationship with the law of kingship, Deuteronomy 17:14-20, and perhaps illustrates how the functioning of such a kingship was thought possible without power.[56] Stoebe thus views the battle as a late theological fiction, and does not regard the miracle of Yahweh as the central historical event of Yahweh's war.[57] Yet this does not prevent him from understanding important aspects of the text: that Samuel exercised in this battle only a prophetic function, that the victory was won by Yahweh's miraculous action, and that this was related to Israel's radical criticism of human kingship (chaps. 8—12).

Stoebe's view of this text as a reconstruction by later theologians is contrary not only to our own interpretation of this particular text, but to the central thesis of this book as well. We have asserted that the theologizing was not a (false) reconstruction of the events of history by a later piety but was rooted in actual events, among which the exodus was foundational.

This event had enough analogies throughout Israel's experience of confrontation with far superior foes that it could be used as the paradigm both in terms of enabling Israel to expect such an intervention in times of difficulty, and as strategy for facing the difficulties themselves. Such an interpretation is credible in an actual life situation only within the context of a prophetic-cultic order as described above, and only if a people are committed to the seeming powerlessness which an order of this nature demands. That Samuel's new order was not without precedent, but was a reflection of that of Deborah and above all, Moses, has been discussed above.[58] The temptation of the heirs of such a tradition is that the enthusiasm of faith may exaggerate Yahweh's victory (vv. 13-14) in the interest of nationalism. A more sober assessment might have resulted in a better discernment of Yahweh's purpose and a realignment of the community to the realism of his rule.

4. *The Issue of Leadership: 1 Samuel 8-12.* First Samuel 8 to 12, one of the most astonishing statements in all of ancient Near Eastern literature, should be approached first of all as a unit. The traditional approach of beginning by dividing the material into anti-kingship (8:4-22; 10:17-27; 11:14—12:25) and pro-kingship sources (9:1—10:16; 11:1-13) is misleading. Seen as a whole the text alternates between a narrative of a meeting (8:4-22), action (9:1—10:16), a meeting (10:17-27), action (11:1-13), and a meeting (11:14—12:25).[59] It is only in the meetings that one would expect issues to be discussed. The records of the meetings should not necessarily be considered unhistorical; rather, the historical veracity should be evaluated following an examination of the issues as they are set forth. The fundamental question is not simply the pro and con of kingship, but how to deal with the whole issue of kingship. This is the case even in the so-called pro-kingship sources.[60] Using traditional materials, the Deuteronomic historian is trying to harmonize the historical fact of Yahweh's covenant with the Davidic dynasty and the older historical tradition that Yahweh's kingship supersedes the human institution of kingship.

This problem is succinctly stated in each of the reports of meetings:

> (Yahweh speaking): " . . . they have not rejected you, but they have rejected me from being king over them" (8:7b).

> (Samuel speaking): "But you have this day rejected your God, who saves you from all your calamities and your distresses; and you have said, 'No! but set a king over us' " (10:10).

> (Samuel speaking): " . . . You said to me, 'No, but a king shall reign over us,' when Yahweh your God was your king" (12:12).

This rejection of Yahweh elicited not only a theological objection, but a political objection as well. The rejection of Yahweh was linked with the rejection of the cultic-prophetic type of political leadership that Samuel represented (8:7b), a leadership that based its authority not upon coercion but upon the people's choice of Yahweh (7:3-4), a leadership without army or police service to enforce Yahweh's will.

The two major responsibilities of the state, internal government and external security or warfare, are underlined in the demand of the people:

> No! but we will have a king over us, that we also may be like all the nations, and that our king may govern us and go out before us and fight our battles (8:19b-20).

Samuel criticizes the usual way human kingship carries out the first function, internal government, in 1 Samuel 8:11-18. Each aspect of this criticism can be documented as characteristic of Canaanite kingship from the Ugaritic texts.[61] Samuel likens kingship to the slavery experienced when Israel was subjected to an outside power (v. 18). The passage thus suggests that Israel learned these "ways of the king" not through her own later experience of kingship but through her periods of subjection to the kingship of outside powers. As early as the reign of Solomon, Israel's kingship incorporated these "ways of the king" which she had experienced from the nations, and it was the very issues set forth by Samuel in chapter 8:11-18 that caused the division of the kingdom under Rehoboam (1 Kings 11:26—12:16).[62] The fact that the tradition of freedom from human kingship was a major causative factor in the early split of the kingdom suggests that such freedom existed in the pre-kingship period. Israel did not need to learn about kingship from her own adoption of the institution. She had learned her lesson well by experience in Egypt and in the city states of Canaan.[63]

The criticism of the internal policy of kingship is closely linked to the criticism of the war policy of kingship (1 Sam. 8:11, 12). Indeed, criticism of the latter is the main thrust of this entire section of 1 Samuel; it is the issue addressed in both of the action narratives (9:1-10:16, see esp. 9:16b and 10:1b; 11:1-13). In the three narratives of meetings (8:4-22; 10:17-27; 11:14—12:25) each of the arguments in response to the people's demand for kingship is linked to the salvation history which sets forth Yahweh as Savior (*môšia'*, 10:19) rather than a human king who would save them.

> (Yahweh speaking): "According to all the deeds which they have done to me, from the day I brought them up out of Egypt even to this day, forsaking me and serving other gods, so they are also doing to you" (8:8).

(Samuel speaking): "Thus says Yahweh . . ., 'I brought up Israel out of Egypt and I delivered you from the hand of the Egyptians and from the hand of all the kingdoms that were oppressing you. But you have this day rejected your God, who saves you from all your calamities and your distresses; and you have said, 'No! but set a king over us' " (10:18-19a).

(Samuel speaking): "When Jacob went into Egypt and the Egyptians oppressed them, then your fathers cried to Yahweh and Yahweh sent Moses and Aaron, who brought forth your fathers out of Egypt, and made them dwell in this place. But they forgot Yahweh their God; and he sold them into the hand of Sisera. . ., and into the hand of the Philistines, and into the hand of the king of Moab. . . . And they cried to Yahweh, and said, 'We have sinned, because we have forsaken Yahweh. . .; but now deliver us out of the hand of our enemies, and we will serve thee.' And Yahweh sent Jerubbaal and Barak, and Jephthah, and Samuel, and delivered you. . . . And when you saw that Nahash the king of the Ammonites came against you, you said to me, 'No, but a king shall reign over us,' when Yahweh your God was your king' " (12:8-12).

It is significant that all three statements of Israel's rejection of Yahweh in favor of the institution of kingship view that rejection in relation to Yahweh's deliverance from Egypt. Yahweh, the war-god, who delivered his people from Egypt, is now rejected in favor of a human deliverer, a human king. We have seen in our discussion of the Song of the Sea how Yahweh's deliverance of his people was the foundation for his kingship.[64] The same point, made in Israel's earliest tradition, is being made here. The new crisis in the history of Israel was that whereas in other crises Israel had repented and had turned back to the kingship of Yahweh, in this new crisis Israel turned to a deliverer of her own devising, a human king. Like other nations, Israel, through political restructuring and the manipulation of power, would now deliver herself. Comparisons with other peoples had made Israel painfully conscious of the differences between her values and those of her enemies, values which affected her political organization and war technique.

The narratives in question consider the problem of political power and direct their criticisms both at internal rule and at warfare. Neither of these general objections are used by the Deuteronomic historian in his criticism of individual kings.[65] Since the Deuteronomic historian is positive in his attitude toward the Davidic dynasty, these objections to kingship can hardly be credited to him.[66] Israel's early poetry and early names in Israel witness to the fact of Yahweh's kingship before Israel had human kings.[67] Israel's relatively late acceptance of the institution of kingship, the conflict between prophet and king throughout Israel's kingship period, and the continuity of

Israel after the collapse of the kingdom all testify to the ancient nature of the anti-kingship tradition. In view of the fact that writing and transmission of the tradition in the ancient Near East was to a large extent dependent upon the structures of kingship, it is remarkable that the anti-kingship tradition was preserved at all.

Today the historical value of the anti-kingship tradition is being reconsidered, and there is increasing agreement that the tradition is not the result of after-the-fact theological reflection but that it was a religious conviction which actually entered into the shaping of Israel's history.[68] We have noticed furthermore that the anti-kingship tradition is closely linked with the tradition of Yahweh as Israel's savior in warfare, and that this is the fundamental argument against human kingship.[69] Therefore the anti-kingship tradition and the tradition of Yahweh as Israel's only savior in battle stand or fall together as historical realities which actually shaped Israel's history.[70] If the anti-kingship tradition is not the result of a mere theological reflection upon Israel's history, the tradition of Yahweh as Israel's only savior is also no mere theological reflection.

The absolute nature of Israel's opposition to kingship is graphically set forth in 1 Samuel 12:16-19. Samuel's problem was to harmonize the will of Yahweh as expressed in this passage and the will of the people, a harmony attempted mainly in the action narratives, but also in the narratives of the meetings. No canonical pro-kingship thought was in favor of accepting what would be, either ideally or in practice, a mere borrowing from the nations. As Roland de Vaux has pointed out, both so-called pro- and anti-kingship lines of thought

> are inspired by the same conception of power, one which is fundamental to Israelite thought, the conception of theocracy: Israel is Yahweh's people and has no other master but him.[71]

The practice of the politics of the nations is seen by the Old Testament as unbelief, in the sense that the state itself is nothing other than an order that mistrusts God and his rule.[72]

Samuel's attempt to harmonize the demand of the people with the will of Yahweh is worked out along the lines of Israel's compromise on the question of Yahweh's war, as set forth in the two action narratives (1 Sam. 9:1—10:16; 11:1-13). The king is to be designated by Yahweh through the prophet, but as "prince" not as "king" (*nāgîd* not *melek*; see 9:16), he is to function in relation to the prophet in holy war.[73] How successfully this solution actually functioned in history will be the subject of the next two chapters.

C. *Jonathan's Attack at Michmash: 1 Samuel 14*

A fourth battle narrative of this period in which Yahweh's intervention is decisive is that of Jonathan's successful attack on the Philistine garrison at Michmash (1 Sam. 14). This narrative is generally accepted as quite accurately revealing the historical background of the conflict.[74] The battle is important to our thesis only as it shows that in the time of Saul, Israel still operated from a position of military weakness and relied upon Yahweh's miracle rather than on military superiority. The theological theme is expressed in 14:6: "Nothing can hinder Yahweh from saving by many or by few." The statement of this conviction, confirmed by a sign (14:9-12), is followed by the account of Jonathan's attack in which about twenty Philistines were killed (v. 14). Following this there was panic and an earthquake (v. 15), a continuing tumult in the camp of the Philistines (v. 19). When Saul and his people entered the battle, among the Philistines "every man's sword was against his fellow, and there was very great confusion" (v. 20). The confusion was taken advantage of by the Israelites who had concealed themselves in the hill country of Ephraim. "So Yahweh delivered Israel that day" (v. 23). If this narrative is seen in isolation, its warfare theology is not particularly different from the warfare mythologies of other Near Eastern states, for no statement is made here about the deliverance from Egypt.[75] But the name Yahweh is used, a name that in the exodus story is closely linked with that liberation. It is likely that in every situation Israel saw Yahweh's intervention to deliver his people in light of the Egyptian experience, even when the connection is not explicit in the narrative.

D. *Minor Local Battles*

In the narratives of the local battles led by Othniel, Ehud, Abimelech, and Jephthah no specific miracles are reported. Except for the account of Abimelech (whose battle against the Shechemites illustrates the developing relationship between the Israelites and certain Canaanite towns)[76] both the ancient narratives and the Deuteronomist relate that the spirit of Yahweh came upon the person and that Yahweh delivered the enemy into Israel's hand.[77] In these battles the human leaders figure prominently, though the theological statements clearly assert that the leader is Yahweh.

E. *The Federation's War Against Benjamin: Judges 19-20*

In addition to these battles led by judges against Israel's enemies, we will consider the war of the federation against the tribe of Benjamin occasioned by the tribe's violation of covenant law (Judg. 19—20).[78] The offense was called "wantonness in Israel" (20:6, 10), a technical term signifying the violation of divine law. This law was especially severe in sexual matters because of Israel's tension with Canaanite practice. Since the crime at Gibeah was not punished locally, the Levite divided the body of his concubine into twelve pieces, sending one piece to each tribe (19:29). In response to this summons the tribes assembled first at Mizpah, perhaps because this was close to the scene of the crime.[79] The assembly, meeting in the presence of Yahweh, decided to avenge the crime. Since the tribe of Benjamin refused to hand over the guilty persons, the tribes waged war against the Benjaminites.

The story reveals the close relationship which existed among federal warfare, the law, and the cult. Because the divine law was broken, Israel assembled "before Yahweh" for discussion and judgment. Afterward the men of Israel "arose and went up to Bethel" where they inquired of Yahweh about the strategy of the battle (20:18; cf. 20:23, 26-28).[80] Directions for the battle were received through the priests by an oracle (see vv. 27, 28), a familiar method in the ancient Near East. The defeat of Benjamin is described as follows: "And Yahweh defeated Benjamin before Israel; and the men of Israel destroyed twenty-five thousand one hundred men of Benjamin that day. . . ." (20:35).

It is significant in terms of our thesis that no single leader is named. Throughout chapter 20, frequent references are made to the "people of Israel," the "people," "tribes of Israel," "men of Israel," and "Israel."[81] The leaders are mentioned only once as the *pinnôt*, literally "the corners," the "chief supports," the prominent men.[82] The lack of emphasis on human leadership is also found in the narrative of the federation's battle against the Philistines, a battle ending in Israel's defeat (1 Sam. 4). Here again the leaders are not named, though the priests, Hophni and Phinehas, accompanied the ark into battle.

F. Two Battles of Saul: 1 Samuel 15 and 17

We close this analysis with a few observations on two battles of Saul. The first battle was an attack on Amalek, a nomadic tribe south of Judah (1 Sam. 15). The battle was sponsored by Samuel, motivated not by immediate provocation, but because the Amalekites had opposed Israel in the desert (15:2).[83] The complete destruction of the enemy *(hērem)*, including the hewing up of the enemy before the divinity, was an ancient Near Eastern practice followed under certain circumstances, and was probably a part of the life of some of the clans before they entered Israel.[84] We can only note what the new organizational structure of kingship made possible in regard to this ancient religious enmity. The earlier battle with the Amalekites in the wilderness (Ex. 17:8-16) was evidently a defensive battle, in which the symbolism of Yahweh's action was seen as the effective agent in the battle. Now it is Saul, the anointed of Yahweh, who as agent of Yahweh and at the command of the prophet attacked an unsuspecting enemy. The new organization and manipulation of political power made possible the use of violent power in support of religious hostility against an unsuspecting enemy.

The writer is not critical of Samuel and the incident must be judged within the context of the religious and ethical perceptions of ancient times. The writer is critical of Saul, however, who bent the tradition of the religious war to suit his own purposes of economic aggrandizement and power. This incident occasioned the final break between Samuel and Saul.

A second battle of Saul is that against the Philistines (1 Sam. 17), in which David's speech states well the theology of Israelite warfare:

> Then David said to the Philistine, "You come to me with a sword and with a spear and with a javelin; but I come to you in the name of Yahweh of hosts, the God of the armies of Israel, whom you have defied. This day Yahweh will deliver you into my hand . . . that all the earth may know that there is a God in Israel, and that all this assembly may know that Yahweh saves not with sword and spear; for the battle is Yahweh's and he will give you into our hand" (1 Sam. 17:45-47).[85]

Here the theology of warfare is expressed both negatively and positively. Although Israel fought, Yahweh did not save with, by, or through Israel's sword or spear. While David used an instrument, a sling, thus making the narrative different from the sea event, Israel nonetheless operated from a position of military weakness, and the disparity is not a mere theological fiction. While this view of warfare has a certain relationship to Near Eastern mythological thought, its specific orientation is Israelite, with its polemic against the military armor and weapons that kingship might provide by its more sophisticated social organization:

> Then Saul clothed David with his armor; he put a helmet of bronze on his head, and clothed him with a coat of mail. And David girded his sword over his armor, and he tried in vain to go, for he was not used to them. Then David said to Saul, "I cannot go with these; for I am not used to them" (1 Sam. 17:38-39).

This polemic is related to the explicit statement of 17:45 ff. which we have just discussed. H. W. Hertzberg aptly states in regard to the description of the ensuing battle:

What is stressed here, and was certainly taken up and celebrated by the community which heard this story and handed it down, was that God had done his saving work without there having been a sword in the hand of his chosen instrument.[86]

G. Conclusion

It is obvious that the traditions of this period are disparate. Of the four battles in which miracles occur, one compares with the event at the sea where the action is all Yahweh's, two tell of miraculous events followed by human fighting, and one shows human participation preceding the miracle. Of the seven battle narratives in which no miracle is reported, four state that Yahweh smote the enemy before Israel, three report a battle involving more than one tribe, one tells of the confederation fighting against a member tribe, another concerns a purely local matter, one is a ruthless battle of Saul against an ancient enemy, while the last tells of unexpected victory by an antiquated weapon, and includes a polemic against contemporary weaponry associated with kingship. This polemic undoubtedly relates to Joshua's destruction of horses and chariots discussed in chapter IV of our work.

We make no attempt to harmonize these accounts, realizing that we are dealing with diverse material. Neither the Bible nor life is made up of closely congruous events which fit neatly into a theological history. But does this lack of consistency imply that neither the ancient sources nor the Deuteronomistic sources had a unified conception of a theological-political order, and thus of warfare within that order? On the contrary, we have noted that there was a theological conception of Yahweh as the sole ruler of Israel, an understanding that all the sources dealing with the question combined with the conception of Yahweh as Israel's only savior in battle. This emphasis on Yahweh as sole savior, characteristic of all the exodus narratives, is expressly tied to the kingship of Yahweh in the Song of the Sea. This tie of Yahweh as savior and king is also made in all three of the narratives which are critical of human kingship (1 Sam. 8:8;10:18 f.; 12:8-12). Thus there is after all something of a sorting out of the war traditions. The theme of Yahweh's intervention, patterned after the intervention of the sea, rather than the theme of Israel's participation in the fighting, is the tradition which is stated as decisive of Israel's peculiar political structure.

On the other hand, the "pro-kingship" narratives of 1 Samuel 8—12 which contribute to an adjustment to human kingship (recognized by the "anti-kingship" narratives as becoming like the nations) are narratives that include no miracles. In the narrative of 9:1—10:17, Samuel anointed Saul because *Saul* would deliver Yahweh's people out of the hand of the Philistines (9:16; 10:1). The narrative of 1 Samuel 11:1-13 bases Saul's kingship squarely upon his victory over the Ammonites in the delivery of Jabesh-Gilead. Whatever controls might be established to keep Saul's kingdom from becoming entirely like the nations, this order is quite in contrast to Yahweh's Sinai order as founded upon his deliverance at the sea. Israel's transition to human kingship followed the change to human participation in warfare that Israel had also experienced. The order founded upon Yahweh's miracle was exchanged for an order that moved toward the human manipulation and control of political resources involving violent power.

Let us now relate this chapter to the issues as set forth in chapter I. In the first place, some of the most ancient as well as the younger holy war materials set forth the present battle in terms of the ancient paradigm of the sea. This result favors Weippert's view that the depiction of Yahweh as the sole agent of holy war, along with the consequent minimizing of human fighting, was not a late theological reflection, but is found in the most ancient narratives. On the other hand, we disagree with Weippert in our finding that Israel's narratives and poetry use not merely generalized motifs of holy war comparable to the Assyrian Annals, but the motif of the ancient sea tradition as the paradigm for subsequent holy war. Thus there is a distinctive Israelite theology in regard to this important emphasis on miracle in holy war.

In the second place, according to these narratives this concept regarding Israel's ancient holy war forms the foundation of Israel's theo-political order, an order in which Yahweh alone is king, grounded in the claim that Yahweh alone is Israel's savior. The tension of Israel's history, as set forth in these narratives, is not a tension between "holy war as Yahweh myth" versus "holy war as Yahweh's action in history" (Miller-Hanson), but between holy war as applied to the historical situation by a prophetic type of leadership that points anew to Yahweh's miracle (Israel), versus holy war as applied to the historical situation by a kingship type of leadership that as servant of divinity exercises the "Enlil" or "warrior" power common to other Near Eastern nations. Thus the tension is similar to that set forth by Smend, except that it is not a result of polarization between two separate traditions of Israel's early history (holy war and covenant). To the contrary, it was grounded in an early tradition of Israel's experience in holy war itself, a tradition that formed the foundation of the new structure for Israel's theo-political existence and set her at variance with her neighbors and at tension within herself when tempted to become like her neighbors.

Chapter VI

A Theology of Defeat

This chapter departs from the linear treatment of history in this book to date, to deal with the concept of defeat, a minor emphasis of the early periods of Israel. We insert this treatment here since the theme of defeat becomes dominant with the narratives of kingship, and it is the major preoccupation of the Deuteronomic historian in his unified work from the Book of Judges through 2 Kings.

A. *Narratives of Defeat*

Accounts of defeat are found as a minor emphasis in the wilderness and conquest periods. The first such relates the defeat at Kadesh-barnea (Num. 14:39-45).[1] After the Israelites had heard Yahweh's judgment for their refusal to occupy Canaan, they changed their minds and decided now to enter the land. But Moses said:

> Do not go up lest you be struck down before your enemies, for Yahweh is not among you. For there the Amalekites and the Canaanites are before you, and you shall fall by the sword; because you have turned back from following Yahweh, and Yahweh will not be with you (Num. 14:42 ff.).

As Yahweh's presence was the important factor in victory, so his absence resulted in defeat.

A second narrative (Josh. 7), recounting Israel's defeat at Ai in the period of the conquest (a consequence of the sin of Achan), presents four aspects of Yahwistic holy war theology:[2]

(1) Yahweh gave Israel into the hands of the Amorites (7:7).
(2) If Israel is destroyed, what will Yahweh do for his great name (7:9)?

(3) Yahweh's action was not arbitrary but was the result of Israel's disobedience to Yahweh's covenant (7:11).

(4) Yahweh would be with Israel no more, unless the things devoted *(ḥērem)* to Yahweh would be destroyed (7:12).[3]

A third narrative of defeat is from the period of the judges, telling about the capture of the ark by the Philistines (1 Sam. 4).[4] The defeat was probably seen as a judgment upon the leadership of Eli and his family, since his progeny was nearly wiped out. The writer's view is that Yahweh himself had defeated Israel before the Philistines (4:3). The document also recognized that the presence of the ark did not insure that Yahweh would fight for Israel (4:3 ff.).

In summary, it is evident that these narratives, all early, represent a reversal of the usual concept of holy war.[5] In one, Yahweh deserts Israel, and so Israel is defeated. In another, Yahweh, in terms of holy war language, gives Israel into the hands of the enemy as punishment for transgression of the covenant. In yet a third, Yahweh smote Israel before the enemy. Thus at least in the last two there is the concept of Yahweh at war against his own people.[6]

B. A Comparative Theology of Defeat

Since these accounts in written form do not precede kingship, we might ask whether this interpretation of defeat was held in the pre-kingship periods or whether it was only the interpretation of the editor at the time of kingship. Comparative ancient Near Eastern thought would support the former view. The concept of a god or goddess fighting against his or her own people reaches back in Mesopotamia to a least the third millennium. One of the most extensive interpretations of a defeat was made by a Sumerian writer who explained why the kingdom of Akkad fell to the barbarous Guti.[7] The document begins by telling how the leadership of Sumer was transferred from the city of Kish and Erech to Akkad. This transfer was made by the god Enlil who put to death the people of Kish, crushed the house of Erech, and gave to Sargon of Akkad "the lordship and kingship from the lands above to the lands below." Under the guidance of Inanna, goddess of Akkad, the city prospered.

Then came catastrophe. Inanna forsook her temple in Akkad.

> Like a maid who forsakes her chamber, the holy Inanna has forsaken her Agade (Akkad) shrine; like a warrior with raised weapons she attacked the city; in fierce battle, made it turn its breast to the enemy.[8]

Thus lordship and kingship departed from Akkad, and the city was destroyed forever.

The document explains this catastrophe by telling how Naram-Sin, fourth ruler of the Akkadian dynasty, had sacked Enlil's city, Nippur, and desecrated his temple, Ekur. Because of this desecration, "counsel left Agade" and "the good sense of Agade turned to folly." "Enlil, the raging flood which has no rival, because of his beloved house which has been attacked . . . destruction wrought." To avenge himself, he brought down the Guti from the mountains, "a people which brooks no controls"; "it covered the earth like the locust."[9] Communications broke down in Sumer:

> the herald could not proceed on his journey; the searider could not sail his boat. . .; brigands dwelt on the roads; the doors of the gates of the land turned to clay; all the surrounding lands were planning evil in their city walls.[10]

This invasion resulted in famine:

> The great fields and meadows produced no grain; the fisheries produced no fish; and the watered gardens produced neither honey nor wine.[11]

To soothe Enlil's rage, eight important gods of the Sumerian pantheon "turn their faces to the city, pronounce (a curse of) destruction upon Agade." The ancient writer concludes by saying that the curses came to pass.[12]

To summarize the narrative's view of divine-human relations:

(1) The invasion of Sumer was due to Naram-Sin's disobedience, his desecration of Enlil's city and temple, Nippur and Ekur, resulting in the alienation of Enlil.
(2) The destruction of Akkad was caused by Enlil and by the curses of eight important Sumerian gods who in this way tried to soothe Enlil's temper.
(3) The goddess Inanna who dwelt in Akkad forsook her temple and city to fight against it.
(4) All action is regarded as that of the gods, except for Naram-Sin's ritualistic violation of Nippur. Even the Guti are seen as the instruments of Enlil.
(5) The punishment by the gods was not immediate but was deferred for several generations (cf. 2 Kings 23:26).

C. The Poetry of Defeat

Apart from the ancient prose narratives, there is evidence supporting the antiquity of a theology of defeat in Israel's ancient poetry, specifically in Deuteronomy 32 and Psalm 78.[13] The poem in Deuteronomy, commonly known as the Song of Moses, follows the "*rîb*" form, in which Yahweh reasons with his people in court. In the trial, an appeal is made to heaven and earth, a demythologized parallel to the international treaty forms that appealed to the gods as witnesses and administrators of the curse.[14] This legal case form was occasioned by the contemporary situation of Israel, oppressed as she was by the Philistine (?) enemy. In court cases such as this, the poet explains the reason for the oppression, exonerating Yahweh and condemning Israel. Following the introduction, the song sets forth the character of Yahweh, concentrating on the recital of his acts (32:4-14). After this, Israel's apostasy is recited (vv. 15-18), which in turn is followed by Yahweh's decision to desert his people and to destroy them with the sword (vv. 19-27). The method of punishment is summed up in verse 31, climaxing a statement (vv. 28-31) that if Israel were wise, she would understand:

> For their rock [i.e., their god] is not as our Rock,
> Even our enemies themselves being judges.

This is followed with the promise that Yahweh will have compassion upon his people and will avenge himself upon a nation which is less righteous than they. A "Leitmotif" appears in the stern, but healing words of Deuteronomy 32:39:

> Behold now, I am I and there is no other God than I;
> I kill and restore to life,
>> After I have smitten I heal,
>> and none can save from my hand![15]

While ancient Near Eastern nations occasionally saw their gods as fighting against their own city or nation, Israel expressed this as a continuing theological principle that ruled both her historical writing and her prophetic thought.[16] The principle is probably rooted in the Mosaic covenant itself, as is suggested by the fact that the covenant form underlies Deuteronomy 32.[17] The specific root is the covenant threat, set forth already in the Ten Words: "for I Yahweh your God am a jealous God, visiting the iniquity of the fathers upon the children to the third and fourth generation of those who hate me . . ." (Ex. 20:5).[18]

We close this discussion with the words of Albright:

> Two main streams of later Israelite religious literature may both be traced through direct borrowing and adaptation back to *Ha'ăzînû* [Deut. 32] and the genre of which it is the chief exemplar; they are Deuteronomic theology and Prophetic theodicy. In *Ha'ăzînû* and Psalm 78 the conquest of Israel by the Philistines and the dramatic fall of Shiloh represent the final and bitterest phase of divine punishment of rebellious Israel. This phase is followed in

Ha'ăzînû by divine punishment of Israel's foes, and in Psalm 78 by the messianic rise of David. The later Prophets learned by bitter experience that the pattern is not so simple, that renewed rebellion would be followed by more punishment, that the "day of the Lord" is "darkness, not light." The burden of the Prophets from Elijah to Micah is then formulated into the sober warnings from generalized experience which we find in the Book of Deuteronomy. The incorporation of *Ha'ăzînû* into the final edition of Deuteronomy is a recognition that the message of the Book is prefigured in the magnificent cadences of the poem.[19]

Chapter VII

Battles, Kings, and Prophets

In this chapter we will survey the pre-Deuteronomic sources relating to warfare and its political context during the kingship period of Israel's history.[1] After an overview of the numerous conflicts during this period, we will note the changes in the mode of warfare that characterized the battles of David. We will then examine the theological changes that kingship effected upon the Yahwist tradition, particularly with regard to the meaning of warfare. Next we will give considerable attention to the "theology of history" of Genesis 1—12:3, in view of its significance as an understanding of history contemporary with kingship, yet markedly different from contemporary kingship views in terms of its understanding of the source and nature of power, and its world view. Finally we will consider the sources that recount the prophets' involvement with kingship in warfare; these are primarily accounts of Yahweh's judgments against the kings through his prophets.

A. Conflicts of the Kingship Period

The most warlike period in Israel's history was that of the kings. Seen in the perspective of the entire period, the aggressive wars of conquest began and ended with David. Warfare after David was mainly defensive, or, if aggressive, was meant to regain what had been lost.[2] David's wars of conquest were waged against the Philistines, against Jerusalem, the Arameans (Syrians, RSV), the Ammonites, the Moabites, and the Edomites.[3]

While Solomon fought no wars, his burdensome domestic and military policy led to the disintegration of his empire, an empire largely lost with the division of the kingdom after his death.[4] Judah and Israel subsequently engaged in wars between themselves: Rehoboam and his son Abijah with Jeroboam, Asa with Baasha, Amaziah with Joash, Ahaz with Pekah.[5]

The divided kingdom was often at war with the surrounding states. Judah fought with Philistia under Jehoram, Uzziah, Ahaz, and Hezekiah.[6] Israel battled with this league of cities under Nadab and Elah-Zimri.[7] Judah warred with Edom, led by her kings Jehoram, Amaziah, and Ahaz.[8] Jehoram of Israel, cooperating with Jehoshaphat of Judah, challenged the rebellion of the king of Moab against Israel.[9] However, the most important conflicts with the smaller states were with Aram (Syria, RSV). Israel warred with the Arameans throughout the entire ninth and into the eighth century under the kings Baasha, Ahab, an unnamed king, Joram, Jehu, Jehoahaz, Joash, and Jeroboam II.[10] Judah was also engaged in this conflict under Jehoash and Ahaz.[11]

The greatest threat to Judah and Israel came with the rise of the Near East empires, beginning in the eighth century. Already in the ninth century Ahab had cooperated with the Palestinian states in the battle of Qarqar, in an attempt to contain the Assyrian Emperor, Shalmanezer III.[12] Jehu paid tribute to this same Shalmanezer who pressed westward to the Phoenician coast.[13] After a period of internal weakness and withdrawal lasting about a century, the Assyrian empire was solidly founded by Tiglath-pileser III. Menahem of Israel became a vassal of this emperor about 738 BC.[14] When Pekah of Israel and Rezin of Damascus tried to force Ahaz of Judah into a coalition against Tiglath-pileser, Ahaz sent to him for help. As a result, Tiglath-pileser occupied the greater part of Israel, leaving intact only a little territory around her capital city, Samaria.[15] Israel's next king, Hoshea, rebelled at the accession of Shalmanezer V, and was attacked by this emperor in 724 BC. It was left for Sargon II to take Samaria in 722 BC.[16]

To the south, Judah became a vassal of Assyria when Ahaz petitioned for the help of Tiglath-pileser III to counter the threat of the Syro-Ephraimite coalition.[17] In 705 BC Hezekiah defied Sennacherib, after which the emperor ravaged the cities of Judah in 701 BC. Sennacherib accepted terms of peace without the capitulation of Jerusalem, and Judah remained a vassal of Assyria until the decline of that empire in the latter quarter of the next century.[18] Josiah took advantage of that decline by annexing the former territory of Samaria.[19]

Concerning relationships with Egypt during this period, only two conflicts are reported. The first was Shishak's invasion of Judah during the reign of Rehoboam.[20] The second was Pharaoh Necho's battle with Josiah at the Megiddo pass.[21]

The Battle of Carchemish in 605 BC established the hegemony of Babylon over Palestine.[22] When after a few years Jehoiakim revolted, Nebuchadnezzar sent against him "bands of the Chaldeans, and bands of the Syrians, and bands of the Moabites, and bands of the Ammonites. . . ."[23] Jehoiachin succeeded to the throne before the full vengeance of Nebuchadnezzar had been accomplished, and was taken captive to Babylon in the first deportation, 597 BC.[24] Jerusalem was destroyed by Nebuchadnezzar ten years later, 587 BC, after a revolt by Judah's last king, Zedekiah.[25]

In addition to these wars with external powers, both Israel and Judah suffered from internal conflicts. David experienced the revolt of Absalom and Sheba.[26] In the Northern Kingdom, Baasha overthrew the dynasty of Jeroboam.[27] Zimri and then Omri usurped the throne from Elah, son of Baasha.[28] By a bloodbath Jehu replaced the dynasty of Omri. Shallum put an end to the dynasty of Jehu, and was himself assassinated by Menahem.[29] Pekah usurped the throne from Pekahiah, the son of Menahem, and was in turn slain by Hoshea, the last king of Israel.[30]

Judah maintained one dynasty to the end, except for the interval under Athaliah.[31] A palace revolt engineered by Jehoida the priest rid the kingdom of this queen mother and reinstated the Davidic dynasty, represented by Joash. Joash was in turn assassinated by members of his court, but his son Amaziah succeeded to the throne.[32] Amaziah also was slain in a palace conspiracy, but the "people of Judah" crowned his son, Uzziah, as king.[33] About a century later Amon, son of Manasseh, was assassinated, again by members of the royal court. Again the "people of the land" took the matter in hand to replace him by his son, Josiah.[34] The final conspiracy was perpetrated by Ishmael "of the seed royal" against Gedaliah, the governor whom Nebuchadnezzar had set over Judah in Mizpah after the destruction of Jerusalem in 587 BC.[35]

There are a few other experiences that, while hardly classed as warfare, may have been regarded by the shapers of Israelite tradition as examples of Yahweh's war. One of these was Elijah's slaughter of the prophets of Baal near Mount Carmel.[36] Another was Elijah's miraculous annihilation of the companies of the Israelite army of king Ahaziah.[37] To these might be added Jehu's massacre of the worshipers of Baal, and Josiah's massacre of the priests of the North.[38]

B. Warfare Under David

As we have seen, an attempt was made to modify kingship in Israel to conform at least partially to the tradition of Yahweh's warfare.[39] But David's use of a private army and the establishment of his own capital city of

Jerusalem, never integrated into the tribal structure, provided a new power base in Israel. This new concentration of power was certain to clash with the older Yahwistic authority represented by the prophets, and if unchecked, would result in selfish misuse of power and personal aggrandizement through conquest.

The Davidic wars, as noted above, were of an aggressive nature. The battle against Jerusalem (2 Sam. 5:6-10) was fought by David with his own personal troops, an innovation in warfare that implied a fundamental change in Israelite political thought.[40] In correspondence with this fact, the emphasis throughout the narrative is upon David rather than Israel. Even here, however, the battle is won by a ruse rather than by the power of the troops.

The narratives of the Philistine wars (2 Sam. 5:17-25; 8:1) report that David inquired of Yahweh as to whether he should fight and as to the nature of the attack.[41] While such inquiries were made of divinity by other Near Eastern rulers, the oracle in Israel was to be founded not upon concepts of Near Eastern power and wisdom but upon the Yahwistic tradition, the foundation of which was Yahweh's deliverance from Egypt and Sinai.[42] This inquiry gives a central position to Yahweh throughout the narratives, placing David in subjection to him (see especially verse 25). But as in the case of the battle against Jerusalem, Israel and Judah are not named at all. Throughout the narratives, David alone is the human representative, except for verse 21 where "David and his men" are spoken of.

The short statement in regard to Moab (2 Sam. 8:2) similarly emphasizes David.[43] In addition, it contains what may have been a variation of the practice of *ḥērem*.[44]

In a summary statement of this pre-Deuteronomic source (2 Sam. 8:9-14), King David "dedicated to Yahweh" both the gifts of the king of Hamath and "the silver and gold . . . from all the nations he subdued," a common practice of the nations of the ancient Near East.[45] This summary, along with the narrative of the defeat of the Arameans (2 Sam. 8:3-8), gives prominence to David, never mentioning Israel, and relegating Yahweh to a sentence: "and Yahweh gave victory to David wherever he went" (8:6, 14). The latter is likely a Deuteronomistic insertion.[46]

Thus the source, in narrating the battles, does not mention the Israelites but exalts David by making him the main character, though recognizing the preeminence of Yahweh.[47] The only exception is the account of the Philistine wars in which Yahweh is given more emphasis because of oracles (2 Sam. 5:17-25; 8:1).

David's conflict with Aram (Syria) and the Ammonites (2 Sam. 10-11;

12:26-31) is further discussed in the ancient source, the "Succession Document."[48] The place of Yahweh as victor and Yahweh's freedom of decision are recognized in the narrative by the statement of Joab (10:12). However, in contrast to the Songs of the Sea and of Deborah, Yahweh is largely lost as subject, as might be expected in view of the rise of kingship and the standing army. David is named throughout the narrative along with his general, Joab, and Abishai the brother of Joab. Israel is mentioned a number of times throughout chapter 10 (vv, 9, 17, 18, 19), but David and his generals remain the central figures.

Significant to our study is the distinction between David's standing army and the militia ("all Israel") as recorded in the account of the Ammonite war (2 Sam. 11:1; 12:26-31). According to the text, David sent Joab out with "his servants," i.e., David's personal army, and "all Israel," i.e., the militia (2 Sam. 11:1). The story of Bathsheba also reveals this dualism (11:11) and indicates that the ark was associated with the militia.[49] While this division between the standing army and militia was not unique to Israel, the text shows the special theological significance of the dualism and related division of labor.[50] This significance is suggested by the way in which the Ammonite city, Rabbah, was taken (12:26-31). Joab had fought the decisive battle with his professionals (v. 26), yet he was careful that the city was taken by David and the militia ("all the people," v. 29). This contrived "division of labor" was no doubt an attempt to tie the new age to the old. In the old tradition a military crisis was responded to by a voluntary militia which depended for victory upon the intervention of the divine. Miracle was now replaced by professional army.[51] The pathetic attempt to preserve the form of the ancient tradition only highlights the fact that this form was emptied of its real content—faith in the decisive act of Yahweh—and replaced by faith in the professional army. The shift is further emphasized by the fact that Yahweh is not mentioned once in the narrative except for the Bathsheba account, where David's treatment of Uriah "displeased Yahweh" (2 Sam. 11:27) and was opposed by the prophet.

David's census (2 Sam. 24) was a part of this same transition from reliance upon miracle and the militia to emphasis upon the standing army. The intent of this census was

> to incorporate the levies into the royal army officered by royal appointees about whose competence and loyalty the king would have no doubts. In contrast, the old folk militia was not reliable, since they would not answer a call to arms issued by an unpopular king, or for a war they felt to be unnecessary (see 1 Kings 12:21-24).[52]

Popular opposition to the census was reinforced by a plague, which according to the oracle of the prophet Gad was Yahweh's judgment upon David's act. This narrative is evidence that the old tradition was far from dead and that the king had to act judiciously in his attempts to break with it.

The civil war of Absalom against David (2 Sam. 15 ff.) was seen by the writer of the "Succession Document" as Yahweh's judgment against David (2 Sam. 12:10, 11).[53] The concept of warfare as Yahweh's judgment against his own people is thus demonstrated in one of Israel's earliest documents.[54]

In summary, our investigation of the Davidic history has shown an increased emphasis upon kingship and a minimization of Israel and even Yahweh.[55] Yahweh was given greatest stress in the narrative of the Philistine battle, while Israel was recognized in the narrative of the Ammonite battle. In comparision with the Song of the Sea and the Song of Deborah, these narratives are clearly more in harmony with the Royal Psalms (2 Sam. 22 and Psalm 18, to be discussed below) in their emphasis upon the king rather than upon Israel, and in their lack of emphasis upon Yahweh's miracle, here replaced by the technology of the professional army. This shift in emphasis suggests a change in theo-politics, to which we now turn.

C. The Theo-Politics of Kingship

The adjustment in theology occasioned by Davidic kingship may be seen in the royal psalms and in the oracle of Nathan (2 Sam. 7:4-17).[56] One of these royal psalms, Psalm 18, was incorporated into the Deuteronomic History (2 Sam. 22), perhaps to set forth the new theology of the Davidic kingship. In this psalm, which betrays strong Canaanite influence, the place given to the king approaches to some degree the place of kingship in the victory hymns of Ramesses II and Tukulti-Ninurta I.[57] In this the psalm is radically different from both the Song of the Sea and the Song of Deborah.[58] As we have observed, Yahweh alone is credited with the fighting in the Song of the Sea. In the Song of Deborah, Yahweh was responsible for the crucial act, while the tribes participated chiefly in the mopping up operation. The main leadership was prophetic (a woman) while insignificant persons are named as participants. In Psalm 18, however, there is no mention of Israel. The personal pronouns are all first person singular and refer to kingship, except for one which is first person plural (v. 31). While it is likely that the king represented the people in the sense that they as a body were incorporated into his "I," this was no point of difference from other cultures. The arming of the king and conquest of the enemy as recounted in Psalm 18:34-42 is a familiar Near Eastern motif. The passage may be compared to the arming of Sennacherib in the annals of his eighth campaign.[59]

Despite its emphasis upon kingship, however, the psalm stresses the leadership of Yahweh throughout and thus if taken seriously would limit the powers of the king.

The limits of kingly power are suggested even more dramatically by Nathan's oracle, the classic expression of royal theology.[60] In this statement, David was not to build a temple because of the ancient belief that Yahweh meets with Israel in a tent (2 Sam. 7:4-7). This tradition, alive among the prophets, may have been activited by Nathan in an attempt to guard against the replacement of the ancient center of the league with a dynastic sanctuary patterned after the Canaanites in which the king would have a dominant role as later happened, for example, with Jeroboam II as represented by Amaziah the priest in his clash with Amos (Amos 7:12 ff.). More important, the covenant with David, while an eternal covenant patterned after the Abrahamic covenant, was subjected to the covenant of Moses in that punishment was threatened for disobedience (2 Sam. 7:14). This primacy of the law of Moses is even more decisive for the Davidic covenant when it is noted that the shrine of the Ark of the Covenant, the link with the ancient Mosaic tradition, is the setting for this promise to the Davidic dynasty.[61] That this primacy of the law of Moses was more than empty form is suggested by Nathan's challenge and judgment following David's sin against Bathsheba and Uriah.[62]

In assessing David's faithfulness to the Yahwistic ideal, a distinction should perhaps be made between his rise and the latter part of his reign. The narrative of his battle with Goliath shows that in the eyes of the narrator David accepted the theology of Yahweh's war in principle (1 Sam. 17).[63] Also, David "seems to have been the last king to consult oracles about when and whether to fight, which is certainly part of primitive Yahwism."[64] His later wars and statecraft, however, reveal an increased reliance upon calculation and worldly wisdom. An example of this is the statement in 2 Samuel 16:23: "Now in those days the counsel which Ahithophel gave was as if one consulted the oracle of God; so was all the counsel of Ahithophel esteemed, both by David and by Absalom." This statement is a harbinger of the direction that war and statecraft would take after the reign of David. The prophetic and priestly oracles were based upon the ancient traditions of Yahweh's sole power and demand, the foundation of which was the exodus and Sinai. The counsel of Ahithophel, however, which toward the end of David's reign was valued equally with the oracle, had its foundations in the statecraft and wisdom of the ancient Near East.[65]

Of such "wise men" as Ahithophel (who later were attacked by Isaiah and Jeremiah),[66] McKane says they are to be equated with a class of officials who existed from the time of David onwards, and the emergence of such a governing and administrative class has been correctly correlated with the fundamental political reorganization of Israel which was carried through by David and Solomon. Israel became a state with a new political structure which demanded the creation of a cadre of royal officers through whom the king governed his people.[67]

Insofar as the Davidic state was informed by the goals and ambitions of a Near Eastern state, it would no longer rely for guidance upon the prophetic oracle, but would rely upon the calculations of wise men who knew the way of Near Eastern warfare and statecraft. Solomon's diplomatic marriages with foreign women is an example of Israel's integration into Near Eastern statecraft, an integration based upon polytheism and a conception of power quite alien to that of ancient Yahwism (1 Kings 11:1-13).

While David was accepted in Israel as the ideal king, yet his kingship and perhaps kingship as an institution came under criticism in the so-called "Succession Document."[68] The purpose of the writer of this document may well have been to shake confidence in the reign of Solomon and to suggest that from the outset it was a disaster to give one man so much power.[69] The "peaceful" reign of Solomon was founded upon a series of murders, beginning with David's adultery with Bathsheba and murder of Uriah, and culminating in Solomon's murders of his brother Adonijah, the commander Joab, and Shimei the relative of Saul.[70] It is entirely appropriate that the writer of this narrative permitted Yahweh to recede into the background as he unfolds an account of human action that was primarily an expression of rebellion. And yet the writer conveys the point, largely through the prophetic oracle and judgment (see 2 Sam. 12:1-23), that Yahweh is still the leader of this sordid political history and that the rebellion of man is not outside his control.

An implied criticism of the Davidic-Solomonic empire may also be found in the theology of history of Genesis 1—12:3, a passage which we will now examine in some detail.

D. A Theology of History: Genesis 1—12:3

We have already noted that the institution of warfare can be understood only in relation to the larger political development of which it is a part.[71] No responsible nation wages war for war's sake, but to help establish what it considers to be "peace" or "shalom." This is especially true of the world's great empires, whether it be the shalom of Assur, the shalom of Marduk (Babylon), or the pax Romana, Brittania, or Americana. It is the purpose of Genesis 1—12:3 to set forth the shalom of Yahweh, his theo-political relationship to the peoples of the world, and the meaning and place of Israel in that relationship. This relationship is quite a different one from that set forth in the Royal Psalms (cf. Ps. 2).

Any interpretation of Genesis 1—11 must take into account the long preliterary history within Israel of the elements in these narratives, as well as the history of analogous materials outside of Israel, reaching back to ancient Akkadian-Sumerian times.[72] Their meaning was transformed significantly when they were attached to the patriarchal history and to the history of Israel.[73] The recasting of these common materials, from the perspective of the central prophetic events of the exodus, Sinai, and Israel's later history, stamped them with Israelite individuality. Israel saw in Yahweh's relationship to her own peoplehood his concern and pattern for working in relationship to the peoples of the world. The transformation of the meaning of this material was probably not the work of one or two writers, but was a gradual community process which no doubt began shortly after the central prophetic events themselves.

1. *The Genealogies.* The unity of Genesis 1—12 material is provided to a large extent by the genealogical lists which are provided by both J and P.[74] These lists, common among primitive tribal types of societies, show relationships between families and groups.[75] The "archaic" character of one side of Israel's life is apparent here when one compares these lists with a similar Near Eastern list also used to unify historical writing, namely, the Sumerian Kingship List. The Sumerian list, dating about 2000 BC, is comprised of the names of kings of the pre-flood and post-flood periods. It begins with the time "when kingship was lowered from heaven," proceeds through eight generations of kings to the time of the flood, after which kingship was again let down from heaven, and continues until the approximate time of the writer. The list tells how kingship passed from city to city in Sumer, the last city being Ur, from which Abraham in the biblical story set forth.[76]

The remarkable aspect of the Israelite writing was the refusal to "modernize" these lists, even though both recensions achieved their present form after kingship was an established fact in Israel.[77] This refusal reflects Israel's bias against kingship as the institution was known in the Near East. Just as Israel experienced the relationship between God and people as decisive, so these genealogies portray the central relationship as between God and mankind, a genuine people's history.

This side of Israel's life, its "archaic" character as manifested in the simple genealogical lists, is united with its unique progressive character which set forth a unified, historical picture of mankind, albeit without the contemporary institution of kingship.[78] A unity of peoples under the leadership of God, without the human institution of kingship, is undoubtedly related to Israel's own historical experience of unity under the kingship of Yahweh after his deliverance at the Sea, and her subsequent rejection of human kingship. What Israel herself rejected, the theological writers of this passage rejected also for Yahweh's relationship to the world.

2. *The Creation Narratives.* The creation narrative of Genesis 1:1— 2:3 tells of the creation of the universe, while that of Genesis 2:4-25 speaks of the creation of mankind.[79] The "archaic" character of both narratives is evident in that they climax in the family rather than in the state, in contrast to both the Babylonian *Enuma Elish* and the Egyptian *Memphite Theology.*[80] The redactors of the biblical narratives rejected any temptation to "modernize" the story of creation in order to make it uphold the coercive powers of the state. This conservatism is remarkable since Genesis 2 achieved its present shape at the beginning of Israel's kingship, when this institution was most successful in the development of an empire, and when one would expect theology to follow this development by undergirding and supporting the new political reality.[81] It was the objective of the *Enuma Elish* to do just that for the Babylonian empire.[82] The *Enuma Elish* attempted not to describe the beginnings of the universe but to present the cosmological reasons why Marduk, god of Babylon, was made king of the pantheon. The priests' purpose in composing this epic was to strengthen Babylon's claim to supremacy over all the cities of the land. This political development was supported by two theses of the *Enuma Elish:* that the god of Babylon, having conquered Tiamat, had given order to the universe, and that the city of Babylon had been founded by the gods themselves at the beginning of time for their own habitation.[83] Similarly, the *Memphite Theology* was composed by the priests of Memphis to justify the emergence of that city as the new theo-political center where the rule of upper and lower Egypt was united in Pharaoh.[84] But the scribes responsible for the Israelite tradition did not take that route; they refused the possible temptation to use religion to undergird contemporary politics by updating these materials. This was true not only at the beginning of kingship as evidenced by Genesis 2, but all the way through the kingship period as evidenced by Genesis 1.[85] The creation narrative is never used in the Bible to undergird the coercive structures of Israelite empire.

On the other hand, these creation narratives do not have a merely archaizing interest in the family. They are not apolitical but have as their chief interest the unity of mankind, and thus portray in the beginning not an Israelite family but the family of mankind (Adam).[86] Thus while not political in the sense of the coercive politics of Babylon or Memphis, they nevertheless demonstrate a new kind of unity, a theo-politics that does not rest on coercion in the usual political sense of that word, but instead assumes the freedom of man.

Genesis 1 uses kingship language in such expressions as "in the image of God" (1:27) and "subdue it and have dominion" (1:28).[87] This kingship language is used of mankind in his cooperation with Yahweh's rule over the earth, and not of man's rule over his fellowman. It is significant that both male and female are partners in this rule over the world, an assertion without parallel in anything that has come down to us elsewhere in the ancient Near East. In this statement the rule of man over woman within the family is rejected. No part of the family of man, whether Babylon or Israel, is to rule over the other, but man and woman are to cooperate as God's representatives in their rule over the earth.

3. *The Fall.* Two narratives from the ancient Near East which in part resemble the fall are the Adapa myth and sections of the Gilgamesh epic.[88] While both of these statements deal with how man lost eternal life, neither deal with the main theme of Genesis 2—3, that man's central problem is his pride and rebellion against divinity. Assuming that the narrative of the fall may be best interpreted by relating it to comparable material in the Old Testament, it is significant that the closest parallel, Ezekiel 28:11-19, has to do with kingship.[89] A comparison of this passage with Genesis 2—3 gives this result:

Genesis 2—3	Ezekiel 28:12-19
Man is formed by God	The king is created by God
Man lives in a garden	The king lives in a garden
The garden is in Eden	The garden is in Eden
Eden is "in the East"	Eden is on the holy mountain of God
Animals are present	A cherub is present
Man is naked	The king wears royal attire
Man is sinless and unashamed	The king is "blameless"
Man desires to become wise	The king rebels through pride of heart
Man rebels to become like God by eating of the tree	The king disobeys through violence and trade

Man knows good and evil	The king's wisdom is corrupted
Man is expelled from the garden	The king is expelled from the mountain
Cherubim guard the way to the tree of life	A cherub expels the king
A flaming sword guards the way	The king is judged by fire
Man is not permitted to eat of the tree of life and live forever	The king is judged by God forever

It may be assumed that Ezekiel 28:11-19 identifies the king of Tyre with the fall of primal man, and that the Ezekiel statement is a variant of Genesis 2—3.[90] In at least two other cases in the literature and art of the Near East, the king was evidently identified with primal man. First, in the story of Adapa, the king of the Mesopotamian city of Eridu was created by the god Ea as the "model of man" and may have been considered as the first man. Eridu itself was valued as the garden of the gods and as the pattern of the cosmic mountain of the gods.[91] Second, a fresco in the palace of Mari, a city on the Middle Euphrates, depicts the investiture of a king with several deities present.[92] The ceremony is held in an idealized garden, whose trees are guarded by cherubim. The garden is watered by four streams which flow from a single source. This fresco is all the more pertinent when it is remembered that the ruling class at Mari were the Amurru, that is, "Westerners," closely related to early Israel and the patriarchal tribes.[93]

It is significant that the Old Testament parallels to the Genesis 2—3 themes of pride, rebellion, and fall are related to the governments of this world, especially as represented by kingship. Ezekiel 28:1-10 is another poem which tells of the fall of the prince of Tyre:

> Because your heart is proud,
>   and you have said, "I am a god,
> I sit in the seat of the gods,
>   in the heart of the seas,"
> Yet you are but a man, and no god ... (28:2).

The prophetic taunt song in Isaiah 14:12-15 sets forth the fall of the king of Babylon:

> How you are fallen from heaven,
>   O Day Star, son of Dawn!

How you are cut down to the ground,
  You who laid the nations low!
You said in your heart,
  "I will ascend to heaven;
above the stars of God
  I will set my throne on high;
I will sit on the mount of assembly
  in the far north;[94]
I will ascend above the heights of the clouds,
  I will make myself like the Most High."
But you are brought down to Sheol,
  to the depths of the Pit.

Isaiah exploits the same theme in regard to the armed forces of Egypt:

Woe to those who go down to Egypt for help
  and rely on horses,
Who trust in chariots because they are many
  and in horsemen because they are very strong,
but do not look to the Holy One of Israel
  or consult Yahweh!

The Egyptians are men, and not God;
  and their horses are flesh, and not spirit.
When Yahweh stretches out his hand,
  the helper will stumble, and he who is helped will fall,
and they will all perish together (31:1, 3).

If the above are parallels to the theme of Genesis 2—3, the story of the fall in Genesis 2—3 is not an isolated criticism by J, but is a part of a major emphasis of the biblical message. The fallen nature of the governments of this world is a significant theme of the Old Testament found in the oldest as well as in the youngest biblical sources.[95] It was this rebellion with which Israel was charged when the people demanded kingship "like all the nations" (1 Sam. 8:5).[96]

How did J develop this theme of rebellion? Obviously his central concern was not the loss of immortal life, as was the case of the Adapa and Gilgamesh epics. His concern was the commandment as typified by the tree of knowledge, good and evil. This phrase "good and evil" is used in the Old Testament of legal decisions made by a king or the head of a patriarchal clan.[97] In 1 Kings 3:9 Solomon prays, "Give thy servant a hearing heart to judge thy people, that I may discern between good and evil." The ability to make such a decision in a judicial situation was thought to be a divine characteristic (see 2 Sam. 14:17). Not only kings but also heads of patriarchal clans were responsible to make such judgments. When Laban overtook Jacob, God warned him not to "speak with Jacob from good unto evil," that is, he was not to prosecute Jacob (Gen. 31:24, 29).

It may be well to remind ourselves here that there is no essential difference between a tribe and a nation, other than one of economic and social development.[98] The rebellion of Israel in demanding kingship was not that the people wished to take the next logical step in the chain of social development, but rather that the people wished to change their theo-political system of government for one that was "like all the nations." This the Yahwist tradition regarded as a move away from theo-politics, towards autonomy from Yahweh.

If there was any temptation for the king of Israel to identify himself with the first man (as in the Adapa myth discussed above), J put that temptation to rest by showing the first man as involved in rebellion against Yahweh.[99] J evidently accepted a modified type of kingship for Israel, but the warning to kingship implied in the story of the fall is indeed profound.

In the fall narrative, J carries further the Genesis 1 concept of kingship expressed in the whole family of mankind ruling over the created order, and sees the first family as representative of every family in rebellion also. Just as woman participates with man in rule over the earth in Genesis 1, so in Genesis 3 woman participates in the fall and shares with her husband the "knowledge, good and evil." The self-proclaimed autonomy of man from the rule of God, usually associated with kingship in the Bible, is here thrust back to the patriarchal family long before the development of kingship. After the fall, the complementary relationship of man and woman (Gen. 2:24) is only a reminder of the past. The patriarchal reality of the writer's present situation was that the man "shall rule over" woman (3:16). In Genesis 2 woman is designated by the same term as man, except that a difference in sex is recognized (2:23). Woman's complementary nature is further emphasized by a possible reference to a matriarchal order (2:24). In Genesis 3, after the fall, woman is named by man just as he has named the animals (3:20; cf. 2:20), an expression of his ownership and rule.

It is obvious that for J mankind's rebellion against Yahweh is not identified with rebellion against the Davidic empire. The unity of mankind is not affirmed by coercive structures but by a theo-political structure quite strange to both ancient and modern man. Its radical nature is suggested by the relationship that J depicts between man and woman. Elsewhere in the literature of the ancient Near East there is no narrative of the creation of woman as such. Also, in Genesis 3 the woman participates in the fall; she too becomes wise, "knowing good and evil." This is quite in contrast to the episode of Enkidu in the Gilgamesh epic where the harlot woman is the means whereby Enkidu receives the gift of wisdom to become "like the gods," yet she in no way participates with him in the experience itself.[100] While J's experience of family was patriarchal, woman nevertheless shared in the divine likeness (in fact, she led in the search for it) and ideally was not to be ruled over by man. This elevation of woman may be related to the Bible's demotion of the martial hero.[101] In this new theo-political order leadership is not given to the martial hero who by physical prowess represents deity, but to the word of Yahweh, to which woman and man as complementary creatures are alike subjected.

4. *The Election of Abraham.* The main point of Genesis 1—12 is not the creation and fall, but the coming of Yahweh to judge and save rebel man. Yahweh came to Adam with his question, "Where are you ?" (3:9). He came to Cain with the question, "Where is Abel your brother?" (4:9). That these questions follow the general pattern of the *Ten Words*, that is, concern for relationship to God (Ex. 20:2-8) coupled with responsibility to the brother (Ex. 20:9-17), suggests the underlying outline that was in the mind of J. The story of Lamech (Gen 4:19-24), with its emphasis on cultural technological advance, is one of the proliferation of violence. The intermarriage of the "sons of God" with the "daughters of men" resulting in a super-race of warriors (Gen. 6:1-4), regarded by Near Eastern literature as a boon to mankind, is regarded by J as the climax of the fall.[102] These incidents result in the coming of Yahweh in the flood to judge mankind, and to save mankind for a new beginning through Noah and his family.

To give man this new beginning, Yahweh removed the curse that he had placed upon the ground and gave to man the promise of his benefaction (Gen. 8:21 f.,J). This promise was not based upon a change in man's attitude toward the rule of Yahweh, but upon the fact that man had not changed—that his thoughts were evil from his youth. This same basic fact of man's nature had moved Yahweh previously to cause the flood.[103] Also, in the statement at 9:12-17 (P) God sets in the cloud his unstrung bow as a sign of his new *shalom* to his enemy man. The war is over and man will not again suffer the violence of Yahweh's overwhelming wrath.[104] But as the narrative continues, Yahweh's new approach does not change the course of the story. As a result of drunkenness and a sex incident, Noah cursed Canaan (9:20-27).[105] The next major event was man's rebellion at Babel (11:1-9), to which Yahweh had only a long-range answer, the election of Abram.[106]

In the story of the election of Abram, the writer again maintained the original character of his material. We have noted above that the Babylonian

Creation Epic was primarily a political document that set forth the election of Marduk as king of the cosmic gods and the political ascendancy of his city, Babylon. The epic assumed the election of a human king who acted as the servant of the god Marduk. A succinct statement of the election of both Marduk and Hammurabi is found in the prologue of Hammurabi's law code.[107] Both Marduk and Hammurabi were chosen by the leading gods, Anu and Enlil. Marduk, god of Babylon, was given the "Enlil" power, the violent power of storm, by which he was to subdue the rebellious will.[108] King Hammurabi was to act as Marduk's servant, as head of the police and armed services in the earthly sphere. He represented the authority of law and order backed by violent power.

In contrast to the Babylonian writers, the writer J made no attempt to modernize his story to make it relevant to the epochal event of his time, the movement of political leadership from the North to Jerusalem and the election of the Davidic dynasty. This is astonishing when we remember that both the cult (cf. Ps. 78) and the prophetic party (cf. 2 Sam. 7) certified this movement as a new act of Yahweh in salvation history. The king of Israel was elected in response to the popular demand for law and order backed by violent power.[109] Despite this, there is no trace of a kingship election in the call of Abram (Gen. 12:1-3). Abram's election fits into a broad category of patriarchal religion to which his experience belonged.[110] The writer J thus refused to update his material to make it fit the nationalism of his times. The ancient election of Abram set forth Yahweh's and Israel's relationship to the nations in a way quite different from that of the election of Marduk and Hammurabi.

At the same time, J does set forth a theme of the unity of mankind, a new kind of unity to which mankind is called through Yahweh's servant. He contrasts this with the old attempt to preserve unity by means of the Babylonian city-state (11:1-9), an attempt which resulted only in confusion and disharmony.[111]

Careful observation would suggest that J makes the following contrasts:

(1) 11:3: and *they* said *one* to *another*   12:1 and *Yahweh* said unto Abram.

(2) 11:2: and it came to pass, when *they* journeyed from the east, that *they* found a valley in the land of Shinar and *they* dwelt there.   12:1 Go from your land and from your kindred and from your father's house to the land which *I* will show you.

(3) 11:4: and *they* said, "Come, let *us*   12:2: And *I* will make you a great

build a city, and a tower with its top
in the heavens . . . lest *we* be
scattered upon the surface of all the
earth."

nation, and *I* will bless you.

(4) 11:4: and let *us* make for *ourselves* a
name.

12:2, 3: and *I* will make great your
name and you shall be a blessing . . .
and all the families of the earth shall
bless themselves in you.

a. *Leadership of the Community*. The primary contrast has to do with
the leadership of the community. J used the third and first person plural
pronouns (they, we, us) for the Babylonians, to indicate that the community
made its own decisions, acting as a sovereign city-state in line with what it
assumed to be its self-interest, without regard to the leadership of Yahweh.
In the new community, on the other hand, the subject throughout is
Yahweh as indicated by his name and the first person singular pronoun.[112]
This suggests that Israel is not a sovereign state but makes its decisions
under the prophetic authority of Yahweh who has determined the fundamental direction of the community in line with his interests for all mankind.
This contrast of leadership corresponds to that set forth by both J and P
throughout the primeval history. The real human problem was not that
mankind worshiped idols, or even other gods, but that, according to the
analysis of the biblical redactors, the worship of such idols and gods was a
false cult that supported the shortsighted, self-interested decisions of the
city-state community.[113] Man's fundamental problem was a self-proclaimed
autonomy from the rule of Yahweh as expressed first in the rebellion of
primeval man (Gen. 3), and finally in the rebellion of the self-proclaimed
autonomy of the Babylonian city-state (Gen. 11).

While it is astonishing that J in his analysis of the problem of mankind
does not mention idolatry, it is equally surprising that he does not see the
city-state's self-proclaimed autonomy in terms of kingship. We have seen
that the autonomy of decision-making by the community is usually
identified by the prophets with the rebellion of kingship.[114] Our redactor,
however, may have had an ancient tradition before him which reflected a
primitive Babylonian democracy, as he uses the plural pronoun ("they,"
"us").[115] J saw the fundamental issue not as "kingship" versus "democracy"
but as the human community, in this case a primitive democracy in rebellious autonomy from Yahweh, making its decisions in terms of a
shortsighted self-interest, versus the human community under Yahweh's
prophetic leadership.

b. *Identity of the Community.* The second contrast between Genesis 12 and Genesis 11 concerns community identity. Both of the peoples involved were in the process of migration. As stated in Genesis 11, when the community migrated from the east "they found a plain in the land of Shinar and settled there" (v. 2). There is an immediacy between community and land in Genesis 11 that is not found in Genesis 12. In Genesis 12 Abram is commanded to abandon all natural roots (v. 1), his land or country as well as his kindred and father's house. Thus, the principle of social structure founded upon territory, the territorial state described in chapter 11, is rejected.

Commanded to turn from his natural "roots," Abram is further told to go to that land which Yahweh would show him (12:1). In this statement land no longer has the same immediacy to the community as it does in chapter 11. Relationship to land continues to be important, but its primacy is replaced by the reality of Yahweh and people. Throughout the Bible the primary relationship is never that of blood and soil but of Yahweh and people.

This relationship between God and people is characteristic of a religious type that Abram shared with other patriarchal clans of his day.[116] Here again the writer refused to "modernize" his material to make it conform with pressure toward a new territorial reality that became manifested in Samuel with the structure of kingship, a relationship of people and land that worked toward the assimilation, elimination, or subjugation of others.

c. *The Community and Nationhood.* The third contrast of the two statements suggests the nature of the two communities. The rebel community attempted to build its own city and tower. The city represents an economic and political power center that attempted to achieve political unity in Mesopotamia by domination and exploitation of village and pastoral life.[117] The tower was undoubtedly the ziggurat. In Mesopotamia the tower was not regarded as an expression of man's rebellion but as the bond between heaven and earth, mankind and the gods, a bond that was essential to the prosperity of the city-state.[118] Our writer was evidently unimpressed with a similar tendency in Israel, the temple on Mount Zion, which was cheek-in-jowl with the palace. For J community and "nation" would develop out of relationship with Yahweh. Like land, it would be Yahweh's gift to his people, and should not be established by the autonomous initiative of the people themselves.

d. *The Community and International Unity.* If J was "archaic" in all three points treated above, he was nevertheless "modern" in that he saw election in terms of a world unity, albeit an alternative kind of unity to that of an empire based on coercive power. Yahweh rather than the organized community would provide Abram's posterity with the fundamental direction of political leadership. Yahweh rather than land would be the basis for Israel's identity, and land would be provided as his gift. Israel was to be a genuine "nation," though its nationhood was to be Yahweh's gift and therefore in a category of its own. And this theo-socio-political structure was to answer the need for international unity.

In the grammatical construction of the election statement, the five imperative-cohortative clauses move toward verse 3b—"and by you all the families of the earth shall bless themselves."[119] This emphasis is enhanced by the fact that in verse 2 there is already an intention clause that changes the subject from Yahweh's blessing to Abram's being a blessing. It is powerfully reinforced by the position of the passage itself as the answer to the problem of primeval history, and more specifically as the answer to the scattering of the nations in 11:1-9.

This blessing to the families of the earth would not be achieved by an act of conquest, but by Yahweh's blessing of Abram and a subsequent free response by the peoples—"by you all families of the earth shall bless themselves."[120] This "volunteerism" of the election corresponds to the prophetic statement of Isaiah 2:2-4 where the nations by their own volition go up to Jerusalem to learn Yahweh's teaching as an alternative to warfare for the resolution of international conflict.

It was a primary importance of J that this blessing of Yahweh could be achieved only by a new kind of election, a new kind of relationship to divinity and land, a kind of nationhood different from that demonstrated by the scattered peoples of the world. Thus the message of J, though making use of archaic patriarchal materials, was not itself archaic. Rather, it points toward a type of theo-political unity that represented an alternative to the coercive empire types of the Near East. The roots of this alternative tradition reached back through the confederacy to the wilderness tradition, and perhaps in a limited measure to the patriarchal period itself.

E. The Prophetic Narratives and Warfare

Other important pre-Deuteronomic sources relating to Israel's kingship era are the prophetic narratives, some of which were available to the Deuteronomic historian as cycles of narratives, others as individual narratives.[121]

1. *Narratives in Which Prophets Confront Kings.* These prophetic narratives are predominantly negative in that most of them contain oracles of judgment involving warfare against Israel, though the oracles are

directed primarily against the king or his dynasty, and only secondarily against Israel. The oracle and its fulfillment in a historical situation is a central characteristic of the Deuteronomic history.[122] Although some scholars suggest that this is a theologizing of history that had little or no relation to political realities in the life of Israel, we should note that the Deuteronomic historian inherited this perspective from the older sources such as the Succession Document, where Nathan delivered an oracle against David that was fulfilled in the subsequent history.[123] This political function of the prophet is also found in the classical prophecy of both Northern and Southern Kingdoms in the eighth to seventh centuries BC, and, as we will note below, is present as well in the Elijah narratives.[124] It would thus appear that in the arrangement of his sources the Deuteronomic historian was only reiterating a common political understanding of the community of Israel both North and South, an understanding presumably based upon experience. A prior conclusion of our study is that this primacy of the prophetic word, while greatly expanded in the time of Samuel in an attempt to control kingship, was characteristic of the pre-kingship league probably going back to the person of Moses himself.[125]

We have already discussed the oracles of Nathan and Gad against David.[126] In other narratives, the legend of Ahijah of Shiloh (who sparked the rebellion of Jeroboam, 1 Kings 11:29-39) tells of the prophetic word directed against the Davidic dynasty.[127] Shemaiah, a prophet of Judah, proclaimed a negative oracle against the war policy of King Rehoboam (1 Kings 12:1-24).[128] Ahijah of Shiloh pronounced a second negative oracle, this time against the dynasty of Jeroboam (14:7-16).[129] An unknown prophet of the Aramean wars declared to Ahab an oracle involving the destruction of both king and people because the king had violated the rule of *ḥērem* of holy war (1 Kings 20:35-43).[130] The prophecy of Jehu ben Hanini was delivered against King Baasha (16:1-4). John Gray holds that the language of 1 Kings 16:3 ff. is likely the remains of a North Israelite source used by the Deuteronomistic compiler. He further states that

> verses 9-12a also may belong to this source, which reflects the same critical view of the monarchy in North Israel as finds expression in Hos. 8:4 and in the tradition of Elijah and part of that of Elisha.[131]

This source may be that designated by 2 Chronicles 20:34 as "the chronicles of Jehu the son of Hanani, which are recorded in the Book of the Kings of Israel" (compare with "the vision of Isaiah the prophet the son of Amoz, in the Book of the Kings of Judah and Israel," 2 Chron. 32:32). It would ap-

pear from this that perhaps there were prophetic chroniclers who presented
not only the deeds of kingship, as did ancient Near Eastern historiography,
but also the political oracles of the prophets in relation to those deeds.

The serious breach within the prophetic office, first encountered in the
narrative of Micaiah, is important to our study.[132] This breach first
developed under the Omride dynasty, which evidently included as its
policy the encouragement of the Baal religion.[133] At issue was a question of
war policy that divided the prophets. The narrative presents two enthrone-
ments, the first that of the kings of Israel and Judah "sitting on their
thrones, arrayed in their robes, at the threshing floor at the entrance of the
gate of Samaria..." (1 Kings 22:10). In the second enthronement, seen in
vision by Micaiah, Yahweh was "sitting on his throne" (22:19). Both have
their "messengers" before them, in the first case the prophets (v. 10), in the
second "all the host of heaven" (v. 19). The issue concerns the relation
between the two thrones. The king of Israel evidently regarded the prophet
as an agent of the community who by sympathetic word and action might
influence the divine will. Jehoshaphat, the king of Judah, on the other
hand, "regarded the prophet not as an agent of the community in its efforts
to influence God by auto-suggestion, but as the instrument of the revelation
of the will of God to the community."[134] The sincerity of the four hundred
prophets is not questioned; rather, their connnection with the throne of
Yahweh is seen as perverted. Walter Eichrodt says of these prophets:°

> It has rightly been stressed that the four hundred prophets of Ahab need not
> in every instance have been lying prophets. Nevertheless it is true that, in
> general, when nabism [prophetism] became a highly regarded and regularly
> consulted political tribunal, it came under *strong pressure from the national
> will to power* embodied in the monarchy; and the successful maintenance of
> its own integrity must have become all the more difficult, the more strongly
> the inflated members of the prophetic guild were influenced by their material
> dependence on the favour of the king, and the more resolutely the latter
> moved toward Oriental despotism. What men wanted from the prophet was
> the word of power which would bring about the *šālôm* of people and state
> without imposing hard and fast limits on political action in the name of
> Yahweh's moral demands (Jer. 23:17). There was here a real danger that un-
> dertakings called for by dynastic interest would be justified by identifying
> them with Yahweh's holy war, and that ruthless imperialist policies, which
> could be forwarded only at the cost of the nation's internal well-being, would
> be exalted as pious zeal for the greatness of the national God. It is food for
> thought that Ahab, who had been so vigorously opposed by Elijah on account

---

°From *The Theology of the Old Testament*, Vol. 1, by Walter Eichrodt. Translated by J.
A. Baker. Published in the U.S.A. by The Westminster Press, 1961. Copyright © 1961 S.C.M.
Press, Ltd. Used by permission.

of his internal policies, could always find prophets, quite apart from the four hundred already mentioned, who were prepared to support his warlike schemes (cf. 1 Kings 20:13, 22, 28), and only reproached him for his inadequate exploitation of his victory. The extent to which the original orientation of nabism had been abandoned may be seen even more clearly in the so-called *Royal Psalms*, which extol the accession of the sovereign as the coming of the God-sent Prince of Peace. The fact that these hymns most probably derive from the court prophets suggests that the divinization of the earthly king which is one of the most prominent features may be regarded as indicative of the attitude of certain prophetic circles to the monarchy and its religious pretensions. The eschatological tension, which looked wholly for the succour promised from God, is here very much weakened in favour of an outlook which sees salvation in the contemporary institution of divine kingship. *Here again institutional religion has repressed the proper prophetic concentration on God's coming.* In addition, the strong emphasis on the military function of the ruler helped to attach a disproportionate importance to an aspect of Yahweh worship which, when placed in false isolation, went more than half-way to meet the nationalistic perversion of the Yahweh religion.[135]

The meaning of the prophetic narratives' emphasis on negative prophecy thus stands out clearly in the account of Micaiah, in which one prophet challenges the nationalism of the four hundred.

The Elijah narratives involved with warfare against kingship and/or Israel are 1 Kings 17:1—19:18; 21.[136] The narrative of the drought, the ordeal, and the flight to Horeb is related to the revolution of Jehu and the Aramean wars (1 Kings 19:15-17).[137] While Elijah is the main human character, he is portrayed in such a way that it is Yahweh himself who is the actor.[138] As the ambassador of Yahweh, the prophet rather than the king is presented in all of these narratives as the decisive political leader in Israel. (George Fohrer, in his penetrating analysis of the Elijah traditions recognizes this fact, but denies that this was true in the actual history.)[139] The community that originated the tradition had maintained that Yahweh alone is the political ruler of Israel and the prophet is his ambassador. This was the essence of Elijah's conflict with the Baal prophets and Ahab. When the Omride dynasty violated this fundamental political policy by recognizing Baalism as well as Yahwism, thus making religion a department of the state rather than coming under the rule of Yahweh as represented by law (Torah) and prophet, Elijah single-handedly opposed this political rebellion by the ordeal at Mount Carmel (1 Kings 18:20-46).[140] As a result of this ordeal, Elijah won over the majority of the people (18:39) and set in motion a movement which, as seen by Elijah's near contemporaries, ended with the revolution of Jehu and the disastrous Aramean wars.

At issue on Mount Carmel was the first commandment. It was Elijah's premise that only Yahweh and not Baal had the character of God.[141] This religious question (mono-Yahwism) was also fundamental to Israel's politics, a fact that becomes clear when one understands the character of Baal and his relation to economics and politics. This relationship is vividly portrayed by "Baal au foudre," a bas-relief found in 1932 at Ras Shamra in a sanctuary west of the temple.[142] In the left hand of the god Baal is a lance which at the top flowers into a plant. This represents Baal as god of fertility and plant life, the foundation of economics. The lance itself symbolizes that Baal unites this economic interest with the coercive, political interest that is further elaborated by his right hand swinging a club over his head. By use of his club and lance, Baal opposes all those forces that interfere with his economic interest.

This Baal was elevated to an official position alongside of Yahweh by Ahab, who had been married by his father Omri to Jezebel, princess of Tyre, in order to seal an economic-political alliance with Ethbaal her father (1 Kings 16:25-33). Elijah confronted Israel on Mount Carmel with a demand to make a choice. Israel must choose between Baal as represented by Ahab-Jezebel and their prophets and Yahweh as represented by the prophet, Elijah. If Baal is God, represented by Israel's economic-religious interests and backed by the coercive power of Ahab-Jezebel, let Israel worship Baal. If Yahweh is God, represented only by the word of Elijah which was dependent for support entirely upon religious tradition and miracle, then let Israel worship Yahweh. The issue was thus between a divinity who represented an alliance of economic and religious interests backed by political coercion, and a divinity who represented the moral-social-spiritual values of Exodus-Sinai, whose economics consisted of faith in his word of promise, and whose politics consisted of obedience to his word through Elijah, a word entirely dependent upon miracle.

The narrative of Ahab's misappropriation of Naboth's vineyard (1 Kings 21) is also connected with warfare or threat of revolution.[143] Elijah's indictment charges Ahab with murder and theft (21:19). Thus the sin and punishment of Omri's dynasty is related to the violation of the first commandment (1 Kings 17—19) as well as Yahweh's social laws (1 Kings 21).

The issue of Naboth's vineyard is clarified only through an understanding of the system of Israel's land tenure.[144] According to Israel's ancient law, all land belonged to Yahweh, who gave to each family a portion to be used as an inalienable heritage (Lev. 25:23). King Ahab, by contrast, was pushing toward the Canaanite tenure system in which land was dispensed by the king, usually as a reward for faithful service in the armed forces. Yahweh's law was designed to protect his people from the very economic dependency upon kingship that Ahab had proposed. Naboth asserted this equality of each Israelite under Yahweh's law by his faithfulness in rejecting Ahab's request. Ahab, also bound by Yahweh's law, recognized Naboth's right by his helplessness in the situation. Jezebel, on the other hand, as a princess of Tyre was psychologically free from such restrictions of Yahwistic law (1 Kings 21:7). Even she, however, could gain control of the property only by subverting Israelite justice.

When Naboth and his heirs were destroyed, the property would have reverted to the crown had Israel followed ancient Near Eastern custom. But according to David N. Freedman, Elijah's objection

> is precisely the issue in Israelite law: the crown has no claims on other people's property, not even by "royal domain" or "eminent domain" as we would say. Only God exercises such rights: Israel is the "divine domain" and the property would have to revert to God, who owns it anyway. Jezebel's counsel to Ahab about seizing the property would be all right according to Canaanite law no doubt, and perhaps Mesopotamian and even Egyptian law, but was it proper according to Israelite law; obviously no law allows a criminal to profit from his crime, but even if the execution of Naboth for *lese majesté* had been on the up-and-up, it would have remained a nice question what would happen to the property. Strictly speaking it would go into the divine domain, but what that would mean in practice would depend. In the time of the monarchy the king would have the strongest claim simply because he had the most authority and power, and it may be that they worked out some rationale for the king to hold such property in trusteeship or the like; but certainly he would not be allowed to confiscate property for his own need and use. I would say it probably was added to the public domain, to be administered by the king.[145]

No passage of scripture reveals more clearly than this narrative that Israel's theo-political system had real meaning in the lives of the people. Yahweh's law severely restricted the powers of the king in favor of the economic freedom and security of the individual. When that law was violated through royal manipulation of the local court, Yahweh's messenger the prophet pronounced Yahweh's indictment. The dynasty, doomed by the indictment, was annihilated by the violence of Jehu several years later.

A prophetic narrative connected with the Aramean wars is that of Elisha and Hazael, who was to become king of Damascus (2 Kings 8:7-15).[146] According to 1 Kings 19:15-18, Elijah had been commissioned to anoint Hazael as king in Damascus, and was thus to interfere with a foreign government. While Hazael was never anointed, the narrative of Elisha tells how this *coup d' état* was set in motion. Not only the revolution of Jehu, but also the Aramean wars were regarded as Yahweh's punishment of Israel. While the concept of Yahweh's enlisting an enemy nation against his own people was a reality in the life of early Israel and thus is not new, the institutionalization of this enlistment in the office of a prophet is a new development, and in the usual state would be regarded as an act of treason.[147] The prophet was commissioned to set in motion Yahweh's judgment. The non-nationalistic character of the Yahwistic faith is nowhere more apparent than here, though the prophet certainly had nationalistic sympathies (2 Kings 8:11 ff.). The Yahwistic faith is an international faith; foreign governments are also Yahweh's agents. This understanding is characteristic of most of the canonical prophets as is evident from their prophecies to the nations.

2. *Narratives in Which Prophets Cooperate with Kings.* In contrast to the above narratives which show the prophet in conflict with kings, a number of Old Testament accounts show the prophet working on the side of the king. One such narrative describes how Elisha by a miracle overcame the Aramean army of chariots and horses (2 Kings 6:8-23). Elisha's servant had his eyes opened to see that "the mountain was full of horses and chariots of fire round about Elisha" (v. 17). Smiting the Aramean army with blindness, Elisha led them into the city, banqueted them, and sent them home. One should not be too quick to reject the possible historical foundation of such a narrative, in light of the charismatic powers of a prophet.[148] Yet regardless of the historicity of the narrative, it certainly reflected the traditional belief about Yahweh's war. As in the exodus, no Israelite army was involved whatsoever, but only a prophetic personality. (There was, however, an unseen army about Elisha, the chariots of Yahweh, so that those who were with Elisha were more than the Arameans; v. 16.) In answer to prayer, the Aramean army was delivered into the power of Elisha (vv. 18 ff.). Up to this point the narrative as an idealization follows the main lines of Israelite holy war. However, in the remainder of the account the king proposed the ancient tradition of the *ḥērem* (v. 21), while the prophet demanded an action quite at variance with this tradition.[149] This demand broke the chain of reaction of violence, at least for a time—"and the Syrians came no more on raids into the land of Israel" (v. 23).

The narrative of the deliverance of the city of Samaria from the Aramean siege (2 Kings 6:24—7:20) has many of the hallmarks of historical authenticity. It

> contains reminiscences at close hand of historical realities; e.g., a siege of Samaria by Aram, the reference to the Hittites and Musrites (7:6), as also minor details, e.g., the harrowing event of mothers eating their children by mutual bargain, with the king's human indignation which he would vent extrava-

WARNER LIBRARY HOLD

Borrower's Name

Morris, Alex

ID# 000614183

Due Date 4/28/15

Date Placed on Hold Shelf 3/31

gantly upon Elisha, and the humorous anecdote of the lepers' discovery of the abandoned camp. Also, Elisha again appears in a political rôle, as in 3:4 ff., here sitting in conclave with the civic elders, and assuming the offensive against the king in the spirit of Elijah and Micaiah.[150]

Assuming that the distress of the city was from Yahweh (i.e., that it was a judgment, v. 33), the king threatened the prophet. Elisha responded with an oracle that could be fulfilled only by an unusual act of Yahweh. The miracle is set forth in absolute terms in that Israel played no part whatsoever. The flight of the Aramean army was first discovered by four lepers who went out to give themselves up to the Aramean camp. Highlighting the effect of the miracle was the lengthy report of the discovery and the incredulity of the king and his officer. The Aramean flight was explained in terms of Yahweh's war:

> For Yahweh had made the army of the Syrians hear the sound of chariots, and of horses, the sound of a great army, so that they said to one another, "Behold, the king of Israel has hired against us the kings of the Hittites and the kings of Egypt to come upon us" (7:6).[151]

The narrative compares with the Song of Deborah in that many Israelities are mentioned: the king, a woman who had experienced an injustice, Elisha, the elders, the king's messenger, the captain, the four lepers, the porters of the city, the king's servants, and the people. Quite unlike the Song of Deborah, however, none of these persons participated in any way in the fighting. In this respect the account is similar to the Song of the Sea. Israel saw the victory as a result of the unilateral action of Yahweh.

A third narrative, in which neither prophet nor miracle are as decisive as in the above account, is that of Elisha and the three kings in the campaign against Moab (2 Kings 3).[152] The account reflects the hostility of the prophet toward King Jehoram (vv. 13 ff.). The prophet promised water without rain as well as victory over the Moabites. The Israelite army evidently approached Moab from the east (v. 22), and the water fell in the mountains of Edom. When the Moabite army rose in the morning they saw the sun shining on the water which was "red as blood." The Moabite's mistaking of water for blood is curious. John Gray suggests that

> the sight of the red light suggesting the semblance of blood might have been taken as a favorable omen to the Moabites, who were obviously poised for attack, such psychological factors being of great importance in warfare of that age.[153]

The three kings themselves withdrew when the king of Moab sacrificed his oldest son upon the wall of the city (v. 27).

The last of the narratives describing Elisha's cooperation with the kings tells of the simple magical act upon his deathbed when he was visited by king Joash (2 Kings 13:14-19).[154] The drama consisted of two acts.

> With his hand on the king's hand, at the *window eastward* (i.e., toward Aram), the prophet bids the king, *Shoot!* accompanying the action with a word of power, *an arrow of victory of YHWH's, and an arrow of victory at Aram!*[155]

As a result of this act the prophet promised victory over the Arameans in Aphek. While the symbolism emphasizes that Yahweh will give the victory, the accompanying action of the king was essential. In fact, in the second act of the drama, when Joash was told to strike the ground with the arrows, it was due to a lack of forcefulness that the king was promised only an inconclusive victory. This emphasis upon the king compares with the Royal Psalms, though it is obvious that Joash was dependent upon the word of the prophet.[156]

In the context of this narrative appears a saying regarding the prophets, used of both Elijah and Elisha: "My father, my father! The chariots of Israel and its horsemen!" (2 Kings 2:12; 13:14). This saying unites the prophet and warfare in Israel. It recognizes the prophet not as peripheral to warfare, but as central to it. Inasmuch as it was used of Elijah, who so far as we know never cooperated with the king in warfare, the saying may have applied to Yahweh's warfare against Israel, as well as to his protection of Israel. In any event this saying, used of the ninth-century prophets, sums up well the concept of Israel's warfare as we have traced it from her ancient beginnings.

Two incidents of unknown prophets who support the Israelite king in warfare are found in 1 Kings 20.[157] In neither case does a miracle occur. Both instances involve oracles promising victory (20:13, 28); the first also gives instructions for the battle (20:14). This more peripheral involvement of the prophet in warfare compares closely with that of the Mari prophets.[158]

In 2 Kings 14:25, the prophet Jonah prophesied that the boundaries of Israel would be enlarged under king Jeroboam of Jehu's dynasty.[159]

The last account of the cooperative action of the prophets and kings is found in the narratives of Isaiah in the account of Hezekiah's battle with Sennacherib (2 Kings 18:13—19:37).[160] Because of difficulty in harmonizing the various sources, a number of proposals have been advanced as to what actually happened.[161] These need not be discussed here, as our purpose is to note the theological thought of the narratives.

The speech of Rabshakeh (18:19-25, 28-35) set forth the alternatives for Judah.[162] Judah might trust in mere "words" (v. 20), in Egypt (vv. 21, 24), Sennacherib (v. 31), or Yahweh (vv. 22, 30). But they could not trust in Yahweh, for they had offended him. Hezekiah had destroyed his high places (v. 22), and Yahweh had sent Sennacherib against Judah in judgment (v. 25). Furthermore, other gods had availed their worshipers nothing. What help could the people expect from Yahweh (v. 35)?

When Hezekiah sent messengers to Isaiah, Isaiah answered him in terms of holy war: "Behold, I will put a spirit in him [the king of Assyria], so that he shall hear a rumor and return to his own land; and I will cause him to fall by the sword in his own land" (19:7).

The taunt song of 19:21-28 and the oracles of 19:29-34 are probably Isaiah's own.[163] Both the taunt and the last oracle promised Yahweh's deliverance. Such a deliverance is described in 19:35:

> And that night the angel of Yahweh went forth, and slew a hundred and eighty-five thousand in the camp of the Assyrians; and when men arose early in the morning, behold, these were all dead bodies.

F. Conclusion

In this chapter we have made a survey of pre-Deuteronomic documents related to warfare and the political context into which warfare must be placed. While this has been varied material—some narratives having moved toward ancient Near Eastern concepts in regard to power—we have found even in the Royal Psalm (Ps. 18) and in the Davidic covenant certain emphases that have withheld identification with Near Eastern concepts of power. David's reliance upon prophetic and priestly oracles in the practice of warfare meant that there was some attempt to keep warfare in line with the ancient concepts rooted in the exodus and Sinai. The development in which the counsel of the wise man rivaled in importance the divine oracle, however, laid the foundation for a conflict between the prophetic concept of reliance upon Yahweh (Isaiah-Jeremiah) and the wisdom concept that counseled integration with the power relationships of the ancient Near East. The Ammonite war, in which the technology of specialized warfare substituted for the militia's dependence upon Yahweh's miracle, established the basis for such counsel, which would later look to the technology of Egypt rather than to Israel's own tradition of Yahweh's miracle (Is. 31:1-5).

A barrier against such alien concepts of power, however, was provided by David's own actions such as the transfer of the ark to Jerusalem and subjection to the dynastic covenant which was related to Mosaic covenant law. These acts tied the empire to the ancient Yahwistic tradition and formed the basis for prophetic criticism and opposition to the power orientation of the ancient Near East. Such criticism arose early, as demonstrated by the Succession Document which exposed the anti-Mosaic roots of Solomon's reign, and condemned both his and his father's murderous acts that had brought him to the throne. In addition, a theology of history was written at this time, setting forth Yahweh's reign in relationship to Israel and the nations, not as patterned after the Near Eastern concept of empire, but as an alternative way that challenged the nationalistic aspirations of the Jerusalem court.

The prophets and allied conservative forces in Israel were a part of this opposition. The prophetic materials in regard to warfare in the Deuteronomic history were predominantly negative; that is, they opposed the various kings, threatening them with Yahweh's judgment. This opposition occasioned the split of the kingdom itself, as the North rejected the Davidic dynasty, and thus brought about the breakup of the empire. By weakening the centralization of political power, the division of the kingdom made possible the survival of prophetic authority, which even throughout the ninth century found its center in the North. There Elijah opposed the Omride dynasty that by its Baalistic policy sought to make Yahwism and the prophets the tool of the state. This opposition was epitomized in the challenge of Micaiah to the four hundred prophets who were the lackeys of a kingship policy that brought Israel ever closer to normal Near Eastern statehood.

Most of the narratives in which the prophets cooperate with kingship in warfare are accounts involving Yahweh's miracle. The few that do not, come closest to the Mari and other Near Eastern examples of relationships between the prophet and warfare.

The fact that ancient Israel was divided between such protagonists as Elijah and Micaiah on the one hand and antagonists such as the king and kingship prophets on the other (1 Kings 20) creates a problem for the modern interpreter who, like the Deuteronomic historian, has his bias and is likely to be just as selective in his own way.

For example, Julius Wellhausen saw the state and its power as the primary agency of God's work in history. For him the "state is always the presupposition of the church. . . ."[164] Reading the history of Israel from this perspective, he could say that, although Moses did not form a state as such, yet it was "the chief task of the age of Moses to bring about. . . the state, in the absence of which the church cannot have any subsistence either."[165]

Thus he concludes that "the nation is more certainly created by God than the church"; "... God works more powerfully in the history of the nations than in church history."[166]

This positive view of conventional political power in relation to God's purpose led to Wellhausen's critical assessment of the exile community; he recognized the genius of Ezekiel, who enclosed "the soul of prophecy in the body of a community which was not political, but founded on the temple and the cultus."[167] But this theocratic creation, "the residuum of a ruined state, is itself not a state at all, but an unpolitical artificial product . . . ; and foreign rule is its necessary counterpart."[168]

For Wellhausen, "every formation of a religious community is a step towards the secularization of religion; the religion of the heart alone remains an inward thing."[169] This negative attitude toward specifically religious institutions, even the voluntary group that would eschew conventional political relevance, parallels the assumption that the power state, with religion supporting it, is God's way of working in the world.

The sacral kingship school of thought also assumes that Israel was essentially a power state.[170] For example, Sigmund Mowinckel, a chastened exponent of this school, attempts to trace in *He That Cometh* the development of the concept of Messiah from sacral kingship, a national, political, this-worldly figure, to a superterrestrial, universal, cosmic religious figure.[171]

If, therefore, the interpreter of the Old Testament sees the power of Yahweh as communicated to the community chiefly through the coercive structures of kingship, thus coinciding essentially with the view of the kingship prophets, will not his or her interpretation be affected by this value judgment? In fact, may not the scientific method itself, as understood by some with their emphasis on analogy and repeatable event, be on the side of kingship and kingship prophets whose mythologies also emphasized the repeatable event? In contrast to this, Israel's orientation was to the unrepeatable event of the exodus and Sinai, which Yahweh by his free act may nevertheless repeat again in history in order to save his people (cf. Jer. 21:2).

As an example of the difficulties of the problem, I cite John Gray, who on the whole is a careful and sympathetic interpreter. He states that

> such passages as 3:4 ff. (2 Kings, Elisha with the three kings who invade Moab) and 9:1-6 (Elisha sends the sons of the prophets to anoint Jehu), which are primarily historical, serve to set Elisha in proper historical perspective and to control the traditions regarding him in the Elisha-saga proper.[172]

Yet one must ask why Gray chose such passages as these for the control group, seeing *them* as "primarily historical," and as setting "Elisha in proper historical perspective." Apparently because they have "the genuine ring of a good historical source" (stated of 3:4-27 minus vv. 11-19),[173] and because "Elisha as a prophet of Israel is mentioned incidentally as any other prophet might have been."[174] This "subsidiary role" of the prophet, however, reflects a "historical perspective" or political viewpoint characteristic of kingship in Israel which compares most closely with the historical viewpoint outside of Israel. The ancient tradition that Yahweh alone is the true king in Israel, that the prophet is his messenger, a view which as we have seen is founded upon Yahweh's unique saving act in the exodus, is contradictory to a view of the prophets' "subsidiary role." Thus the "proper historical perspective" according to Gray is in contradiction to the traditional prophetic view which saw the exodus-Sinai event as the archetypal tradition (witness the emphasis on the Moses tradition in the Elijah-Elisha narratives) rather than the "repeatable events" upon which the order of Near Eastern kingship was based.

It remains to relate the results of this chapter to the issues as set forth in chapter I. It is evident from this study that a major issue of Israel's pre-Deuteronomic documents in the Deuteronomic History had to do with the question of political power. The issue is joined between those forces that would propel Israelite kingship toward a typical Near Eastern state, and those forces that emphasized the ancient tradition. The tension was not between "myth" and history but between two ways in which "myth" relates itself to history. While the Jerusalem court moved far in the direction of Near Eastern power, certain elements of the Mosaic tradition were still residual in it; these provided a base for prophetic opposition, and for opposition from conservative quarters closely allied to prophecy. The ancient proverb as applied to Elijah and Elisha is instructive here: "My father, my father! the chariots of Israel and its horsemen!" (2 Kings 2:12; 13:14). This identification of prophet and holy war provided the tension with Near Eastern concepts of political power not only in the North but also in the South as revealed by the oracles of Isaiah, a prophet who opposed the counsel of the wise, and to whom Hezekiah came for help as he faced the superior forces of Sennacherib.

Chapter VIII

Warfare Theology in the
Deuteronomic Writings

The concept of the Deuteronomic history as proposed by Martin Noth is that Deuteronomy-Kings in their original form were one unified historical work.[1] This work, as understood by Noth, was written about the middle of the sixth century BC[2] from the perspective of the catastrophes of 722 and 587, and in the light of the book of the law (essentially Deut. 4:44—30:20) found in the temple during the reign of Josiah.[3] The historian included this book of the law at the beginning of his work. For historical content he used the disparate traditional materials which were at hand, and unified the chronology of the kingship period borrowed from the chronicles of the kings of Israel and of Judah.[4] He worked out his own chronology from the building of the temple back to the exodus, a period which he totaled at 480 years.[5] According to Noth, the writer was an "honest broker" in regard to the traditions, incorporating into his work large complexes of material such as the Deuteronomic law, the occupation of West Jordan, the histories of King Saul and of David, and the prophetic cycles of narratives.[6] While the writer was on the whole faithful to the tradition, he conveyed through the work his own overall impression (an impression justified by the course of history) by his selection of materials, by insertions of his own such as the introduction (Deut. 1—4), and by monotonously repeated judgments regarding the apostasy of Israel and her kings.[7]

While the view of Noth is essentially correct, it may be improved in some of its details. The Deuteronomic historian may have composed his work approximately 615 BC, presupposing the earlier history, but beginning his work with Moses' farewell speech. A second editor was responsible for the epilogue (from the death of Josiah to the end of the kingdom and the

exile, 2 Kings 23:26—25:26), and attached the earlier part of the Primary
History (Genesis through Numbers) to the work. He also may have incorporated the materials from that earlier work which extended beyond Numbers. David Noel Freedman writes of this second editor:

> This person is responsible for the work in its present form; I think I can locate
> his fingerprint, in a nearly incredible "echo" or inclusio which I believe I
> have identified: we all know about the anachronistic reference to
> "Chaldeans" in "Ur of the Chaldeans"...in Gen. 11, and 15. There is no
> further mention of the "Chaldeans" anywhere in the Primary History until
> we reach the end of 2 Kings (in the Epilogue). As though to say: the whole
> story has come full circle, and we are back where the ancient forefather
> started from, the land of the Chaldeans. I think this is deliberate, and the
> work of the final redactor.[8]

Yet a third person appended the final footnote about Jehoiachin (2 Kings
25:27—30).

We will begin this chapter with an attempt to discover the theology of
warfare of the Deuteronomic historian's foundational theological document, the book of the Torah found in the temple, which we presume to be
essentially our Deuteronomy 5—26; 28. Second, we will ask what specifically was the Deuteronomic historian's own theology of warfare.

A. *Theology of Warfare of the Book of the Torah (Deut. 4:40—26:19; 28)*
    The original Book of Deuteronomy is saturated with numerous exam-
ples of the aggressive spirit of holy war.[9] The older introduction to the book
(4:40—11:32) includes two extended statements on warfare, chapter 7
(especially vv. 16-26) and 9:1-6.[10] Kingship, the prophetic office, and the
laws of warfare are treated in the legal section of the book, from chapter 12
onward.

    In our analysis of these chapters, we are aware that some exegetes
regard use of the singular pronoun and verb with respect to Israel as characteristic of the original Book of Deuteronomy, while the plural usage is later,
perhaps an addition by the Deuteronomic historian.[11] While this may not
necessarily be the case, the statements below deal with passages in the singular, except where the plural is identified.

    1. *The Homiletical Introduction (Deut. 4:40—11:32).* The primary
passages, 7:16-26 and 9:1-6, refer to Israel with the singular pronoun and
verb, except for a short statement which does not concern us in 7:25a where
the plural verb is used. Plurals occur somewhat more frequently in the rest
of the material (7:1-15).[12]

    a. *Israel's Powerlessness.* Both passages emphasize the comparative

powerlessness of Israel, and the means by which Israel is to deal with her
resulting psychological problem:

> If you say in your heart, "These nations are greater than I; how can I dis-
> possess them?..." (7:17).

> Hear, O Israel; you are to pass over the Jordan this day, to go in to dispossess
> nations greater and mightier than yourselves, cities great and fortified up to
> heaven, a people great and tall, the sons of Anakim, whom you know, and of
> whom you have heard it said, "Who can stand before the sons of Anak?" (9:1,
> 2).[13]

An emphasis upon the superior power of the enemy is found also in the
first part of chapter 7:

> When Yahweh your God...clears away many nations before you, the Hit-
> tites, the Girgashites, the Amorites, the Canaanites, the Perizzites, the
> Hivites, and the Jebusites, seven nations greater and mightier than
> yourselves ... (7:1).

Israel's relative inferiority is further developed in a passage that uses
the plural pronoun and verb:[14]

> It was not because you were more in number than any other people that
> Yahweh set his love upon you and chose you, for you were the fewest of all
> peoples; but it is because Yahweh loves you, and is keeping the oath which he
> swore to your fathers, that Yahweh has brought you out with a mighty hand
> (7:7, 8a).

Thus all of the extensive passages dealing with holy war in the oldest
introduction to Deuteronomy emphasize the weakness of Israel.
Deuteronomy 7:7, 8a, a plural passage, says that this choice of the least of
peoples was deliberate on the part of Yahweh. Thus the Deuteronomist sees
the position of Israel as first among the nations (7:6) not as related to superior military power but to military weakness, a position due solely to
Yahweh's moral character and action. This is quite different from
Babylonian thought where the elected Marduk is given the "Enlil" power
and his earthly representative rules over the nations in exercise of that
power.[15] In contrast, Yahweh the ruler of all the nations chose a politically
powerless people to be his representative as leader of the nations.

b. *Reliance upon Yahweh's Miracle.* How was this powerless people to
deal with the powerful nations about them? The Deuteronomist had no
new message, no new weapon to suggest for his generation. They were to
remember the past:

> You shall not be afraid of them, but you shall remember what Yahweh your God did to Pharaoh and to all Egypt, the great trials which your eyes saw, the signs, the wonders, the mighty hand, and the outstretched arm, by which Yahweh your God brought you out; so will Yahweh your God do to all the peoples of whom you are afraid (7:18, 19; cf. 7:8b).

Yahweh's act at the exodus was to serve as the pattern for the conquest. But history would not repeat itself exactly. For the enemy who might hide themselves among the Israelities,

> Yahweh your God will send hornets among them, until those who are left. . . are destroyed (7:20).

The fact that Yahweh did not put an end to the nations at the beginning is explained in verse 22. But the Deuteronomist promises that gradually

> Yahweh your God will give them over to you, and throw them into great confusion *(wĕhāmām mĕhûmâ gĕdōlâ)*, until they are destroyed. And he will give their kings into your hand . . . (7:23).

The Deuteronomy 9:1-6 passage promises similar miraculous action on the part of Yahweh:[16]

> Know therefore this day that he who goes over before you as a devouring fire is Yahweh your God; he will destroy them and subdue them before you. . .(9:3).

c. *Israel's Participation in Warfare.* While Israel was required to wait upon Yahweh's miracle, and until then had to be content to live among the Canaanites, Israel was to wipe out the Canaanites after Yahweh's miracle occurred (7:16, 24; 9:3). Through the practice of the *ḥērem*, Israel was to "utterly destroy them."[17] The Deuteronomist thus sees the conquest in terms of the ancient tradition of the Song of Deborah. Yahweh's miracle, comparable to that of the exodus, would be decisive. Nevertheless, Israel would destroy the enemy which Yahweh had given into her hand.

d. *Yahweh's Choice of Israel.* The Deuteronomist dealt not only with Israel's political powerlessness, but also with the moral problem posed by Yahweh's choice of Israel rather than the Canaanites. It was not because of her righteousness that Israel was to possess the land (9:5). On the contrary, Israel was a stubborn people (9:6). Rather, Israel was chosen for two reasons: first, because of the wickedness of the Canaanites Yahweh was driving them out (9:5a); and second, by so doing Yahweh confirmed the word which he had sworn to Israel's patriarchal fathers (9:5b).

The J source had long before mentioned Noah's curse as a reason for the dispossession of the Canaanites (Gen. 9:20-27).[18] Such explanations are also found in the literature of Israel's ancient neighbors.[19] In the passages on warfare in Deuteronomy 7, the Deuteronomist states that Israel too is subject to Yahweh's judgment (7:4, 10, 11).[20]

The editor-writer of Deuteronomy in discussing holy war does not reflect the irenical spirit of the J writer who shows the patriarch Abraham as withstanding Yahweh's judgment upon the Canaanite cities of Sodom and Gomorrah (Gen. 18:22 ff.). Perhaps the Deuteronomist's times were too threatening for him to express such a spirit. Nevertheless, one should note that the editor did not try to harmonize with the practice of *ḥērem* such statements as Deuteronomy 10:18, 19: Yahweh "executes justice for the fatherless and the widow, and loves the sojourner, giving him food and clothing. Love the sojourner therefore; for you were sojourners in the land of Egypt." Even though the Deuteronomist lived in threatening times, he counseled that Israel meet those times, not through the modernization of her weaponry and political organization but through the ancient institution of holy war. We shall see this more clearly as we look at the Deuteronomic law.

2. *The Laws of Kingship, Prophetic Office, and Warfare in the Torah (Deut. 12—26; 28).*The office of kingship is part of a discussion of the three offices in Israel: kingship, the Levitical priesthood, and the prophet (17:14—18:22), the only such discussion in the Old Testament. Especially pertinent to our study at this point are the discussions on kingship and the prophet.

a. *The Law of Kingship (Deut. 17:14—20).* Although there are critical debates over the sources underlying this passage, its essential unity is suggested by the fact that it emphasizes a central theme, this being the transformation of the office of kingship as it was known in the ancient Near East.[21] The passage is hardly the work of the Deuteronomic historian for had he applied its message consistently, it would have condemned even his favorite kings. Though in part it resembles apodictic law, its genre is not law, but the hortatory or parenetic statement.[22] Its life situation may have been the Northern prophetic party, which evidently came South with priestly Levites after 722 BC.[23]

(1) *The Demand for Kingship: A Break with the Mosaic Tradition.* The discussion of kingship begins by recognizing that kingship dated not from wilderness times but from the period after the settlement (v. 14). Furthermore, the people's demand for kingship represented a serious break with the tradition of Moses, a renunciation of Yahwism. The apostasy may

be shown partially by the apparent fact that the demand for kingship was a decision of the people, though this is uncertain.[24] More important, the apostasy is indicated by the specific wording of the demand: "I will set a king over me, *like all the nations* that are round about me." "Like all the nations" may have been a cliché of Israel's ancient tradition. For the Deuteronomist "nations" often had a negative connotation, something like the English word "heathen." When used as it is in this passage the phrase meant "the way of the nations" in contrast to "the way of Yahweh."[25] Thus Deuteronomy was essentially negative toward kingship. Israel could not have a king "like all the nations" and remain the people of Yahweh. The demand was the essence of apostasy.

(2) *The Transformation of Kingship.* Even though the Deuteronomist had a negative attitude toward kingship, he nevertheless assented to it.[26] The solution of this apparent contradiction was that Israel could not have a king like all the nations, but a transformed kingship, a king "whom Yahweh your God will choose" *(yibḥar).* 'Choose' occurs thirty-one times in Deuteronomy, and is used for the first time by this book of the election, perhaps as a technical term.[27] This election was to be made by Yahweh through the prophet; thus the ascendancy of the word of Yahweh over the kingly office was to be maintained.[28] The intended result of Yahweh's election is obedience and loyalty to Yahweh.[29] "You may indeed set as king over you him whom Yahweh your God will choose" (v. 15) is thus the opposite of the statement "I will set a king over me, like all the nations that are round about me" (v. 14).[30]

The fundamental characteristic of this one whom Yahweh will choose is that he is to be a brother *('āḥ)* and not a foreigner *(nokrî,* v. 15). This contrast suggests the idea of citizen, an equal who is under covenant law. The word for "brother," occurring twenty-five times in Deuteronomy, is used especially in the legal section, where the goal is to assure equality. A brother is one who in the year of release frees his fellow Israelite from slavery (15:1 ff.), rescues him from poverty (15:7, 9, 11), helps him maintain his property (22:1-4), lends him money without interest (23:19), deals honestly with him (19:18-19). If the king is under the covenant rule of Yahweh and observes the fraternal law of brotherhood, the theocratic rule of Yahweh is maintained. Kingship is permitted only if it is thus transformed.[31]

(3) *The Rejection of a Kingship Based upon Military, Political, and Economic Power.* The demand for brotherhood is followed by five negative apodictic type commands that were designed to preserve equality in Israel (16-17):[32]

He shall not increase for himself horses.
He shall not make the people return to Egypt in order to increase horses.
He shall not increase to himself wives.
He shall not turn aside his heart.
He shall not increase for himself over-much silver and gold.

As we have already observed, the first command was the expression of an ancient Israelite tradition against a "modernized," standing army (Josh. 11:4, 6, 9; 2 Sam. 8:4; Is. 30:1-4, 7; 31:1-3; Hos. 14:4; Mic. 5:9).[33] This law was designed to protect Israelite brotherhood against the development of a military caste. Reliance on a well-equipped, professional army was regarded as a denial of trust in Yahweh and in his miracle.

The second command may have been directed against the slave trade and might be interpreted, "Do not sell your brothers as slaves." This interpretation is suggested by the Amarna Tablets in which Canaanite kings were said to have purchased troops in exchange for slaves.[34] Thus, this command as well was intended to preserve Israelite brotherhood.

The third negative command was directed primarily against the reliance upon foreign alliances. Such alliances were considered wrong in themselves as they represented a trust in man and would lock Israel into the economic-socio-political structure of the ancient Near Eastern nations. Furthermore, the gods of the king's wives would have to be recognized by Israel, thus forcing Israel into the polytheistic theo-political structure of her times. This was also the point of the fourth command, which is obviously closely joined to the third (cf. 11:1 ff.). The RSV translates, ". . . lest his heart turn away" (v. 17).

The fifth command was directed against royal ostentation and wealth. Again, its purpose was to protect the brotherhood of Israel against the encroachment of the power of kingship. It was a common practice of Canaanite kings to amass wealth and property and to use it to reward their servants who had served them faithfully in battle.[35]

As noted above, all these negative laws were designed to protect the concept of brotherhood as set forth in verse 15 and to prevent a kingship which was "like all the nations" (v. 14). The radical character of this attempt to transform kingship should not be overlooked. As Neher has stated:

> In the community of the covenant, God alone is king; in order that a human king be able to assume this office, it is necessary that he renounce the essence of his existence—his power. It was this requirement of renunciation which the prophets renewed without respite; it was this requirement which made them strike out against the monarch and those who, along with the monarch, held the power.[36]

(4) *Reliance upon Yahweh and Obedience to Torah as a Power Base (vv. 18-20).* If the king of Israel was not to rely upon military, economic, and diplomatic power like the nations, what was to be his power base? Verses 18 and 19 provide the answer in a positive statement:

> . . .he shall write for himself in a book a copy of this law . . . and he shall read in it all the days of his life, that he may learn to fear Yahweh his God, by keeping all the words of this law and these statutes, and doing them. . . .[37]

Here again an allusion is made to the principle of brotherhood of verse 15: "that his heart may not be lifted up above his brethren" (v. 20a). Faith in and obedience to Yahweh and his way were considered by the Deuteronomist as the only base for the preservation of equality in Israel. That he considered this an adequate power base for Israelite kingship and not a "spiritualization," is indicated by the promise: "so that he may continue long in his kingdom, he and his children, in Israel" (v. 20).

b. *The Law of the Prophetic Office (18:9-22).* The law concerning the prophetic office is stated throughout using the second person singular pronoun and verb, except for the one inconsequential phrase at the end of verse 15.[38] There is thus little reason to see this law as other than essentially a part of the text of the original Deuteronomy, that is, the book found in the temple.[39]

(1) *The Practices of the Nations: Discontinuity with Moses (18:9-14).* The law of the prophet begins essentially like the law of kingship, with the recognition that the practices of the nations regarding prophets or wisemen are in discontinuity with Moses. To understand the close relationship between the kingship and the prophetic laws, it is necessary to note the significance to kingship and to matters of state of the prophetic or diviner's office as practiced by the nations. For example, when the king of Moab was faced with military defeat, he sacrificed his son upon the city wall, and thus achieved a reversal of the military situation (2 Kings 3:27). King Saul, in order to avoid a military disaster, sought out a medium through whom he inquired of the dead (1 Sam. 28:3 ff.).[40] Such practices were the stock-in-trade of the wise men who counseled royalty in the ancient Near East. They were based upon a pseudoscience which demanded a great deal of knowledge.

Pharaoh, seeking an interpretation to his dream, called "all the magicians of Egypt and all its wise men."[41] Joseph interpreted the dream but indicated that it was not on the basis of his own wisdom that he did so (Gen. 41:16). The difference between Israel and the nations in this matter is even more clear in the story of Daniel's interpretation of Nebuchadnezzar's dream. Daniel said, "No wise men, enchanters, magicians, or astrologers can show to the king the mystery which the king has asked" (Dan. 2:27).[42] His own ability to interpret was not based on wisdom ("not because of any wisdom that I have...," Dan. 2:30), but upon a prophetic revelation.[43]

The writer of Deuteronomy called those who practiced sorcery or magic "an abomination to Yahweh" *(tô'ăbat YHWH, 18:12)*.[44] The meaning of this expression is indicated by its opposite, stated in verse 13: "You shall be blameless *(tāmîm)* before Yahweh your God." This should be translated "whole," and means wholehearted, undivided loyalty.[45] In other words, the issue relates to the first and second commandments. The radical transformation which denied kingship its traditional power base also denied to Israel the traditional wisdom, the means by which decisions of state were usually made. Israel must be whole with Yahweh; she must desert the way of the nations entirely for the way of Yahweh.

(2) *The Prophetic Office: Continuity with Moses.* The writer of Deuteronomy was convinced that kingship "like the nations" was fundamentally discontinuous with Moses. On the other hand, he states that the one raised up to the prophetic office is the successor to Moses (18:15). This similarity to Moses is based upon the central feature of Moses' office, his role as mediator of the covenant and the covenantal law at Horeb (18:16). The importance of the prophetic office is all the more striking when it is noted that Moses as covenant speaker was the one who addressed Israel throughout the Book of Deuteronomy. The prophet rather than the king, or even the Levitical priest, filled this highest of offices, according to the writer of Deuteronomy.

Like Moses, the prophet was to be covenant mediator. Israel's experience at Horeb on "the day of assembly" was thus decisive for the prophetic office and message. Perhaps this is further expressed by the fact that the prophet, like the king, was to be taken from among his brethren (v. 18).[46] This meant that his words must be words which promoted the rule of Yahweh in his kingdom of brotherhood.

As covenant mediator, the prophet spoke not mainly to the king, but to all the people. The characters throughout this passage are Yahweh and people. Yahweh will raise up a prophet for *them* ("you," vv. 15, 18); the prophet will speak to *them* what Yahweh had commanded. This relationship between Yahweh and people was so foundational that originally, according to the text, there was no mediator. Only at the request of the people did Yahweh give an intermediary to the people.[47] This too suggests the importance of brotherliness to Israel's faith.

(3) *Yahweh's Word as the Power Base of the Prophetic Office.* We

have noted that the political power base for kingship was to be Yahweh's word as found in the law or Torah. That word had been stated in the past and related to the foundational accounts of election, covenant, and covenant law. The prophet, on the other hand, was to speak the contemporary word. The only basis for his power was the word which Yahweh would put in his mouth (v. 18).[48] It was not the prophetic office that would validate the word, but the prophetic word that would validate the office (v. 22).

> The word of Yahweh has nothing to safeguard it. It rests solely on its having been transmitted to the messenger who brings it to the people. What is proclaimed will be fulfilled, but the people have the possibility of acceptance or rejection. The prophet has immense power, because he is the chosen messenger of Yahweh. He sets forth the word of Yahweh—a word of power. His claim is that Yahweh, as ruler of the universe, as king of Israel, controls and decides the destinies of mankind. It is the prophet, not the king or the priest, who plays the fundamental political role as the messenger of Yahweh. The politics of Yahweh are pronounced by his messenger—the prophet. Yet the prophet in his own person and office is a powerless man. It is only as the word has power that he shows himself true.[49]

c. *The Laws of Warfare (20:1-20; 21:10-14; 23:9-14; 25:17-19).*

(1) *Military Protection Promised by Yahweh.* The laws of warfare contained in parts of chapters 20, 21, 23, and 25 are of ancient pre-kingship vintage, and are the only laws of holy war in the Old Testament. They are homiletical in form and do not mention any obligation of Israel to come to the aid of Yahweh.[50] The absence of a covenant formulary within the Bible which includes participation in warfare as an obligation of Israel represents an important difference from the international treaty pattern which the biblical form to some extent parallels.[51] Since military protection was the promise of Yahweh and since he alone held the monopoly of political power in Israel, warfare was never accommodated to the theo-political structure as Israel's obligation.

The first laws of holy war, and the only ones that in their individuality are relevant to our discussion, are included in a ceremony which was to be used prior to battle. (Deut. 20:1-9). Verses 2 to 4 speak of Israel in the plural pronoun and verb, and may therefore be secondary.[52] Verse 1, undoubtedly from the original Deuteronomy, deals with the problem of Israel's psychological readiness in the light of her comparative powerlessness. Not only does Israel face an army greater than her own, but an army of horses and chariots as well, implements prohibited to Israel because of her faith.[53] Thus the Deuteronomist emphasizes that Israel is a relatively powerless people politically, a powerlessness increased by her own choice of faith, her rejection of a "modernized" army and of a kingship like the nations. In this connection, we notice that kingship is in no way invoked in these laws of holy war. If the Deuteronomist was attempting to revive ancient holy war practice to meet the present military crisis, he evidently did not think it important that he relate the king to that law.[54] This is astonishing in light of the fact that warfare was the king's chief reason for existence in Israel, as in the rest of the ancient Near East.[55]

Deuteronomy sets forth the basis for Israel's fearlessness in the face of overwhelming military superiority. Israel's power base was Yahweh, not Yahweh as he fought through Israel's army but Yahweh as he worked by miracle. The paradigm for Israel's faith remained the experience in Egypt: "for Yahweh your God is with you, who brought you up out of the land of Egypt" (v. 1b).

(2) *Liberal Exemptions from Military Service.* Because of this reliance upon Yahweh's miracle, the writer of Deuteronomy was also able to set forth the ancient laws of exemption from the militia, laws that protected the individual's freedom. In the speech of the officers before battle it was stated that the man who had built a new house and had not yet dedicated it should "go back to his house, lest he die in battle and another man dedicate it" (v. 5).[56] The man who had planted a vineyard and had not enjoyed its fruit should "go back to his house, lest he die in the battle and another man enjoy its fruit" (v. 6). The man who had betrothed a wife and had not lived with her was to "go back to his house, lest he die in the battle and another man take her" (v. 7). The final law in this series exempted the man who was afraid: "What man is there that is fearful and fainthearted? Let him go back to his house, lest the heart of his fellows melt as his heart" (v. 8).[57] The net result was nothing less than volunteerism. Anyone who did not wish to fight could be exempt from the militia.[58] Such sweeping exemption could be tolerated only in the light of the belief that Yahweh held a monopoly on military power, that he fought not through his people, but for them, that he would give them the victory according to the pattern of the redemption from Egypt. The one instance when this law of conscription was applied shows that precisely this faith in Yahweh's action was the basis for the law (cf. Judg. 7:2 ff.). Its radical character, if obeyed, would have the effect of protecting the citizen from the encroaching, coercive power of the state, from the way of kingship as set forth in 1 Samuel 8:11-18.

d. *The Blessing and Curse (Deut. 28).* The legal section ends with a blessing and curse formulary which involves warfare.[59] Nearly the entire chapter uses the second person singular pronoun and verb in reference to Israel, and is thus probably primary material.[60] The blessings consist of *shalom* and a lack of war (vv. 7, 10). The curses include natural calamities, and a strong emphasis upon military defeat by the enemy (vv. 25-26, 29-37, 41, 48-57, 64-68). Some of the natural calamities are compared to the plagues of Egypt (vv. 27, 60); thus the curses may have been regarded as Yahweh's war against his own people. The threat of the captivity is represented as Yahweh's sending them back to Egypt (v. 68).

The blessings are promised if Israel obeys Yahweh's commandments, and the curses are threatened if she disobeys. Thus the foundation for Israel's *shalom* is not her armaments and fortifications. These are false securities (v. 52). Israel's foundation for *shalom* is the way of Yahweh, faith in his promise and obedience to his word (vv. 1 f., 15, etc.).

3. *Summary: Theology of Warfare in the Torah.* The statements on warfare in the original introduction to Deuteronomy emphasize Israel's powerlessness. Israel was the least of all peoples, and as the least was chosen by Yahweh. This is in contrast to the mythology of Babylon where the divinity and his representative were chosen to exercise the coercive "Enlil" power over the nations. As the least of all peoples, Israel's power base was to be a reliance upon Yahweh's miracle. The Yahweh of the exodus was with them. He would deal with Israel's militarily superior enemies, and Israel had only to avoid being assimilated by them. Yahweh is a righteous God who dispossessed the Canaanites because of their wickedness, and who favored the Israelites, not because of their righteousness but because of his promise to the patriarchs. Israel herself must respond with obedience or Yahweh would drive her out as he had driven out the Canaanites.

In the law of kingship we have seen that Israel's military weakness was not to be considered a problem that Israel was to correct by any means possible. Rather, it was to be a deliberate choice for her present existence, a rejection of a social organization "like the nations" that would have made her militarily equal, or even superior. Kingship "like the nations" meant discontinuity with Moses and as such was a denial of Israel's roots. Israel might have a king, but only if he renounced the essence of a king's existence, his power. This meant renouncing ancient Near Eastern concepts of wisdom. Instead of this wisdom, Israel was to rely upon Yahweh's word through the prophet for her decision-making in the immediate situation. This demanded of the community the responsibility of discernment, for the prophet's authority did not lie in his office as such but in Yahweh's political leadership and the communication of his word as his messenger. Like Moses, the prophet was powerless in himself. His word was self-authenticating in that it came to pass as did that of Moses, and furthered the kingship of Yahweh and the brotherhood for which that kingship stood.

The laws of warfare emphasized the same point, that is, that Israel though relatively powerless in the face of a well-equipped, militarily superior enemy was not to fear. This confidence was not to be based upon her own superior organizational structure or armaments. Astonishingly, the writer of Deuteronomy made no attempt to modernize the ancient law of warfare to accommodate the contemporary structure of kingship. Israel's fearlessness was to be based upon Yahweh's word and miracle. This power base, Yahweh's word and miracle, which in the law of kingship resulted in the prohibition of a standing army, in the laws of warfare eventuated in the voluntary character of the militia. Neither a standing army nor a militia were necessary for Israel's protection, but only a few fearless volunteers who would believe in Yahweh's miracle.

The blessing and curse formulary that concludes the legal section of Deuteronomy continues this same emphasis on obedience to Yahweh's word, rather than self-help by fortification of cities. *Shalom* is not based upon "peace forces" but upon the obedience of all Israel to Yahweh's word.

The emphasis of Deuteronomy obviously assumed a different kind of kingdom than that experienced by the ancient Near Eastern states. Unlike the kingship of the nations, the kingship of Yahweh was founded not upon military power, nor upon a manipulation of power through diplomacy, nor upon a concentration of wealth that husbanded national and social resources, nor upon human wisdom that enabled a people to make decisions in regard to all the above for their own national advantage. It was founded rather upon Yahweh's covenant word, a word that provided structure for Yahweh's kingdom as witnessed by the covenant structure of the book of Deuteronomy itself.[61] It consisted of the word of promise fulfilled in the paradigmatic act of the exodus, the word of Torah for general orientation, and the word of the prophet for contemporary decision-making. The Israelite problem of faith addressed by the writer of Deuteronomy concerned the choice between two ways, the way of all the nations or the way of the kingdom of Yahweh.

B. *Theology of Warfare of the Deuteronomic Historian*

We turn now to the question posed at the beginning of this chapter: What was the Deuteronomic historian's theology of warfare? This is a difficult question since he was only the editor of this great work. One cannot know for certain where he may have added speeches of his own and where he was merely putting older material into his own words. Nor can it be ascertained whether his editorial comment, apart from the older material, represented all of his theology. As a result we can only try to assess the impression that the Deuteronomic historian has given this material by examining some of his insertions, and particularly by his repeated value judgments regarding the apostasy of Israel and her kings.

1. *Deuteronomy 1:1—4:44.* We will begin by examining Deuteronomy 1:1—4:44 to discover how it may relate to the rest of the historian's work.[62] The advantage of starting with this passage is that it introduces nearly all of his thought, and that there is wide agreement that it was written by either the Deuteronomic historian or a Deuteronomic editor.[63]

a. *The Uniqueness of Israel as Yahweh's Chosen People.* We note initially that in the thought of the Deuteronomic historian the relationship of Israel to the nations was grounded upon the monotheistic conviction that ". . . Yahweh is God in heaven above and on the earth beneath; there is no other" (4:39).[64] In relation to this one God, Israel was not merely one nation among many equals, but was unique. Her uniqueness consisted not in some special characteristic of her own being, but in the fact that Yahweh was nearer to Israel, to help and to save ("whenever we call upon him," 4:7), than to any other nation, and that the law of Israel was more righteous than the law of any other nation (4:8). These two points are essentially repeated in verses 33 and 34.[65] No other people had heard the voice of God speaking from the midst of a fire, as did Israel, and lived (4:33), and in no other instance had God come to take for himself a people from the midst of a nation "with testings, with signs and wonders, and with war, and with a strong hand and an outstretched arm, and with great terrors," as God had done to Israel in Egypt (4:34). These two aspects of uniqueness correspond to the two main parts of the covenant, Yahweh's protection of Israel (war) and Israel's responsibility to Yahweh (law).

Yahweh with whom Israel had a special relationship was also in relationship to other peoples.[66] He had "allotted to all the peoples under the whole heaven" the sun, moon and stars, and all the host of heaven (4:19).[67] Yahweh thus did not have an immediate relationship with the nations, but one mediated through the natural powers of this world. In addition Yahweh had allotted specific lands to Israel's brethren (Edom, Moab, and Ammon). Israel was therefore not to fight with these brethren, for Yahweh would not give their land to Israel (2:5, 9-12, 19). The Deuteronomic historian viewed the wars of these peoples as of the same order as Israel's wars (2:21, 22). On the other hand, the enemies of Israel, Sihon and Og, were seen as aggressors who insisted on fighting with Israel (2:26-30; 3:1).[68] Sihon had acted so unreasonably because "Yahweh . . . hardened his spirit and made his heart obstinate" in order that he might give Sihon into Israel's hand (2:30).

Yahweh's further relationship to the nations is set forth by the

Deuteronomic historian only in 1 Kings 8:41-43.[69] Here is expressed the hope that all the peoples of the earth might know Yahweh's name and fear him, even as does Israel. In the thought of the Deuteronomic historian this universal worship of Yahweh was tied closely to the institution of the temple. The foreigner, having heard of Yahweh's great person and his saving deeds, would come from a far country for Yahweh's name's sake, to pray toward the temple. While this universal goal of Yahwism is mentioned only once by the Deuteronomic historian and was by no means central to the historian's purpose in editing his history, it should be remembered that this history was likely prefaced by J E, and thus included J's primeval history, which would have given an orientation of a universal purpose to the entire work.[70] It is of primary importance to note that this universal purpose, according to the Deuteronomic historian, is not to be accomplished by warfare or Israel's empire building, but by the free response of the peoples when they hear of Yahweh's "great name," and "mighty hand," and "outstretched arm" (1 Kings 8:42; cf. Gen. 12: 1-3; Is. 2:1-4).

b. *The Occupation of Canaan: A Result of Obedience to Yahweh.* We can further observe that the Deuteronomic historian recognized the occupation of Canaan as a response of obedience to Yahweh. He began his work with Yahweh's command to leave Horeb and to occupy the land (1:7). This, however, was essentially a command to trust Yahweh, for Yahweh had promised Canaan to the patriarchs (1:6-8). Thus the Deuteronomic historian considered the patriarchal covenant to be the motivation and justification for the occupation. Yahweh's love for the patriarchs and his election of their seed was his motivation for bringing Israel out of Egypt, for driving out nations before her, and for bringing her in to give her the land (4:37-38).[71] The patriarchal covenant was also a major reason for Yahweh's forgiveness of Israel and for his permitting Israel to remain in the land (4:31; cf. 2 Kings 13:22-23).[72]

The fact that the Deuteronomic historian began with the occupation rather than with the exodus may have been due to the peculiar function of the Deuteronomy 1:1—4:44 material. It was probably meant to be a bridge between J E and the history rather than an introduction to an independent work. In any case, the Deuteronomic historian was thoroughly acquainted with the exodus tradition and referred to it no less than five times in this "introduction" (1:27, 30; 4:20, 34, 37).

The Song of the Sea presented the saving action of Yahweh as the reason the nations should fear before Israel. Similarly, the Deuteronomic historian saw the exodus as the pattern of Yahweh's action during the conquest: "Yahweh your God who goes before you will himself fight for you, just as he did for you in Egypt before your eyes..." (1:30; cf. 4:34). The land was Yahweh's gift to Israel. Yahweh would go before Israel and fight for her; she was to "fear not" (1:20, 21, 29). The kings of East Jordan were delivered into Israel's hand. With the defeat of Sihon, Yahweh would place the dread and fear of Israel upon "the peoples that are under the whole heaven" (2:24, 25, 29, 31, 33; 3:2, 21).

Only in the light of this ideal experience of Israel's escape from Egypt can the command to "go in and take possession of the land" (1:8) be understood. For it is found not among the stipulations (Deut. 4) in the covenant formula, where it might be expected following the analogy of the international treaties from the second millennium, but in the historical introduction (Deut. 1—3).[73] The command was therefore seen not primarily as an order to fight but as a command to trust and to have confidence in Yahweh "who goes before you" and who "will himself fight for you" (1:30). None of the commands in the stipulations (chapter 4), if one follows the analysis of Klaus Baltzer, deals with holy war, though the possession of the land was dependent upon obedience, as we shall see.[74]

c. *Israel's Rebellion and Yahweh's Judgment: A Recurring Theme.* A final observation regarding the Deuteronomy 1:1—4:44 introduction is that the Deuteronomic historian devotes a great deal of space to the discussion of Israel's rebellion and subsequent judgment by Yahweh. This theme is the heart of his work, for his purpose was to teach the meaning of Israel's history from the occupation to the collapse.[75] In order to show this rebellion as characteristic of Israel's response from wilderness times, the Deuteronomic historian expanded upon the story of the spies (1:19-46).[76] The command to possess the land, as noted above, was a command to trust. Rebellion against this command was rooted in disbelief in the goodness of Yahweh:

> And you murmured in your tents and said, "Because Yahweh hated us he has brought us forth out of the land of Egypt, to give us into the hand of the Amorites, to destroy us" (1:27; cf. v. 32).

When Israel, contrary to Yahweh's command, presumed to fight without Yahweh's presence, she was defeated by the enemy.

Israel was again warned against rebellion in the stipulations of Deuteronomy 4:1-24.[77] The first and second commandment are emphasized; Israel at Baal-peor (4:3) and Yahweh's judgment against Moses, who suffered for Israel's sake (4:21-22), serve as warnings. The threat follows the stipulations (4:25-28), threatening Israel with "utter destruction" (v. 26). Israel would be dispersed among the nations, there to serve idols, the "work of men's hands."[78]

2. *Joshua to 2 Kings*. This emphasis upon Israel's rebellion and judgment can be traced throughout the Deuteronomic historian's larger work by noting especially the structure of the history and the editor's comment. According to the Deuteronomic historian, the apostasy of Israel began in earnest after the conquest in the period of the judges. The Deuteronomic historian ended his history of the conquest period with the concluding statement of Judges 2:6-10, a statement that immediately followed Joshua's speech (Josh. 23). He began the period of the judges with a theological introduction, Judges 2:11-19, and ended the same period with the speech of Samuel (1 Sam. 12).[79] Both speeches, those of Joshua and Samuel, end with the threat of judgment. Thus the entire judges' period is "framed" with this thought.

a. *Rebellion, Judgment, and Salvation in the Period of the Judges*. The theological introduction, Judges 2:11-3:6, outlines the cycle that functions as a framework for the entire period: (1) Israel's rebellion against Yahweh (vv. 11-13); (2) Yahweh's judgment of Israel by warfare (vv. 14-15); (3) Yahweh's salvation in response to Israel's "groaning" (vv. 16-18).[80] In verses 19 ff. the cycle is repeated with Yahweh testing Israel by not driving out the enemy before her.[81] The idea of judgment following apostasy was a traditional one, rooted as we have seen, in the covenant curse.[82] The recurrent, cyclical pattern may have been a lesson from history, learned already by the prophets of the ninth and eighth centuries.[83] The new contribution of the Deuteronomic historian may be the idea of the progressive growth of the rebellion, though the J writer already in the tenth century saw a progressively growing cleft between man and Yahweh as a part of the primeval history.[84]

The growing apostasy of Israel throughout the period of the judges was portrayed by the Deuteronomic historian through the framework in which he placed his individual narratives.[85] This framework is first used in the case of Israel's conflict with Cushan-rishathaim, king of Aram-naharaim (Judg. 3:7-11).[86] Next follows the introduction and closing statement of the Ehud narrative against Moab (3:12-15a, 30b),[87] of the narrative and poem of Deborah and Barak against Sisera (4:1a, 2, 3a; 5:31b),[88] of the narrative of Gideon against Midian (6:1, 6b-10 [an insertion]; 8:28), and of Jephthah against the Ammonites (10:6-16; 12:7).[89] As Noth points out, the apostasy was renewed from time to time, always in heightened measure. It may be that the word "again" *(wayyōsīpû)*, which introduces most narratives (Judg. 3:12; 4:1; 10:6; 13:1), is to be understood in the sense of "they still added" (their abominations), as the Deuteronomic historian noted that the succeeding generations "behaved worse than their fathers" (2:19).[90]

The growing apostasy came to a climax in the lengthy introduction to the narrative of Jephthah (10:6—16). In this introduction the apostasy of Israel was especially great in that they worshiped not only the gods of the land, but also of all the neighboring peoples: Aram, Sidon, Moab, Ammon, and the Philistines (10:6). They were therefore oppressed in increasing measure on both sides of the Jordan by the Ammonites (10:8—9). To Israel's cry for help, the Deuteronomic historian added Israel's confessional (v. 10) which Yahweh rejected because of their continued rebellion (vv. 11-14).[91] Finally, because of Israel's continued petition and complete turning away from other gods, Yahweh "became indignant over the misery of Israel" (v. 16), and he delivered her. In this last historical example of the movement of history outlined in Judges 2:11 ff., the breach had been nearly final between Israel and Yahweh.[92]

   b. *The Apostasy of Kingship.* The crisis of the Ammonite war was followed by that of the Philistine conflict in which the high-priesthood was all but wiped out and the ark was lost to the enemy. Israel was saved only through the rise of Samuel. The Deuteronomic historian allowed this story to speak for itself, and added no editorial comment. The historian was building toward the crisis of a new rebellion that would alter the character of covenant and thus usher in a new age in Israel. For the Deuteronomic historian, by his use of traditional material,[93] saw in Israel's demand for kingship the high point of Israel's rebellion, as it conflicted with the central Yahwistic principle that violent political power was the prerogative of Yahweh alone.[94] The fact that the Deuteronomic historian interwove the two so-called pro-kingship sources with the three so-called anti-kingship sources and used the whole to suggest the divine permission for a transformed kingship indicates that the Deuteronomic historian was following the law of kingship of the Book of Deuteronomy, a law that itself was based on an older historical reality.[95] The demand for kingship was seen by the Deuteronomic historian's sources not only as Israel's rebellion, but also as judgment upon Israel, or as judgment Israel was bringing upon herself (1 Sam. 8:10-18). The Deuteronomic historian agreed with his conception.

   (1) *The Historian's Acceptance of the Davidic Dynasty.* While the Deuteronomic historian may have agreed with the Deuteronomic law of kingship, he did not apply it in a stringent way as a measurement of the performance of the various kings. Had he done so, even his favored kings would have stood condemned. In contrast to Deuteronomy, the Deuteronomic historian reveals his southern origins by his acceptance of the Davidic dynasty as an act of Yahweh.[96] Thus the Deuteronomic historian was less radical on the question of kingship than was the Book of Deuteronomy. (His work may have been to some extent a sermon to the

North in support of Josiah's reformation and program of empire, asserting the claims of the Davidic dynasty upon all Israel.)[97]

However, the Deuteronomic historian was essentially negative about kingship as a whole. David was his standard by which later Judean kings were measured (2 Kings 14:3; 16:2; 18:3; 22:2), and a symbol of hope for the future. While approving the first part of Solomon's reign (1 Kings 3:3), the Deuteronomic historian exposed Solomon's rebellion against Yahweh in the later part of his reign as a rebellion that brought judgment in the form of the division of the kingdom (1 Kings 11:1-13). The division of the kingdom meant the demise of the empire and a challenge to the tyrannical power of kingship as experienced under Solomon. This division saved Israel for Yahwism.

(2) *The Assessment of Kingship in the North.* As David was the ideal standard for the measurement of the Southern kings, Jeroboam I was the standard of measurement for the apostasy of the Northern kings (cf. 1 Kings 12:25-33; 13:33-34). The typical judgment throughout the Deuteronomic historian's framework is: "He did what was evil in the sight of Yahweh, and walked in the way of Jeroboam and in his sin which he made Israel to sin."[98] This sin of Jeroboam was his breaking of the unity of Yahweh-worship by establishing worship centers in the North to compete with those of the South (1 Kings 12:25-33). In this act Jeroboam challenged the ancient Yahwistic faith, that Israel was to find its unity in the common worship of Yahweh, as he manipulated the religious system to make it support the political reality of a divided kingdom. It is significant that for this historian the political division of the kingdom occasioned no problem; but the division of Yahweh worship was a grievous sin as it challenged the ancient theopolitical unity of Israel in the worship of Yahweh.

But it was possible for other kings to do even worse than Jeroboam, and the apostasy may have been seen as progressive, although the process was reversed at certain points. Omri as well as Ahab "did evil above all who were before him" (1 Kings 16:25, 30, 33). Their particular "progress" was the introduction of Baalism. Ahab's son, Ahaziah, followed a dual pattern: he "walked in the way of his father, and in the way of his mother, and in the way of Jeroboam the son of Nebat, who made Israel to sin" (1 Kings 22:52). The second son of Ahab to become king of Israel, Jehoram, put away "the pillar of Baal" but "clung to the sin of Jeroboam the son of Nebat . . ." (2 Kings 3:2, 3). The revolutionary Jehu came nearest to the Deuteronomic historian's approval of any Northern king because of his part in Baal's rejection (2 Kings 10:28-30).

In his editorial comment on the fall of Samaria, the Deuteronomic his-

torian was negative toward the Northern kingship as a whole. He states that
the collapse of the North occurred

> because the people of Israel had sinned against Yahweh their God, who had
> brought them up out of the land of Egypt from under the hand of Pharoah
> king of Egypt, and had feared other gods and walked in the customs of the
> nations whom Yahweh drove out before the people of Israel, and in the cus-
> toms which the kings of Israel had introduced (2 Kings 17:7, 8).

On the other hand, his attitude toward the prophets was positive in that
they were messengers by whom Yahweh had communicated his warnings
to Israel (17:13). This criticism corresponds to the total structure of his work
after the beginning of kingship. Yahweh was the leader of Israel by means
of his prophetic word that was usually one of judgment upon the kings.

(3) *The Assessment of Kingship in Judah.* Of the kings of Judah, the
Deuteronomic historian gave qualified approval to six, while only two
besides David received wholehearted approval.[99] We probably misjudge
the Deuteronomic historian if we assume that his standard of measurement
for these kings had only to do with worship reform and centralization of the
cult. Some version of the refrain that the king "did what was right (*yāšār*) in
the eyes of Yahweh, as David his father had done" is used of four kings: Asa
(1 Kings 15:11), Jehoshaphat (22:43), Hezekiah (2 Kings 18:3), and Josiah
(22:2). This "*yāšār*" probably meant that these kings proclaimed the law of
"*mišarum*" or "liberty" (*děrôr,* Lev. 25:10).[100] With this proclamation
every Israelite who was a slave returned to his own family and to his own
property (Lev. 25:8 ff.).

The worst of the Southern kings was Manasseh who "did what was evil
in the sight of Yahweh, according to the abominable practices of the nations
whom Yahweh drove out before the people of Israel" (2 Kings 21:2). Because of Manasseh's seduction, Israel did more evil than the nations that
Yahweh had destroyed before them (21:9). Other than this, the judgments
of the Deuteronomic historian against the kings of Judah were nearly as
monotonous as those against the kings of the North.[101] This monotony may
be evidence that the judgment of the Deuteronomic historian was leveled
not merely at individual kings, but at kingship as a whole. The exceptions
only show that the individual king had a chance to prove himself a positive
factor in Israel's history, in line with Yahweh's covenant promise to David,
if the individual king obeyed Yahweh.[102] A later epilogue beginning with 2
Kings 23:26, however, showed that even the pious king Josiah could not
redeem Israel, because of the sin of Manasseh.[103] The kingdom therefore
continued to move toward its collapse.

(4) *Yahweh, King, and People: Historiography*. That the Deuteronomic historian accepted kingship in Israel, not only as a historical but also as a theological fact, is shown by the change of the historian's framework after the inauguration of Saul. In the period of the judges he had traced the apostasy and judgment of *Israel* (Judg. 2:11 ff.; 3:7, 12; 4:1; 6:1; 10:6; 13:1).[104] After the establishment of kingship, he traced the apostasy and judgment of *the kings* (1 Kings 15:3, 26, 34; 16:18-19; etc.). Already in the time of the judges the Israelite people had, by continued apostasy, moved to the very edge of the abyss (Judg. 10: 6-16). Thus kingship took over the responsibility of obedience to Yahweh, with the result that the Israelite people were finally pushed over the edge by their kings.[105]

At the same time it is evident that the objective of the Deuteronomic historian was chiefly to present the history of the people of Israel themselves. The first part of his work on the period of the judges, was concerned expressly with the whole people, Israel. If the framework of the second part followed the kingship lists, it is clear that each king was accountable to the rule of Yahweh, whose concern was for all Israel. The framework statements themselves reflect this fundamental concern for Israel in that the first statement has Judah rather than Rehoboam as its subject (1 Kings 14:22-24), and the statements throughout maintain that the king "made Israel to sin" (15:26, etc.). More important is the Deuteronomic historian's extended homily on the history of the Northern Kingdom which he inserted after the account of its collapse. In this homily the subject is Israel as a whole people, rather than the kings (2 Kings 17:7 ff.).[106] In verse 8 Israel and her kings are named together, with Israel named first. It is clear that the place of the king in relation to Yahweh was regarded as secondary to that of the people. The responsibility of the king for administrative leadership was recognized, but Israel herself was held responsible for her apostasy and bore the consequences of it:

> . . .Yahweh removed Israel out of his sight, as he had spoken by all his servants the prophets. So Israel was exiled from their own land to Assyria until this day (2 Kings 17:23).

c. *Hope of Future Deliverance*. In addition to the emphasis upon apostasy and judgment by the Deuteronomic historian, there is finally some suggestion of hope and deliverance. The Deuteronomic historian held that Yahweh had pity upon his people, in the North because of his covenant with Abraham (2 Kings 13:22-23; cf. 14:25-27), and in the South because of the promise to David (2 Kings 8:18, 19). This hope for a king like David, who would stem the tide of apostasy and judgment, was for the

Deuteronomic historian fulfilled in Josiah who "did what was right in the eyes of Yahweh, and walked in all the way of David his father, and he did not turn aside to the right hand or to the left" (2 Kings 22:2). Josiah's reform described in 2 Kings 22—23 is the climax of the Deuteronomic history. All that follows is tragic epilogue.

David Noel Freedman says of this history:

> The Deuteronomic historian was inspired by the conviction that Josiah was the long-awaited scion of David who in his work and life would fulfill the ideals of kingship, restore the empire of his illustrious ancestor, and also lead his people to renewal of life in obedience to the terms of the ancient Mosaic covenant. The entire history aims at this conclusion, the happy climax of the biblical story. At the same time the Deuteronomic discourses of Moses and the disastrous experience of the N Kingdom served as a warning of another denouement, so that the catastrophe which actually ensued was not entirely unprepared. All along there had been two possibilities. With the tragic death of Josiah, it became clearer which alternative was the more likely. It is probable that the Deuteronomic history originally ended with the successful reformation of Josiah, and was subsequently revised to accord with the somber facts of history. . . . [107]

But did the Deuteronomic historian and/or the editors who supplemented him have no hope that after the collapse Yahweh would again act in holy war for his people? In the light of the message of the prophets, it is surprising that this was not the historian's emphasis. The Deuteronomic historian left only a few hints of hope for the future. The first he included in his introduction (Deut. 4:29 ff.). When Israel is scattered among the peoples, then she will seek Yahweh and find him, for "Yahweh your God is a merciful God; he will not fail you or destroy you or forget the covenant with your fathers which he swore to them." He included a second note of hope in the prayer of Solomon at the dedication of the temple. If the people, having sinned against Yahweh and having been carried away captive by the enemy, repent and pray toward the land to Yahweh, then may Yahweh hear in heaven and forgive, and cause their enemies to have compassion upon them (1 Kings 8:46-53; cf. vv. 33-34).[108] The Deuteronomic historian evidently does not anticipate a new act of Yahweh through holy war, but a new act of Yahweh upon the heart of the enemy. Finally, the editor who added the supplement telling of the elevation of Jehoiachin by Evil-merodach of Babylon (2 Kings 25:27-30), sees stirrings of hope in terms of the Davidic promise, a promise that had been an emphasis of the Deuteronomic historian.

3. *Summary: Theology of Warfare of the Deuteronomic Historian.* As

we have seen, the Deuteronomic historian held that Israel had a direct relationship with Yahweh, while Yahweh's relationship to the nations was
mediated through the impersonal powers. Israel's superiority lay not in
herself but in Yahweh's miraculous deliverance and his law. The
Deuteronomic historian looked for the time when the foreigner also would
worship Yahweh in the temple. Israel's command to fight, found among the
acts of Yahweh in the covenant introduction rather than the stipulations,
was related by the Deuteronomic historian to the patriarchal promise. His
pattern for the conquest was the exodus.

The main emphasis of the Deuteronomic historian, both in his introduction and throughout his work, was Yahweh's warfare against his own
people as his act of judgment. The Deuteronomic historian's editorializing
in the period of the judges portrayed a cyclical, progressive development of
rebellion, a rebellion that climaxed in Israel's demand for a king "like all the
nations." The Deuteronomic historian, like the editor-writer of the Book of
Deuteronomy, accepted a transformed kingship. Unlike the writer of
Deuteronomy, however, being a Southerner, he accepted the Davidic
promise as the hope for the future. Most of the kings he condemned, but
those who were obedient to Yahweh and did "right" (*yāšār*) he praised. His
hope lay in the great king Josiah to whom he looked for a reversal of Israel's
decline.

C. *Conclusion*

We will now relate the results of this chapter to the issues as set forth in
chapter I. The message of the Deuteronomist is something of an anomaly.
His threat of war as punishment for Israel's sin is obviously a major motif of
his work. At the same time the Deuteronomist is strongly set against the
concept of Israel as representing the "Enlil" power of divinity, both in his
statements regarding the institution of holy war and in his statements regarding the offices of Israel. He held Israel to be comparatively powerless,
and he directs no message to Israel that they should try to change this situation. In fact, his message is the opposite. Israel's power base is faith in
Yahweh's miracle and obedience to his word. The prophet rather than the
king is seen as the successor of Moses. While kingship is permitted, its
conventional Near Eastern power base is denied and replaced by obedience
to Yahweh's law. Wisdom which in the Near East determined the course of
statecraft and of warfare is rejected in favor of the prophetic word, which
was closely related to the office of Moses. The laws of warfare are not accommodated to kingship; the militia is to rely on Yahweh's promise and
miracle. For the Deuteronomist, Yahweh's kingdom is founded not upon

military power, nor upon manipulation of power through diplomacy, nor upon concentration of wealth that husbands national and social resources, nor upon human wisdom that enables one to make decisions in relation to all the above for one's national advantage. Yahweh's kingdom is founded rather upon Yahweh's promise and miraculous act, upon his covenant structure of Torah and prophetic word; and Israel's future depends solely upon her present faith and obedience to this structure. Thus the tension between the way of the nations and the way of Yahweh in regard to the question of political power is at the heart of the Deuteronomist's message.

The Deuteronomic historian accepted the theology of the Deuteronomist for his own. The difference was that that message which in Deuteronomy was posed as future threat became for the Deuteronomic historian the basis for the interpretation of Israel's and Judah's past. His harmony of the dynastic promise to David and the ancient traditions which had rejected human kingship seems to have followed along the same lines as the Deuteronomist's law of kingship. However, it may be significant that none of his criticisms of individual kings is based upon this Deuteronomic law. Was he evading this fundamental issue of power by criticizing the kings mainly on the basis of whether or not they promoted the centralization of worship? On the other hand, was he saying, by his criticism of Jeroboam's policy of setting up rival Northern centers of worship, that the unity of Yahweh's kingdom was not to be expressed by kingship (which was divided) but by the centrality of Yahweh-worship (as in the ancient confederacy), a worship that was not to be the handmaiden of kingly decision and power? In any case, his concept of the sovereignty and independence of Yahweh's rule from the human institution of kingship is shown by the place that he gives to the prophetic figure in his outline, for the prophet, usually opposed to the king, is concerned not only with centralized worship, but also works against national aggrandizement. On this basic understanding of Israel's power base, the historian was no different from the Deuteronomist. He too shows the tension of Israel's and Judah's history as a struggle between adherence to the way of Yahweh and acceptance of those forces that would make of them merely another Near Eastern state.

Was the historian interpreting Deuteronomy correctly in his mistaken enthusiasm for Josiah's reform? Or was his contemporary, Jeremiah, closer to Deuteronomy in criticizing the reform (Jer. 3:6-10)? Both the historian and Jeremiah were positive toward Josiah (cf. Jer. 22:15-16), yet Jeremiah may have had a deeper insight into the meaning of the Torah, into the incorrigible character of Israel, and into what would be required to bring Israel's history to a favorable conclusion (Jer. 31:31 ff.).

Chapter IX

Retrospect and Prospect

It is our purpose in this chapter to summarize the long way that we have come, and within that summary to make a short analysis in line with the questions raised in Chapter I.

From every period of ancient Israel's existence, the Hebrew literature presents battle reports, in both poetry and prose, that unite the divine and human dimensions. The literature of the patriarchal period, however, while it reports that the clans were occasionally involved with the military culture of their time, is essentially pacifistic in character. This perspective was no doubt nurtured in a period of political weakness, when the patriarchal clans sojourned among the Canaanite city states. The uncertainties involved in this time of political weakness were mitigated and made bearable by the religious experience of election and covenant, involving the clans in a novel "politics of promise" with regard to the human concerns of community, land, and national significance. All this of course is prolegomenous to the story of Israel that follows. But because of what followed, this "politics of promise," born in a time of weakness but grounded in the unconditional and unilateral promise of God (especially in relationship to land), could be promoted as the true way for Israel even in her time of political strength.

In contrast to the passive nature of many of the patriarchal narratives, the exodus poetry and narratives portray a passionate and aggressive concern for justice in the midst of conflict. The uniqueness of the exodus material, however, is that the Hebrew clans were not called to do battle in the usual sense of the word, but to respond to and trust in Yahweh as sole warrior against the military might of Egypt. The Hebrew freedom movement experienced Yahweh as the sole bearer of a unique political power and authority addressed both to themselves and their enemy through a prophetic personality. In the human arena the leadership of the warrior was replaced by the leadership of the prophet, one who spoke the word of Yahweh both to the Hebrews and to Egypt. Contrary to the four "Type A" scholars referred to in Chapter I who held that Israel's emphasis on the lack of human participation in battle was a late theological reflection, we have shown that the unilateral role of Yahweh as warrior in freeing the Hebrews from Egypt is the emphasis of all of Israel's relevant literature, the earliest as well as the latest.

This unique experience of deliverance from Egypt by a prophetic personality rather than by a warrior hero was not an ephemeral event, but was the foundation for a new type of theo-political order, the kingship of Yahweh. He who had been Israel's only warrior was now her only king. It is significant that the Sinai event happened outside the promised land and prior to the fulfillment of the promise of land. The political existence of the people of Yahweh, even their relationship to the land, was dependent upon their relation to the person of Yahweh, and not vice versa.

The radical impact of the exodus event upon Israel's theo-political structure created within Israel a fundamental tension. As we noted in the first chapter, this was not so much a tension between myth and history (Hanson), as it was a tension between the way of Yahweh and the way of the nations. It was caused, not by a polarity between Israel's ancient covenant tradition and her ancient war tradition (Smend), but by an event within the war tradition itself, that is, the deliverance from Egypt. This peculiar way in which mythic experience was mediated to history, through prophecy and miracle, contrasted sharply with the way of warfare and kingship as known among the nations. The testimony to this event, inserted into the covenant tradition, was seen as Yahweh's foundational act of grace upon which Israel's government was to be based.

Significantly, the Song of the Sea, which celebrates Yahweh's victory in the exodus, does not exhibit this tension, but it is apparent in Israel's other ancient war poem, the Song of Deborah. No doubt the event glorified by the Song of the Sea focused the issue for the writer of the Song of Deborah. Both songs proclaim victory, not through human fighting, but through a nature miracle of Yahweh. The Song of Deborah, however, also celebrates Israel's participation in warfare; there is present not only the prophetic personality but also the war leader. For how long would the primacy of the prophetic element over the warrior, so evident in the Song of Deborah, be maintained in Israel?

It should be noted that in the account of the battle, the relationship between Yahweh and his people is not synergistic. The miracle of Yahweh alone is acclaimed as decisive; the human fighting is not described and the human war leader is not made a hero. The apparent influence of the tradition of the sea in this poem as well as in later narratives, suggests that the mind of the poet was guided not merely by a generalized Near Eastern mythology (Weippert) but by the specifics of the exodus event.

The primacy of the sea event is also recognized by the narratives of the conquest; they are introduced by the premonarchic liturgy of the Jordan crossing, a transparent reminder of the sea event that proclaimed the occupation as the gift of Yahweh. The ancient narrative of the fall of Jericho has the same emphasis, though as in the Song of Deborah the people participated, but only after the defeat had been accomplished. The varied narratives of the Judges, especially those that include miracle, maintain this same tension. The tension is found also in the Shechem covenant which, unlike that of Sinai, introduced human fighting into its introductory history. Yet the Shechem covenant, influenced by its earlier recital of the sea experience, denied the efficacy of human fighting.

The ancient tradition of Israel thus proclaimed its distinctive theology of warfare—that obedience to Yahweh's word and trust in his miracle are alone decisive. Israel's faith in Yahweh as warrior led her to reject the military expediency of developing sophisticated weaponry such as horses and chariots even to the time of David, weapons that would have made Israel competitive with her Philistine and Canaanite enemies, not merely on the hills and mountains, but on the lowlands and plains where competition finally counted.

More fundamental than Israel's military inexpediency, though closely related to it, was Israel's political inexpediency with regard to her own theopolitical structure and organization. It is at the point of the Philistine threat that the implicit tension focused by the exodus and Sinai event became explicit in Israel's literature, in the records of an open debate in the central councils of Israel, as Samuel and the people deliberated the issue of kingship. Although the outcome of the three debates is the rejection of the ancient tradition in favor of the institution of kingship, all three statements tie the tradition of Yahweh as the only savior in battle to that of Yahweh as the sole ruler of Israel.

The narratives on the problem of political power thus coincide with the ancient Song of the Sea, in which earlier the same connection was made. It would seem that these two themes, Yahweh as sole warrior and sole king, stand or fall together in their reflection of Israel's early history, for those accounts that speak to the subject unanimously base the latter upon the former. It is significant that Saul's coronation is closely connected with his military deliverance of Jabesh-Gilead, a battle in which no miracle is recorded. The political order founded upon the prophetic personality and Yahweh's miracle was exchanged for an order which was moving toward military and political expediency, the human manipulation and control of the social and political resources involved in the violent use of power.

David's rise began auspiciously as symbolized by the tale of his battle with Goliath, a battle in which David did not rely upon modern instruments of warfare but upon Yahweh and a stratagem born out of political weakness. In the first part of his reign, though his battles were fought by his own personal troops, he nevertheless went into battle only in response to Yahweh's oracle, an oracle based not upon the traditional concepts of Near Eastern power, but upon the tradition of the exodus and Sinai. This dependence upon oracle was qualified, however, as both David and his son Absalom esteemed the counsel of the wise men, based on Near Eastern concepts of calculation and power, as equal in value with the oracle. Such calculation was inevitable when reliance upon a modernized army displaced the traditional reliance upon Yahweh's prophet and miracle. The acceptance of an alien concept of power was not without its limitations, however; the pull of the ancient tradition is seen in David's own act of bringing the ark of the covenant to Jerusalem, and in the formulation of a dynastic covenant that maintained elements of the Mosaic covenant.

Criticism and opposition to this power orientation arose early, as demonstrated by the Succession Document, which exposed the anti-Mosaic rootage of Solomon's reign and the murderous acts that secured his throne. At the same time, the redaction of the ancient theology of history (Gen. 1—12) set forth Yahweh's rule in relation to Israel and the nations, not in the pattern of the Near Eastern theo-political concept of empire (i.e., as represented by the *Enuma Elish* or the *Memphite Theology*) but as an alternative way in line with Israel's ancient heritage. This testimony no doubt was shunted aside by the nationalistic aspirations of the Jerusalem court.

The critical materials, such as the Succession Document and the later prophetic narratives opposing kingship policy, picked up a minor element from the earlier periods—the theme of Yahweh's judgment against faithless Israel—and made it a major concern. A negative oracle from one such prophet touched off the split of the kingdom itself, in which the North rejected the Davidic dynasty. This division broke up the concentration of political power and brought about the collapse of the empire, thus facilitating the survival of prophetic authority.

In the North, Elijah opposed the Omride dynasty and its Baalistic policy that sought to make Yahwism and the prophets into tools of the state. The issue, as posed by Elijah, was between a divinity who represented an alliance of economic and religious interests backed by political coercion, and a divinity who represented the moral, social, and spiritual values of exodus-Sinai, whose economics consisted of faith in his word of promise and whose politics consisted of obedience to his word through the prophet. The conflict between prophet and kingship was also expressed within the prophetic party and Yahwistic tradition itself, as seen in the narrative of Micaiah's confrontation with the four hundred prophets who as lackeys of kingship policy pushed Israel ever further toward typical Near Eastern statehood. The prophets, as represented by Elijah and Elisha, were seen as the protectors of Israel (rather than the kings); thus the striking proverb: "My father, my father! the chariots of Israel and its horsemen!" This division of the prophets in ancient Israel creates a problem for modern interpreters who, divided in their own way over the fundamental questions of loyalty and power that divided the ancient prophets, are apt to bring their own interpretive prejudices to the text.

The Deuteronomic historian held that Israel's difference from the nations was not due to an innate superiority, but lay in Yahweh's miraculous deliverance and in Torah. While he evidently accepted the Northern reorientation of kingship as set forth in the Book of Deuteronomy—from a foundation upon wordly power to a foundation upon Torah—the historian also accepted the Davidic covenant and the dynastic principle of the South. Following the lead of the prophets, one of his main emphases was Yahweh's warfare against his own people, especially against kingship, as an act of judgment. While he recognized kingship on the whole as a failure, his faith in the Davidic promise and the reforms of individual kings made him place his hope in Josiah as one who would turn the tide. It was a vain hope (as he or his successor later observed) due to the cumulative weight of the sin of the dynasty; Judah collapsed, as the Northern Kingdom had done before it.

But was 587 the last word for the meaning of Israel's history? Was Israel elected by Yahweh only for this negative result? Was the vision of the Deuteronomic historian that all nations would one day serve Yahweh to be frustrated? For an answer to these questions we must go beyond the Primary History to the message of the great prophets. Most of the major pre-exilic prophets prophesied on the basis of Yahweh's promise that beyond judgment Yahweh would again act to gather his people to their own land. Perhaps more important than any of these, the exilic prophet known as Deutero-Isaiah proclaimed a second exodus in which Yahweh would again return his people to Zion. Ambiguous as her history had been, Israel would yet go forth not as a conqueror with an army but in the tradition of the prophets to proclaim Yahweh's Torah to the nations. In this experience, resulting in suffering and death, the servant would know Yahweh's new act of resurrection and exaltation to kingly power.

On the issue of Yahweh's decisive act for Israel, the message of the prophets was not essentially different from that of the later apocalypticists, especially as set forth by the Book of Daniel. As Yahweh had intervened throughout Israel's history in terms of the paradigm of the exodus, so he would intervene again at the end of history in judgment and resurrection for the victorious denouement of his kingdom. Daniel and the Wise, rather than the violent Maccabees, were the suffering representatives of this kingdom.[1]

It appears therefore, that just as the Zealots of the first century AD found their antecedent in the Maccabees, so Jesus and his followers, who opposed the Zealots, had their antecedents in the alternative movement of the writer of the Book of Daniel and the Wise.[2] As "Son of Man," as "Messiah," as Prophet and Suffering Servant, and as a second Moses, Jesus was declared by himself and by the ecclesia as fulfilling the promise of the Old Testament, a promise that pointed from the way of the nations to the way of Yahweh.

The root of this vision of the way of Yahweh, a way that alienated Israel from her own environment and made her a suffering people, was not a late spiritualization but an event happening at the beginning of Israel's existence, an event that transformed warfare itself from a manipulation of power to a prophetic act and a patient waiting upon Yahweh's deliverance. It is too much to hope that the way mapped out by such an event can be lived without suffering and contradiction; its goal can be achieved only by new acts of Yahweh, who sustains and leads the faithful into the future.

Notes

Notes

Chapter One

1. For a discussion of the centrality of the theme "God as Warrior" to biblical theology see Patrick D. Miller, Jr., *The Divine Warrior in Early Israel* (Cambridge, Mass.: Harvard University Press, 1973), p. 174.

2. My use of the term "theo-political" is derived from Martin Buber; it points to the distinctive character of divine rulership found in ancient Israel. See his *Kingship of God*, trans. by Richard Scheimann (3rd ed. enlarged; London: George Allen and Unwin Ltd., 1967), pp. 56-57, 126, 139-140.

3. The work of Gerhard von Rad, *Der heilige Krieg im alten Israel* (Göttingen: Vandenhoeck & Ruprecht, 1952) has been pivotal in this discussion. For a survey of the issues, see the essay by L. E. Toombs, "War, Ideas of," *The Interpreter's Dictionary of the Bible*, Vol. IV, ed. by George Arthur Buttrick (New York, Nashville: Abingdon Press, 1962), pp. 796-801, and the updating of the discussion by N. K. Gottwald, "War, Holy," *IDB*, Supplementary Volume (Nashville: 1976), pp. 942-944.

4. Friedrich Schwally, *Der heilige Krieg im alten Israel* (Leipzig: Dieterich'sche Verlagsbuchhandlung, Theodor Weicher, 1901).

5. *Ibid.*, pp. 27 f.

6. Johs. Pedersen, *Israel, Its Life and Culture*, III-IV (London: Cumberlege, Oxford University Press, 1947; first published in Danish, 1934), pp. 1-32.

7. *Ibid.*, p. 18.

8. *Ibid.*, p. 21.

9. Gerhard von Rad, *Der heilige Krieg im alten Israel* (Göttingen: Vandenhoeck & Ruprecht, 1952).

10. *Ibid.*, pp. 33 ff.

11. *Ibid.*, pp. 43-50.

12. *Ibid.*, p. 48.

13. *Ibid.*, pp. 56 ff.

14. *Ibid.*, p. 67.

15. *Ibid.*, pp. 50 ff.

16. *Ibid.*, p. 79.

17. Patrick D. Miller, Jr., *The Divine Warrior in Early Israel* (Cambridge, Mass.: Harvard University Press, 1973).

18. *Ibid.*, p. 156. Granted their presuppositions, the results of the first three writers are logical. But I cannot understand the logic of Miller who holds to the ancient character of such texts as the Song of the Sea (Ex. 15), yet holds that ascription of victory solely to the miraculous intervention of Yahweh apart from any participation of the people is late thought. See *Ibid.*, p. 209, n. 1.

19. Schwally roots Israel's early history in magical thought. Schwally, *op. cit.*, pp. 9 ff. Pedersen rejects magic but emphasizes psychic strength. Pedersen, *op. cit.*, p. 18. Von Rad rejects both of these, but he challenges the historicity of the period of the conquest as a time of holy war. Von Rad, *op. cit.*, pp. 15 ff. Miller, rejecting von Rad, holds that the conquest was the time of holy war par excellence. Miller, *op. cit.*, p. 160.

20. Rudolf Smend, *Jahwekrieg und Stämmebund: Erwägungen zur ältesten Geschichte Israels* (Göttingen: Vandenhoeck & Ruprecht, 1963). See the English translation by M. G. Rogers, *Yahweh War and Tribal Confederation* (Nashville, New York: Abingdon Press, 1970).

21. Smend, *Yahweh War. . .*, pp. 134 f.

22. *Ibid.*, pp. 28 ff.

23. *Ibid.*, pp. 43-75.

24. *Ibid.*, "Rachel Tribes and Leah Tribes," pp. 98-108.

25. *Ibid.*, "The Exodus from Egypt and the Formation of the Covenant at Sinai," pp. 109-119.

26. *Ibid.*, "Moses During the Exodus and at Sinai," pp. 120-135.

27. *Ibid.*, p. 38.

28. A Glock, "Warfare in Mari and Early Israel" (PhD dissertation, University of Michigan, 1968, University Microfilms, Inc., Ann Arbor, Mich.).

29. *Ibid.*, pp. 189-190.

30. *Ibid.*, p. 190.

31. *Ibid.*, pp. 191-192.

32. *Ibid.*, pp. 209-213.

33. *Ibid.*, p. 213.

34. *Ibid.*, p. 234, n. 136.

35. *Ibid.*, pp. 13; 19, n. 48; 213. Cf. *Abstract* at beginning of his work.

36. Fritz Stolz, *Jahwes und Israels Kriege* (Zürich: Theologischer Verlag, 1972). See p. 7. Skeptical of the ancient character of the biblical texts, Stolz places the J and E sources relatively late (p. 7), regards a large part of the Gideon narrative as a reflection of the later Jerusalem celebration of theophany (p. 121, Judg. 7:2 ff.), the greater part of the Song of Deborah as reflecting the time of Saul and the even later Jerusalem cult (pp. 102-113), and the Song of the Sea as a very late composition (p. 91, Ex. 15:1-18). Exodus 15:20-21, however, he considered authentic and contemporary with the sea event (p. 90).

37. *Ibid.*, pp. 196-198.

38. *Ibid.*, pp. 198-202. This could of course be held only by rejecting the early unity of the Song of Deborah. Cf. Note 36.

39. *Ibid.*, pp. 201-202.

40. See the discussion of Deuteronomic literature at beginning of Chapter VIII.

41. *Ibid.*, pp. 204-205.

42. *Ibid.*, pp. 19, 20, 108, 115-123, 141, 151-152, 153-154, 160, 172-173, 187-191, 204.

43. *Ibid.*, pp. 115-123.

44. *Ibid.*, pp. 153-154.

45. *Ibid.*, pp. 187-191.

46. Manfred Weippert, " 'Heiliger Krieg' in Israel und Assyrien: Kritische Anmerkungen zu Gerhard von Rads Konzept des 'Heiligen Krieges im alten Israel,' " *Zeitschrift für die alttestamentliche Wissenschaft*, 84 (1972), 460-493.

47. *Ibid.*, p. 465.

48. *Ibid.*, p. 485.

49. *Ibid.*, pp. 482-483.

50. *Ibid.*, p. 483. My translation. Weippert translates: "Nicht durch meine eigene Kraft, nicht durch die Stärke meines Bogens—durch die Kraft meiner Götter, durch die Stärke meiner Göttinnen beugte ich die Länder... unter das Joch Assurs."

51. *Ibid.*, p. 488.

52. *Ibid.*, p. 492.

53. Ibid., p. 485.

54. Miller, *op. cit.*, p. 165.

55. See above, note 18.

56. Paul D. Hanson, *The Dawn of Apocalyptic* (Philadelphia: Fortress Press, 1975), pp. 1-31, esp. p. 29, note 26.

57. See above, notes 20-27.

58. I reserve the discussion of the primeval history to the time of David as this is assumed to be, for the most part, the compilation of J. For the significance of the Deuteronomic historian, see beginning of chapter VIII.

59. I am indebted in this entire concept of the Primary History to David Noel Freedman. The main lines of the history as here set forth are based on a personal note, Sept. 11, 1977. See also his essay "Pentateuch," *The Interpreter's Dictionary of the Bible*, Vol. III, ed. by G. A. Buttrick (New York, Nashville: Abingdon Press, 1962), pp. 711-727.

Chapter Two

1. See Julius Wellhausen, *Prolegomena to the History of Ancient Israel* (New York: Meridian Books, 1957), pp. 320 f.

2. Hermann Gunkel, *The Legends of Genesis*, trans. by W. H. Carruth (Chicago: The Open Court Publishing Co., 1901), pp. 91 f.

3. For a literary analysis of this text, attributed to J, see E. A. Speiser, *Genesis*, The Anchor Bible (Garden City, N.Y · Doubleday & Co., Inc., 1964), p. 85.

4. Cf. Ex. 12:25; 13:11, 12. Cf. S. R. Driver, *An Introduction to the Literature of the Old Testament* (New York: Meridian Books, 1956), p. 29: "[These materials] may be referred either to J (Dillm.) or to the compiler of JE expanding materials derived from J (so Wellh., at least for 13:3-16)."

5. Speiser, *op. cit.*, p. 111.

6. Cf. Driver, *op. cit.*, p. 72. See also Deut. 1:8, 35; 4:21; 6:10, 23; 7:13; 8:1; 9:5; 10:11; 11:9, 21; 19:8; 26:3, 15; 27:3; 28:11; 30:20; 31:7; Josh. 1:6; 5:6; 21:43-45.

7. *Ibid.*, p. 27. See also Ex. 2:24. E does not connect the patriarchal covenant with the conquest unless Gen. 15:15-16 is credited to E.

8. See "A Letter to Ashurbanipal" in *Ancient Near Eastern Texts*, ed. by James B. Pritchard (Princeton, N.J.: Princeton University Press, 1955), p. 450. For a situation more closely related to the patriarchs see the "Mari Letters," *ibid.*, p. 482, where seers accompany the troops and give directions for the battle, etc. They do not give examples, however, for legitimizing the battle itself. For further discussion, see Manfred Weippert, " 'Heiliger Krieg' in Israel und Assyrien...," *Zeitschrift für die alttestamentliche Wissenschaft*, 84 (1972), 487-490.

9. Gerhard von Rad, *Genesis*, trans. by John H. Marks (London: SCM Press Ltd., 1961), p. 21. See Gen. 12:7; 13:14 ff.; 15:18; 24:7; 26:2 ff.; 28:13; 50:24.

10. Albrecht Alt, "Der Gott der Väter," 1929, *Kleine Schriften zur Geschichte des Volkes Israel*, Band I (München: C. H. Beck'sche Verlagsbuchhandlung, 1953), pp. 1-78. While Alt did his research on the basis of Nabatean and Palmyrene monuments of the first century BC to the fourth century AD, evidences of the same type of religion are found in the Cappadocian tablets and in the Mari texts. Cf. J. Lewy, "Les textes paléo-assyriens et l'Ancien Testament," *Revue de l'histoire des religions*, CX (1934), 29-65; A. Malamat, "Mari," *The Biblical Archaeologist*, XXXIV (February 1971), 2-22. For a gathering up of the evidence of the historicity of the patriarchs see John Bright, *A History of Israel*, 2nd ed. (Philadelphia: The Westminster Press, 1972), pp. 67-102; Roland de Vaux, *Die Patriarchenerzählungen und die Geschichte*

(Stuttgart: Verlag Katholisches Bibelwerk, 1967). It is surprising to see the appearance of the book *The Historicity of the Patriarchal Narratives* by Thomas L. Thompson (Berlin, New York: Walter de Gruyter, 1974), reviving the Wellhausen view that the patriarchs were figures taken up into the Yahwistic tradition in the time of kingship from the contemporary Canaanite/Israelite milieu.

11. Von Rad (*Genesis*, p. 177) emphasizes the disunity of the chapter, vv. 1-6 belonging mainly to E, vv. 7-18 (less vv. 13-16) to J. Norbert Lohfink in *Die Landverheissung als Eid* (Stuttgart: Verlag Katholisches Bibelwerk, 1967), p. 114, accepts the essential unity of the chapter, vv. 1 f., 3-12, 17-21 as J. He also regards this chapter as the oldest text to contain the oath of the promise of land, pp. 11 ff.

12. Lohfink sees three separate traditions behind the account, the promise of a son (2-4), progeny (5), and land (7-21), *ibid.*, p. 35. To separate the promise of progeny from that of a son may be a bit pedantic.

13. See Lohfink's analysis, *ibid.*, p. 48.

14. In the Jeremiah passage the people and their officers have passed between the parts and thus have taken the oath. In the symbolism of Genesis 15 only Yahweh passes between the parts. For the meaning of this ceremony in terms of ancient Near East culture, see E. A. Speiser, *Genesis* (Garden City, Doubleday & Company, Inc., 1964), pp. 112-114; M. Weinfeld, "The Covenant of Grant in the Old Testament and in the Ancient Near East," *Journal of the American Oriental Society*, 90 (1970), 184-203; W. von Soden, "Zum akkadischen Worterbuch, 88-96," *Orientalia*, 26 (1957), 127-138.

15. David Noel Freedman, "The Slave of Yahweh," *Western Watch*, X (March, 1959), 19.

16. See especially Romans 4:13 where, far from spiritualizing, Paul says that the promise consists of inheriting the world.

17. The letter may be dated AD 57-58. See *The Jerusalem Bible*, Reader's Edition, The New Testament (Garden City, N.Y.: Doubleday & Doubleday, Inc., 1966), p. 195.

18. L. A. Snijders, "Genesis XV. The Covenant with Abram" *Studies on the Book of Genesis*, Oudtestamentische Studiën, (Leiden: E. J. Brill, 1958) Deel XII, p. 278.

19. Lohfink, *op. cit.*, p. 108.

20. *Ibid* ., p. 102.

21. Weinfeld, *op. cit.*

22. Von Rad, *Genesis*, p. 183.

23. Ronald E. Clements, *Abraham and David* (Naperville, Ill.: Alec R. Allenson, 1967).

24. George E. Mendenhall, *Law and Covenant in Israel and the Ancient Near East* (Pittsburgh: The Biblical Colloquium, 1955), pp. 46 ff.

25. David Noel Freedman, personal note, Sept. 11, 1977.

26. The Neturei Karta is a small group of Jews in present-day Israel who refuse to recognize the Zionist state on the grounds that the Messiah, whom they await, will *give* them the land. They thus represent the position of older Jewish orthodoxy. See "Statement by the Holy Gerer Rebbe, the Sfas Emes, on Zionism" (1901) in *Zionism Reconsidered*, edited by Michael Selzer (London: The Macmillan Company, 1970), p. 16.

27. In both cases J was working with traditional material. For a Sumerian tradition of the confusion of tongues see Samuel Noah Kramer, "The 'Babel of Tongues': A Sumerian Version," *Journal of the American Oriental Society*, 88 (1968) 108-111. As to the Abramic call tradition, von Rad held that this was a free composition of J. See von Rad, *Genesis*, p. 160. That he is using traditional material, however, is suggested by the fact that we have here ancient poetry. See David Noel Freedman, "Notes on Genesis," *Zeitschrift für die alttestamentliche Wissenschaft*, 64 (1952), 193. Freedman deals here with only verses 1-2, and it may be that verse 3 is J's own forming out of the material. J obviously contrasted Abram's migration with the migration of the city-state (11:1-9), perhaps by reshaping the latter tradition more than the former.

28. "Early Israel was contemporary in what she rejected and ancient in what she ac-

cepted. This is the creative aspect of the culture-dynamic of an archaic society rooted in religious conviction." A. Glock, "Warfare in Mari and Early Israel" (PhD dissertation, University of Michigan, 1968, University Microfilms, Inc., Ann Arbor, Mich.), p. 213.

29. This cosmic mountain was identified with the temple and even with the divinity:

Haus, grosser "Mast" des Landes Sumer,

mit Himmel und Erde zusammen gewachsen,

Eninnu, gutes Ziegelwerk, dem Enlil gutes Schicksal bestimmt,

schöner Berg, der zu (aller) Staunen dasteht,

der aus allen Ländern hervorragt:

Das Haus ist ein grosser Berg, reicht bis an dem Himmel,

ist (wie) der Sonnengott, erfüllt das Innere des Himmels,

das "Eninnu-Imdugud-strahlt" hat im Feindland zahlreiche

(Menschen) getötet,

hat die Menschen (fest) wohnen lassen, hat das Land Sumer geleitet:

Die Anunna-Götter gehen staunend dahin. A. Falkenstein and W. von Soden, *Sumerische und akkadische Hymnen und Gebete* (Zürich, Stuttgart: Artemis-Verlag, 1953, p. 166.

30. For a simple but accurate exposition of the Peniel event in its present context see B. W. Anderson, "An Exposition of Genesis XXXII," *Australian Biblical Review*, XVII (Oct. 1969), 21-26.

31. See UT 67 II 12 where Baal says to Mot: 'bdk. an . wd'lmk. Jonas C. Greenfield translates this, "I am your bondsman forever." Greenfield comments that here "Ba'al declared himself Mot's eternal vassal, hoping thereby to escape from the death that awaited him at Mot's hand." (Jonas C. Greenfield, "Some Aspects of Treaty Terminology in the Bible," *Fourth World Congress of Jewish Studies, Papers*, Vol. I, Jerusalem: World Union of Jewish Studies, 1967, p. 117.) See also UT 137:36-38 where Ba'al is called 'bd ('servant') and asr ('captive'). Greenfield points out that Ba'al here is on the "same level as the other gods, the ilm and bn qds who bring argmn and mnh as vassals of Yam. Yam had previously declared himself their b'l and adn. Ibid. On the human side 'bd designates the vassal of the great king in the Ugaritic nonliterary texts (PRU II 18, 3 [UT 1018, 3]) "just as Ba'al is called by El the 'bd of Yam and had declared himseof the 'bd of Mot." *Ibid.*

32. In UT 137:37, 38 the ilm and bn qds bring argmn and mnh as Yam's vassals. *Ibid.*

33. See Pritchard, *ANET*, pp. 277b-281. These lists are varied, often consisting of silver, gold, large and small cattle, wine, with occasional additions. See pp. 277b, 278a. The tribute given by Jehu, son of Omri, is as follows: silver, gold, a golden saplu-bowl, a gold vase with pointed bottom, golden tumblers, golden buckets, tin, a staff for a king, (and) wooden puruhtu, P. 281a. Another list consists entirely of animals: camels, a hippopotamus, a rhinoceros, a type of antelope, elephants, and monkeys. P. 281ab. Here again it is Greenfield who pointed out to me that this is a tribute list. Greenfield, *op. cit.*, p. 118.

34. Rib-Addi, prince of Byblos, wrote to Akh-en-Aton (Amen-hotep IV) about 1370 BC or a little later: "Rib-Ad [di spoke] to the king, [his] lor[d, the Sun-god of the lands.] Beneath the feet [of the king, my lord,] seven times, and seven times [I fall.]" EA, No. 137, Pritchard, *ANET*, p. 483. That it was a cliché can be seen by its repetition in EA, Nos. 254, 270, 271, 280, 286, 287, 288, 289, 290, 292, 297, 298, Pritchard, *ANET*, pp. 486-490.

35. H. Freedman and Maurice Simon, eds., *Midrash Rabbah, Genesis II* (London: Soncino Press, 1961), 75:11, p. 697.

36. See John Hayward, "The Classical Greek Hero and the Biblical Anti-Hero," unpublished paper read at Tantur, Jerusalem, Spring, 1976.

37. See 2 Sam. 15-19; 20; 1 Kings 12.

38. See the analysis of Hayim Tadmor, " 'The People' and the Kingship in Ancient Israel: the Role of Political Institutions in the Biblical Period," *Journal of World History* 11 (1968), 48 f., 54 f.

39. See Speiser, *op. cit.*, pp. 287 f.

40. See *ibid.*, pp. 288 f.

41. See *ibid.*, pp. 332 f., 335 ff.
42. See *ibid.*, pp. 336 f., 341.
43. This is the only mention of Dinah in Genesis except for two genealogical entries: Gen. 30:21; 46:15.
44. Speiser suggests that this chapter is essentially the work of J, *op. cit.*, pp. 266 f.
45. For a discussion of the date of this pre-kingship poetry embedded in the Pentateuch see chap. III on the Song of the Sea, note 16. The translation is from D. N. Freedman, personal note, September 11, 1977.
46. Speiser places this event in pre-exodus times, favoring even a pre-Amarna date. *Op. cit.*, p. 267.
47. The sexual sins are called by the same term, *nblh*. See Judg. 19:23, 24; 20:6, 10.
48. See 2 Sam. 13, especially v. 12.
49. Speiser notes this difference in the generations. He writes, "There is also a marked difference between the generations. Hamor and Jacob are peace-loving and conciliatory; their sons are impetuous and heedless of the consequences that their acts must entail." Speiser, *op. cit.*, p. 268.
50. *The Testaments of the Twelve Patriarchs*, "The Testament of Levi, 6:8": ". . .for they sought to do to Sarah and Rebecca as they had done to Dinah our sister, but the Lord prevented them." R. H. Charles, *The Apocrypha and Pseudepigrapha of the Old Testament*, Vol. II (Oxford, at the Clarendon Press, 1913), p. 308. Charles sets the date of this writing between 109-106 BC *Ibid.*, p. 282.
51. See above, note 36, for the contrasting concepts of honor.
52. See Speiser's long explanation, based on Hurrian custom, how the narratives originally were interested, like biblical genealogies, to "establish the superior strain of the line through which the biblical way of life was transmitted from generation to generation." Speiser, *op. cit.*, pp. 91-94.
53. Cf. von Rad's comment, *Genesis*, p. 328.
54. *The Book of Jubilees* 30:23. Charles, *op. cit.*, p. 59. R. H. Charles holds that *The Book of Jubilees* was written between 153 and 105 BC, Charles, *op. cit.*, p. 6.
55. *The Book of Jubilees* 30:17, 18. Charles, *op. cit.*, p. 59.
56. *The Testaments of the Twelve Patriarchs*, "The Testament of Levi, 5:3." Charles, *op. cit.*, p. 307.
57. *The Testaments . . .*, "The Testament of Levi, 6:8." Charles, *op. cit.*, p. 308.
58. For a discussion of the characteristics of holy war and of holy war language, see Gerhard von Rad, *Der heilige Krieg im alten Israel* (Göttingen: Vandenhoeck & Ruprecht, 1952), pp. 6-14. Although recent research has challenged the uniqueness of Israel's holy war, and has questioned the standardization of holy war traits as set forth by von Rad, his descriptive presentation is still by and large valid. See also the discussion of holy war scholarship in chapter I, A., and the essays in *IDB* cited in note 3 of chapter I above.
59. Von Rad, *Genesis*, p. 332.
60. Cf. Ex. 15:14; 23:27; Josh. 10:10; Judg. 4:15, etc. For Assyrian and Hittite parallels see below on the Song of the Sea, chap. III, A. I.
61. Speiser, *op. cit.*, p. 356.
62. *Ibid.*, p. 358.
63. This was pointed out to me by Freedman, personal note, September 11, 1977.
64. Both von Rad and Speiser are agreed on this point. Von Rad says, "It is substantially, generically, and literarily completely isolated and was apparently first incorporated into its present context by a redactor. . . . Any hasty combination with the historical view or chronology of the other Hexateuchal sources can only cause great confusion." Von Rad, *Genesis*, p. 170. Speiser writes, "On one point, however, the critics are virtually unanimous: the familiar touches of the established sources of Genesis are absent in this instance. For all these reasons the chapter has to be ascribed to an isolated source, here marked X." Speiser, *op. cit.*, p. 105.

Apart from this negative point, however, these two interpreters disagree. Von Rad holds that the chapter is "composed of two parts quite distinct from each other as to origin and nature," with the seam occurring between v. 11 and v. 12. Von Rad, *Genesis*, p. 173. He sees this literary unification as an attempt on the part of someone to give additional theological support to Davidic dynasty, and as directed against the "liberty-minded population in Judah." *Ibid.*, p. 176. Speiser, on the other hand, argues that this chapter had a foreign source "from which the present narrative was either excerpted or adapted." Speiser, *op. cit.*, p. 108. D. N. Freedman points out that Gen. 14 is based on an old poem, with excerpts still partly embedded in the prose text. Freedman, "Notes on Genesis," pp. 193 f. These three positions are the basic ones taken by recent scholars. For a survey of the latter two positions (exemplified by Speiser, Freedman) see J. A. Emerton, "Some False Clues in the Study of Genesis XIV," *Vetus Testamentum*, XXI 1971), 24-47. He demolishes both positions, though he admits that he is not an Assyriologist! For a survey of the first position (exemplified by von Rad) see J. A. Emerton, "The Riddle of Genesis XIV," *Vetus Testamentum*, XXI (1971), 403-439.

Emerton agrees that most scholars hold that Gen. 14 has no affinity with the sources of Genesis. It is curious, therefore, that a recent work has appeared which argues that no less than the authors of the three pentateuchal sources were involved in the production of the chapter, J, P, D! Werner Schatz, *Genesis 14, Eine Untersuchung* (Bern: Herbert Lang and Frankfurt/M: Peter Lang, 1972), pp. 321-323. He bases his argument on the basis of a few words which are also found in J, E, or P, and an insistence on fitting the main pentateuchal sources into his theory of a tradition history of chapter 14. Cf. *ibid.*, p. 319. He finds nothing of D in the chapter and yet argues that the chapter was reedited by the Deuteronomist about 550 BC. *Ibid.*, p. 323.

65. Freedman, personal note, September 11, 1977. Later retracted.

66. This suggestion was made to me by Ronald Guengerich, September 19, 1977.

67. Gen. 14:20a, the translation in RSV except for the name ʾĒl ʾElyôn. The decisive expression is "*mggn ṣryk bydk.*" See note 58 above.

68. For uses with the verb "*ntn,*" see Num. 21:2 ff. Occurrences of the phrase include: Gen. 14:20; Num. 21:2, 34; Deut. 2:24, 30; 3:2, 3; 7:24; 21:10; 30:13; Josh. 2:24; 6:2; 8:1, 7, 18; 10:8, 19, 30, 32; 11:8, 21:44; 24:8, 11; Judg. 1:2, 4; 2:23; 3:10, 28; 4:7, 13; 7:2, 7, 9, 14, 15; 8:3, 7; 11:21, 30, 32; 12:3; 13:1; 18:10; 20:28; 1 Sam. 14:10, 12, 37; 17:46, 47; 23:4, 7, 14; 24:4, 18; 26:8; 2 Sam. 5:19; 1 Kings 20:13, 28; 22:6, 12, 15; 2 Kings 3:18; 10·24; 1 Chron. 5:20; 14:10; 22:10; 2 Chron. 13:16; 16:8; 18:14; 28:5, 9; Dan. 2:38; 7:25. (There is also the state ment, "You will be delivered into the hand of the enemy," Lev. 26:25; Deut. 1:27, etc.)

69. ". . .*bel nakrika ana qataka limnu.*" See Robert Pfeiffer, *State Letters of Assyria, A Transliteration of 355 Official Assyrian Letters Dating from the Sargonid Period* (722-625 BC) (New Haven: American Oriental Society, 1935), p. 220, No. 324. See also *ibid.*, p. 217, No. 323: "Shamash and Marduk are giving into the hands of the king my lord a passage through the land, which you have seized by force of arms, from the upper to the lower sea . . . (*ana qata sarri beli-ia in [d]ami*).

Chapter Three

1. While this conflict is not corroborated directly by archaeology, nevertheless because of its fundamental importance to the biblical story, its essential authenticity can hardly be doubted. For a discussion of the indirect evidence see John Bright, *A History of Israel* (2nd ed.; Philadelphia: The Westminster Press, 1972), pp. 119-122.

2. For examples in the Pentateuch, see Ex. 32:12 (J); Ex. 33:1 (E); Lev. 11:45 (P); Deut. 6:21 ff. (D), etc.; in the prophetic books: Josh. 24:4-6; Judg. 2:12; 1 Sam. 6:6; 1 Kings 8:9; Mic. 6:4; Hos. 11:1; Amos 3:1; Jer. 2:6; Zech. 10:10; etc.; and in the Writings: Ps. 18:12 ff.; 81:11 (Eng. 10); 105:23 ff.; Dan. 9:15; Neh. 9:9 ff.; etc.

3. Ex. 29:45, 46, etc. This was a radical shift from the central emphasis upon the creation myth of other Near Eastern peoples. The passover, celebrating the theme of the exodus, may

be contrasted with the New Year's festival of Babylon, whose central theme was creation. For the program of this festival which included the reading of the *Enuma Elish* see James B. Pritchard, *Ancient Near Eastern Texts* (Princeton, New Jersey: Princeton University Press, 1955), pp. 331 ff. Also Henri Frankfort, *Kingship and the Gods* (Chicago: University of Chicago Press, 1948), pp. 313 ff.

4. Ex. 19:4-6; 20:2-3; Lev. 25:54-55; Josh. 24:2-15; Deut. 4:37-40; 26:5-11. See further Kl. Wessel, "Durchzug durch das Rote Meer," *Reallexikon für Antike und Christentum: Sachwörterbuch zur Auseinandersetzung des Christentums mit der antiken Welt*, hsg. von Theodor Klauser, IV (1959), 370-389.

5. Hos. 11:1; Amos 3:1-2, etc. Cf. Rudolf Schmid, "Meerwunder-und Landnahme-Traditionen," *Theologische Zeitschrift*, 21 (1965), 260.

6. Rudolf Schmid points out how the various accounts seem reticent to give the details of the exodus. Evidently the chosen people were little concerned about the details. What counted was the fact: Yahweh led his people from the slavery of Egypt by his mighty deed. *Ibid.*, pp. 260 f.

7. Johannes Pedersen regards Ex. 1—15 as having a cultic character, used at the paschal feast to glorify Yahweh "through an exposition of the historical event that created the people." The events were "re-lived in the Paschal night by the whole of the festival legend being reviewed." While these materials no doubt did have a cultic preliterary history, Pedersen gives to the cult such formative power that there would seem to be very little history left. See Johannes Pedersen, *Israel, Its Life and Culture*, III, IV (London: Cumberlege, Oxford University Press, 1947; first published in Danish, 1934), pp. 728 ff. Sigmund Mowinckel points out that while the sagas were not "history" as an end to and for itself, but *Heilsgeschichte*, the message of the great deeds and victory of Yahweh upon which the existence and salvation of the people was grounded and which was again experienced in the festival cult, nevertheless they are not merely *Heils*geschichte but also Heils*geschichte* for Israel in that they go back to a historical occasion. Cf. Sigmund Mowinckel, "Die vermeintliche 'Passahlegende' Ex. 1—15 in Bezug auf die Frage: Literarkritik und Traditionskritik," *Studia Theologica*, V (1951), 66-68. One might go farther than Mowinckel in emphasizing the original element of *Geschichte*.

8. See chapter I where I set forth the positions of both von Rad and Miller. See also chap. I, note 19.

9. For a discussion of the various exodus traditions through the Talmudic period see Samuel E. Loewenstamm, *mṣwrt yṣy't mṣrym bhštlšlwth (hwṣ't sprym 'l-šm ' 'l m'gns, h'wnybrsyth l'bryt, yrwšlym, išk''t)*. This includes an English summary.

10. See my article "Paradigm of Holy War in the Old Testament," *Biblical Research*, XVI (1971), 16-31. Robert Boling writes, "The holy war par excellence was the one at the Reed Sea in which Yahweh and his heavenly army defeated the hosts of Egypt (Israelites did no fighting) and thus laid the basis (Exod 1—15) for Israel's acknowledgement of his total sovereignty (Exod 18—24). So holy was that one 'war' that it provided the organizing principle for the first half of Gideon's story (6:11—7:22), where Yahweh did it again." Robert Boling, *Judges* (Garden City, New York: Doubleday & Company, Inc., 1975), p. 28. We will discuss this question further in the argument below.

11. A. Lauha criticizes correctly, in my opinion, the attempt of Pedersen to do away with the various literary sources. A. Lauha, "Das Schilfmeermotiv im Alten Testament," *Supplements to Vetus Testamentum*, Congress Volume, Bonn, 1962 (Leiden: E. J. Brill, 1963) pp. 32-46.

12. Martin Noth holds that the sea event is the climax of the exodus theme. See Martin Noth, *Exodus*, trans. by J. S. Bowden (Philadelphia: The Westminster Press, 1962), pp. 104 f. Samuel E. Loewenstamm also holds that the splitting of the sea is the grand finale which concludes the story of the exodus in all sources, including the homiletical summaries. Samuel E. Loewenstamm, *op. cit.*, p. 8. George W. Coats challenges this, holding that both J and P regard the sea tradition not as the nucleus of the exodus theme but as the beginning of the wilderness theme. See George W. Coats, "The Traditio-Historical Character of the Reed Sea

Motif," *Vetus Testamentum* XVII (1967), 258. Brevard S. Childs agrees with Coats in regard to JE, but holds that P places the sea event with the exodus tradition. See Brevard S. Childs, "A Traditio-Historical Study of the Reed Sea Tradition," *Vetus Testamentum*, XX (1970), 407. Thomas W. Mann holds that the view of Coats does not adequately deal with the complexities of the tradition and that "while the Jordan crossing (Josh. 3—4) and the Reed Sea event (Ex. 14) are dependent in their transmission on other traditions, they became of such individual importance that neither could be subsumed under one tradition." Thus each comprised "*both the beginning and the end* of a crucial segment of Israel's history." See Thomas W. Mann, "The Pillar of Cloud in the Reed Sea Narrative," *Journal of Biblical Literature*, XC (1971), 27 f. (underlining mine).

13. For an overall statement see David Noel Freedman, "Prolegomenon"in George Buchanan Gray, *The Forms of Hebrew Poetry* ([New York]: Ktav Publishing House, 1972), pp. vii-lvi. Albright, Freedman, and Cross were pioneers in this work. See also David A. Robertson, *Linguistic Evidence in Dating Early Hebrew Poetry* (Missoula, Mont.: Society of Biblical Literature, 1972).

14. David Noel Freedman, "Early Israelite Poetry and Historical Reconstructions" (unpublished paper, 1975).

15. *Ibid.*, pp. 3 f.

16. This is Freedman's date in *ibid.*, p. 5. Albright dated the song a century earlier, but to do this he had to regard the reference to the Philistines (15:14) as an anachronism. Cf. Frank M. Cross, Jr., and David Noel Freedman, "The Song of Miriam," *Journal of Near Eastern Studies*, XIV (1955), 237-250. Frank M. Cross says that the poem is to be dated by "(1) the typology of its language, (2) the typology of its prosody, (3) orthographic analysis, (4) the typology of the development of Israel's religion, (5) the history of tradition, and (6) historical allusions." Frank M. Cross, "The Song of the Sea and Canaanite Myth" in *Canaanite Myth and Hebrew Epic* (Cambridge, Mass.: Harvard University Press, 1973), p. 121. He feels that all evidence points to a premonarchic date, in the late twelfth or early eleventh century BC. *Ibid.*, p. 124. This is an impressive study, and Cross is quite confident of his results. David A. Robertson (*op. cit.*, p. 155) places Ex. 15 in the twelfth century. While he is cautious about his results in regard to the other poems, he is quite confident of the early dating of Ex. 15. Oswald Loretz disagrees with this early dating. Oswald Loretz, "Ugarit-texte und Israelitische Religionsgeschichte," (2) The Song of the Sea, Ex. 15:1-18, *Ugarit-Forschungen*, B and 6 (Verlag Butzon & Bercker Krevelaer, 1974), 245-247. However, his only given reason was that it was possible for Canaanite myth to be worked into Israel only in Canaan. He does not take into account the influence of Baalism in Egypt, especially among Semitic groups found there. Cf. Frank E. Eakin, Jr., "The Reed Sea and Baalism," *Journal of Biblical Literature*, LXXXVI (1967), 381, n. 9. Childs on the basis of tradition-historical criticism dates the poem, with Mowinckel, in the ninth century. Childs, "A Traditio-Historical Study of the Reed Sea Tradition," *op. cit.*, 411, n. 1. However, Childs holds that a common tradition lies behind J and the poem and that the sea tradition was therefore ancient: ". . . the fact that in the prose account the sea was transmitted with the wilderness tradition while in the poetic account with the exodus would point to the antiquity of the sea tradition. The common tradition preceded the period in which the prose tradition was transmitted within a larger traditional complex." *Ibid.*, p. 412. Noth also saw the poem as relatively late, but takes no account of the evidence of the Ugaritic literature. Noth, *op. cit.*, p. 123. Dillman saw the poem as having a genuine Mosaic kernel. But Bruno Baentsch held that it was hardly written before Deuteronomic times because of what he considered to be a reference to the Jerusalem temple. See Bruno Baentsch, *Exodus, Leviticus, Numeri, Handkommentar zum alten Testament* (Göttingen: Vandenhoeck & Ruprecht, 1903), pp. 128 f.

17. See James Henry Breasted, *Ancient Records of Egypt* (New York: Russell & Russell, Inc., 1962), III, pp. 135-141. For Tukulti-Ninurta, see P. C. Craigie's analysis of this epic, "The Song of Deborah and the Epic of Tukulti-Ninurta," *Journal of Biblical Literature*, LXXXVIII (1969), 253-265.

18. This is the suggestion of Freedman in "Strophe and Meter in Exodus 15" from *A Light unto My Path: Old Testament Studies in Honor of Jacob M. Myers,* ed. by Howard N. Bream, Ralph D. Heim, Carey A. Moore (Philadelphia: Temple University Press, 1974), pp. 170 f. This seems to me to be the best solution of the relationship of v. 21 to the longer poem. Cross explains this verse as embedded in recension E, while the longer poem was a part of J. Cross, "The Song of the Sea and Canaanite Myth," *Canaanite Myth and Hebrew Epic,* p. 123. Older critical scholarship held that this short statement was ancient, and the older poem was a late expansion. This typical position is still represented by Fritz Stolz, *Jahwes und Israels Kriege* (Zürich: Theologischer Verlag, 1972), pp. 90 f. This position is based upon the old form critical principle that the short piece is ancient while the longer piece must be late. Today we know that the opposite is more likely true.

19. See Freedman, "Strophe and Meter in Exodus 15," *op. cit.,* p. 181. The mythological background of these terms in the Baal epic are either Baal's messengers or personified weapons. Here the use is merely figurative.

20. *Ibid.,* p. 193.

21. For comments on the use of this tradition in the Old Testament, see A. Lauha, *op. cit.*

22. See our discussion of Weippert, chap. I.A.2.

23. See chap. I, notes 17 and 18.

24. There is a difference of opinion between Cross and Freedman on this question. Cross holds that the march was to Canaan, thus uniting the exodus and conquest, while Freedman considers it as a march to Sinai. See Cross, "The Song of the Sea and Canaanite Myth," *Canaanite Myth and Hebrew Epic,* p. 123. For Freedman's view see "Early Israelite History in the Light of Early Israelite Poetry," *op. cit.,* pp. 5-7. This represents a recent change in Freedman's thought. Cf. Freedman, "Strophe and Meter in Exodus 15," *op. cit.,* p. 193.

25. See Norbert Lohfink, "Das Siegeslied am Schilfmeer" in *Das Siegeslied am Schilfmeer* (Frankfurt am Main: Josef Knecht, 1965), pp. 125 f.

26. For holy war language, see chap. II, note 58.

27. Cf. Freedman, "Strophe and Meter in Exodus 15," *op. cit.,* pp. 169, 192.

28. See the Baal Epic in Pritchard, *ANET,* pp. 129 ff. For a discussion of the comparison see Cross, "The Song of the Sea and Canaanite Myth" in *Canaanite Myth and Hebrew Epic,* pp. 113-120.

29. For evidence that Near Eastern gods were also involved in history, see Bertil Albrektson, *History and the Gods* (Lund, Gleerup, 1967).

30. See the two reliefs, British Museum Nos. 124540 and 124555. These are reproduced by George E. Mendenhall in his book, *The Tenth Generation* (Baltimore, London: Johns Hopkins University Press, 1973), p. 46, figs. 11, 12.

31. *Ibid.,* p. 47, fig. 13.

32. *Ibid.,* p. 47.

33. For a discussion of this unique concept of politics in ancient Israel see my article, "The Concept of Political Power in Ancient Israel," *Annual of the Swedish Theological Institute,* VII (1970), 4-24. I deal with the question of Yahweh's kingship at greater length below, chap. V.

34. See Friedrich Hrozny, *Hethitische Keilschrifttexte aus Boghazköi* (Leipzig: J. C. Hinrichs'sche Buchhandlung, 1919), Nr. VI, K Bo. III, Col. II (16).

35. *Ibid.,* Nr. VIII, K Bo. II, Nr. 5, 5a, Col. IV (11-15).

36. See Albrecht Götze, *Die Annalen des Mursilis* (Leipzig: J. C. Hinrichs'sche Buchhandlung, 1933), p. 193.

37. *Ibid.,* p. 195.

38. See below, Ch. V, A.

39. For a review of interpretations see John Gray, *The Krt Text in the Literature of Ras Shamra: A Social Myth of Ancient Canaan* (Leiden: E. J. Brill, 1955), pp. 1 f. For the text see *ibid.* pp. 7 ff. Also, see Pritchard, *ANET* pp. 142 ff.

40. John Gray, *op. cit.,* p. 8.

41. John Gray, *op. cit.,* p. 3.

42. James B. Pritchard, *The Ancient Near East in Pictures* (Princeton, N.J.: Princeton University Press, 1954), p. 92, no. 296.
43. Cf. John A. Wilson, *The Burden of Egypt* (Chicago: The University of Chicago Press, 1951), p. 49, and Henri Frankfort, *Ancient Egyptian Religion* (New York: Harper & Brothers, 1961), p. 42.
44. For a translation of this hymn see John A. Wilson, "The Texts of the Battle of Kadesh" (unpublished PhD dissertation, University of Chicago, 1926), p. 63. This supporting action of the gods is especially evident in the narrative where Ramses prays to Amon. *Ibid.*, pp. 77 ff.
45. This hymn is transcribed and translated by R. Campbell Thompson, *Annals of Archaeology*, XX (1933), 118-126. For a discussion on the hymn see P. C. Craigie, *op. cit.*
46. See Pritchard, *ANET*, pp. 227 ff.
47. The Hebrew word "$y\check{s}by$" in vv. 14 and 15 should probably be translated "enthroned" rather than "inhabitants."
48. See Brevard S. Childs, *The Book of Exodus* (Philadelphia: Westminster Press, 1974), p. 14.
49. See Bertil Albrektson, *History and the Gods* (Lund, Sweden: C. W. K. Gleerup, 1967), pp. 115 ff.
50. Cf. Freedman, "Strophe and Meter in Exodus 15," *op. cit.*, pp. 170 f.
51. His analysis is as follows: J: Ex. 13:20-22; 14:5b, 6 (or 7), 9aa, 10bb, 13, 14, 19b, 20, 21ab, 24, 25b, 27abb. E is fragmentary: Ex. 13:17-19; 14:5a, 6 (or 7), 19a. P: 14:1-4, 8, 9abb, 10abb. 15-18, 21aab, 22, 23, 26, 27aa, 28, 29. Noth, *op. cit.*, pp. 105 f.
52. For holy war terminology, see note 58 in chap. II.
53. See the analyses of Lauha, *op. cit.*; Cross, "The Song of the Sea and Canaanite Myth," *Canaanite Myth and Hebrew Epic*, pp. 132-137; and Loewenstamm, *op. cit.*, chapter 7 (Hebrew). This latter reference discusses also the post Old Testament traditions in the Jewish literature.
54. Noth, *op. cit.*, p. 119.
55. *Ibid.*, p. 113.
56. Gerhard von Rad, *Old Testament Theology*, Vol. I, trans. by D. M. G. Stalker (Edinburgh, London: Oliver and Boyd, 1962), p. 107, esp. n. 3.
57. See chapter I.A.1.
58. J. Philip Hyatt, *Commentary on Exodus* (London: Oliphants, 1971), p. 157.
59. Lewis S. Hay, "What Really Happened at the Sea of Reeds," *Journal of Biblical Literature*, 83 (1964), 397-403.
60. *Ibid.*, pp. 402 f.
61. Manfred Weippert, " 'Heiliger Krieg' in Israel und Assyrien: Kritische Anmerkungen zu Gerhard von Rads Konzept des 'Heiligen Krieges im alten Israel,' " *Zeitschrift für die alttestamentliche Wissenschaft*, 84 (1972), 460-493. See my discussion in chapter I,A.
62. Loewenstamm, *op. cit.*, chap. 7.
63. Cross, "The Cultus of the Israelite League," *Canaanite Myth and Hebrew Epic*, pp. 77-144.
64. See above (A.1.d.) where I discuss what appear to be Hittite "miracles."
65. See Josh. 24:5 ff. I will discuss this in the next chapter.
66. Martin Noth, *The History of Israel* (2nd ed., rev. Eng. trans.; New York: Harper & Brothers, 1960), pp. 2 f.
67. Cf. Freedman, "Strophe and Meter in Exodus 14," *op. cit.*, pp. 170 f. While Freedman dates the poem itself to the twelfth century, he sees its final liturgical form as dated in the time of the United Kingdom.
68. See E. W. Nicholson, *Exodus and Sinai in History and Tradition* (Oxford: Basil Blackwell, 1973), pp. 58-61. He challenges Noth's theory that Moses was not connected with the exodus tradition, a point which we will discuss below in connection with the plagues. See also Bright, *op. cit.*, pp. 123-125.

69. Hyatt, *op. cit.*, pp. 96-99; Childs, *The Book of Exodus*, pp. 133-142. Neither of them agree with Noth that only J (with supplements) and P tell of the plagues. Noth, *Exodus*, pp. 69-71.

70. See Psalm 78:42-51, where there are seven plagues rather than the ten of exodus. For the dating of this psalm see Otto Eissfeldt, *Das Lied Moses Deuteronomium 32:1-43 und das Lehrgedicht Asaphs Psalm 78 samt einer Analyse der Umgebung des Moses-Liedes* (Berlin: Academie-Verlag, 1958).

71. See Loewenstamm, *op. cit.*, chap. 4.

72. For a discussion of the problems involved in the relationship of these traditions to the passover and the various solutions see Childs, *The Book of Exodus*, pp. 186 ff. Cross holds that the passover was celebrated at the Gilgal sanctuary at an early date on the basis of the material in Josh. 3—5. According to him, however, the celebration centered mainly around the crossing of the sea (Jordan) and march through the wilderness. Cross, "The Divine Warrior," in *Canaanite Myth and Hebrew Epic*, pp. 103-105 and "The Song of the Sea and Canaanite Myth" in *ibid.*, pp. 138 ff.

73. This is Childs' suggestion. Childs, *The Book of Exodus*, p. 177. However, see David Daube, *The Exodus Pattern in the Bible* (London: Faber and Faber, 1963), pp. 55 ff., who has other ideas. Also see George W. Coats, "Despoiling the Egyptians," *Vetus Testamentum*, 18 (1968), 450-457; Julian Morgenstern, "The Despoiling of the Egyptians," *Journal of Biblical Literature*, 68 (1949), 1-28.

74. The exodus occurrences are 1:15, 16, 19; 2:6, 7, 11, 13; 3:18; 5:3; 7:16; 9:1, 13; 10:3. Other usages: six times in Genesis; eight in 1 Samuel; twice in Jeremiah; once in Jonah; and twice in legal material, Ex. 21:2 and Deut. 15:12.

75. These references are usually in J, although Ex. 1:15, 16, and 19 are regarded as E by Noth in *Exodus*, p. 23.

76. See Moshe Greenberg, *The Hab/piru* (New Haven, Connecticut: American Oriental Society, 1955), pp. 55-58. For summary statement see Hyatt, *op. cit.*, pp. 39, 56 f. For references to "ḫabiru" in the Amarna letters, see Mendenhall, *op. cit.*, p. 123. In cuneiform materials outside of the Amarna letters the ḫabiru are referred to from the end of the third millennium BC to the seventh century BC. Mary P. Gray, "The Ḫâbirū-Hebrew Problem in the Light of the Source Material Available at Present" in *Hebrew Union College Annual* (New York: Ktav Publishing House, Inc., 1958), Vol. 29, p. 137.

77. The letter read as follows:

   1 All of my cities, which are (situated) in (20) the mountain(s)
   2 and on the shore of the sea, have turned themselves over to the
   3 'Apiru host. (Only) Byb[los], together with two (other) cities,
   4 remain to me. Moreover, behold, now 'Abdi-Ashirta has taken
   5 Shigata for himself, (25) and he has said to the people of Ammiya,
   6 " Kill your [l]ord so that you may be like us and be at peace!" So
   7 they turned themselves over according to his [wo]rds, and they became
   8 like the 'Apiru. And behold, now (30) 'Abdi-Ashirta has written
   9 to the host in the temple of Ninurta, "Muster yourselves, and let
  10 us attack Byblos—behold, th[ere is no] man who can rescue [i]t
  11 from ou[r] power—and let us drive the mayors from (35) the midst
  12 of the lands, and let all the lands turn themselves over to the
  13 'Ap[i]ru, and let an [al]liance be formed for all the lands so that
  14 the sons and daughters may have peace forever. And even if the
  15 king comes out,(40) as for all the lands there will be hostility
  16 toward him, so what can he do to us?" Thus they took an oa[t]h
  17 among themselves, and thus I am very much afraid, for there is no
  18 one who can rescue me (45) [fr]om their power. Like a bird that lies
  19 in a snare, so am I in By[b]los.

This letter was translated by Ronald Fred Youngblood, "The Amarna Correspondence of Rib-Haddi, Prince of Byblos" (unpublished PhD dissertation, Dropsie College for Hebrew and Cognate Learning, Philadelphia, 1961), pp. 127 f.

78. E is fragmentary. See the discussion of Childs on the various recensions, *The Book of Exodus*, pp. 133-142.

79. Noth held that Moses was not the leader of the exodus, and cites Ex. 5:6-19 as an example of the older tradition in which the elders rather than Moses were the main figures. Noth, *Exodus*, pp. 53 ff. However, this passage in Exodus is Pharaoh's attempt to discredit Moses' leadership by dealing with the elders. See Nicholson, *op. cit.*, pp. 58-61. There are no solid grounds for denying the leadership of Moses in the exodus. See Hyatt's criticism of Noth's and von Rad's positions. Hyatt, *op. cit.*, pp. 34 ff.

80. Pritchard, *ANET*, p. 119.

81. For a further discussion see Childs, *The Book of Exodus*, pp. 8 ff.

82. Quoted by Mendenhall, *op. cit.*, p. 21.

83. See chapter II,D.

84. Compare Gen. 49:5-7 with Deut. 33:8-11.

85. See Otto Eissfeldt, "Jacob's Begegnung mit El und Moses' Begegnung mit Jahwe," *Kleine Schriften*, Vierter Band, Herausgegeben von Rudolf Sellheim und Fritz Maass (J. C. B. Mohr [Paul Siebeck], Tübingen, 1968), pp. 92-98.

86. The RSV here follows the Greek and Vulgate text. The Hebrew text reads "no, not by a mighty hand." In the context of what follows in v. 20, however, the meaning of the Hebrew may be little different from the Greek.

87. See Thorkild Jacobsen, "Mesopotamia" in *Before Philosophy*, Frankfort, *et. al.* (Baltimore, Md.: Penguin Books, 1961), p. 208. See above, A.1.d, where I discuss the concept of warfare as depicted in art.

88. See Martin Noth, *A History of Pentateuchal Traditions* trans. by Bernhard W. Anderson (Englewood Cliffs, N.J.: Prentice-Hall, Inc., 1972), p. 39.

89. Klaus Baltzer, for example, compares the prophetic call with Pharaoh's commission to his vizier. "Considerations Regarding the Office and Calling of the Prophet," *Harvard Theological Review*, 61 (1968), 567-581.

90. Pritchard, *ANET*, pp. 446 f.

91. *Ibid.*, p. 164.

92. For the prophetic speech as that of a messenger see Claus Westermann, *Basic Forms of Prophetic Speech*, trans. by Hugh Clayton White (Philadelphia: The Westminster Press, 1967), pp. 98-128.

93. I deal with Gideon in chap. V,A.

94. I do not include here any discussion of the battle narratives of the wilderness and East Jordan since these add little to our treatment beyond the analysis of the conquest narratives in the next chapter. For further discussion of this material, see my dissertation, "The Theology of Warfare in the Old Testament" (Pittsburgh: Pittsburgh Theological Seminary, 1963).

95. George E. Mendenhall, *Law and Covenant in Israel and the Ancient Near East* (Pittsburgh, Pa.: The Biblical Colloquium, 1955); Walter Beyerlin, *Origins and History of the Oldest Sinaitic Traditions*, trans. by S. Rudman (Oxford: Basil Blackwell, 1965). Dennis McCarthy in *Treaty and Covenant* (Rome: Pontifical Biblical Institute, 1963, pp. 160 f.) sees the reference to Egypt not as a historical introduction but as an identification of Yahweh, though he holds that the probability is that it was original. The identification of Yahweh does not make it less of a historical statement, for that is the purpose of much history in the Old Testament. Klaus Baltzer hesitates to work with the Ten Words because of their difficulties, but he sees in Ex. 19:3-8 a short parallel form used to introduce the Exodus experience. Klaus Baltzer, *The Covenant Formulary*, trans. by David E. Green (Oxford: Basil Blackwell, 1971), pp. 28 f.

96. See Martin Noth, *The Laws in the Pentateuch and Other Studies* (Edinburgh and London: Oliver & Boyd, 1966) pp. 1-107.

97. Martin Buber, *Kingship of God*, trans. by Richard Scheimann (London: George Allen & Unwin Ltd., 1967), pp. 121-135.

Chapter Four

1. See Albrecht Alt, "Erwägungen über die Landnahme der Israeliten in Palästina," 1939, *Kleine Schriften zur Geschichte des Volkes Israel*, Band I (München: C. H. Beck'sche Verlagsbuchhandlung, 1953), pp. 126-175. Gerhard von Rad's *Der heilige Krieg im alten Israel* (Göttingen: Vandenhoeck & Ruprecht, 1952) begins holy war with the period of the Judges. For the view of Martin Noth see *The History of Israel*, (2nd ed., rev. Eng. transl.; New York: Harper and Brothers, 1960), pp. 73 ff. and *Das Buch Josua* (Tübingen: Verlag von J. C. B. Mohr [Paul Siebeck], 1953), pp. 7-13. Noth holds that the narratives in Joshua 2—12 were originally separate etiological tales arising about the holy place of Gilgal of the tribe of Benjamin, and independent war narratives from Judah and Galilee, which like the later acts of the Judges were made the concerns of all Israel and attached to the Ephramite leader. *Ibid.*, pp. 11 ff. It is questionable whether Judges 1 presents the settlement as "peaceful"; it is rather presented as "piece-meal."

2. For a summary of the archaeological evidence see John Bright, *A History of Israel* (2nd ed.; Philadelphia: The Westminster Press, 1972), pp. 127-130.

3. See George E. Mendenhall, "The Hebrew Conquest of Palestine," *The Biblical Archaeologist*, XXV (1962), 74. Also Norman K. Gottwald, "Domain Assumptions and Societal Models in the Study of Pre-monarchic Israel," *Supplements to Vetus Testamentum XXVIII*, (Congress Volume, 1974 [Leiden: E.J. Brill, 1975], pp. 89-100).

4. This song was probably written between 1150 and 1125. Cf. David Noel Freedman, "Early Israelite History in the Light of Early Israelite Poetry" in *Unity and Diversity: Essays in the History, Literature, and Religion of the Ancient Near East*, ed. by Hans Goedicke and J. J. M. Roberts (Baltimore, London: The Johns Hopkins University Press, 1975), p. 13; Alexander Globe, "The Literary Structure and Unity of the Song of Deborah," *Journal of Biblical Literature*, 93 (1974), 495 ff.

5. See Globe, *op. cit.*, p. 509.

6. See J. Blenkinsopp, "Ballad Style and Psalm Style in the Song of Deborah: A Discussion," *Biblica*, 42 (1961), 69.

7. See chapter III, note 17.

8. See Globe, *op. cit.*, p. 497.

9. See Blenkinsopp, *op. cit.*, p. 69. Otherwise, he makes an excellent analysis. For a more radical treatment see Hans-Peter Müller, "Der Aufbau des Deboraliedes," *Vetus Testamentum*, XVI (1966), 446-459.

10. Globe, *op. cit.*, p. 497.

11. For a structural analysis see Globe, *op. cit.*, pp. 499 ff. and P. C. Craigie, "The Song of Deborah and the Epic of Tukulti-Ninurta," *Journal of Biblical Literature*, LXXXVIII (1969), 261 ff.

12. The relation between this and the presumably earlier battle for Hazor under Joshua need not concern us here. However one may see this relationship, it is evident that the battle of Deborah was the more decisive politically. Yohanan Aharoni sees this as the battle of Hazor and places it no later than 1200 BC. Yohanan Aharoni, "Hazor and the Battle of Deborah—Is Judges Wrong?" *The Biblical Archaeological Review*, I (1975), 3, 4, 26. The battle is usually placed in the last half of the 12th century. See Robert G. Boling, *Judges* (Garden City, N.Y.: Doubleday & Company, Inc., 1975), p. 116.

13. See chapter III, A.1.d.

14. See vv. 2, 3, 5, 7, 7, 8, 9, 11. The earliest reference to Israel is the Egyptian victory stela of Merneptah. See James B. Pritchard, *Ancient Near Eastern Texts* (Princeton, N.J.: Princeton University Press, 1955), pp. 376-378. It is curious that Israel is not mentioned in the Song of Miriam. May this mean that Israel was an early patriarchal confederation which as such did not enter Egypt, but was converted to Yahwism by the invading Yahwists from the South? See Freedman, *op. cit.*, p. 21.

15. For an excellent summary of the discussion and argument against the federation see Georg Fohrer, *History of Israelite Religion*, trans. by David E. Green (Nashville, New York:

Abingdon Press, 1972), pp. 89 ff. The book by Fritz Stoltz, *Jahwes und Israels Kriege* (Zürich: Theologischer Verlag, 1972) presupposes that there was no federation. See chapter 1 of Stoltz.

16. See Freedman, *op. cit.*, pp. 19 ff.

17. There are analogies for such a confederation not only in the old Thessalian league (Boling, *op. cit*, pp. 20 f.), but also in an ancient Sumerian league of cities *(ibid.*, p. 21). Cultic centers found in Shechem and Amman might also be interpreted as pre-Yahwistic examples of centers of confederation. See Edward F. Campbell, Jr., and G. Ernest Wright, "Tribal League Shrines in Amman and Shechem," *Biblical Archaeologist*, XXXII (1969), 104-116.

18. See chap. II, D. on Gen. 34 and 49.

19. See Freedman, *op. cit.*, pp. 15 ff.

20. See vv. 2, 3, 3, 4, 5, 5, 9, 11, 11, 13, 23, 23, 31; the angel of Yahweh, v. 23.

21. P. C. Craigie, "Some Further Notes on the Song of Deborah," *Vetus Testamentum*, XXII (1972), 352. In the light of Craigie's recognition of the fact of miracle here, it is difficult for me to understand his statement suggesting that God's meeting with man in terms of the miraculous would not be meeting man in the world as it is. P.C. Craigie, "Yahweh is a Man of Wars," *Scottish Journal of Theology*, 22 (1969), 186. Israel understood all of Yahweh's relationship to the world in terms of creation or of the "miraculous."

22. Thus substantiating my disagreement with the "Type A" scholars—Schwally, Pedersen, von Rad, and Miller. See chap. I. A. 1.

23. Von Rad sees this coming "to the help of Yahweh" *(l'zrt YHWH)* as the ancient reality of holy war, a reality which was later changed by theological reflection. Von Rad, *op. cit.*, pp. 12 f. The opposite statement, that Yahweh is the help or comes to the help of man, occurs exclusively in the Psalms: 46:2 (46:1, Eng.); 27:9; 40:18 (40:17, Eng.); 35:2; 22:20 (22:19, Eng.); 38:23 (38:22, Eng.); 40:14 (40:13, Eng.); 70:2 (70:1, Eng.); 71:12; 60:13 (60:11, Eng.); 108:13 (108:12, Eng.); 44:27 (44:26, Eng.) 63:8 (63:7, Eng.); 94:17.

24. "i-na tukulti-(ti) *da*šš*ur* bêli-ia it-ti-šu-un- am-da-hi-is-ma...." From Daniel David Luckenbill, "The Oriental Institute Prism Inscription (H2)," Col. III, 1, 2, *The Annals of Sennacherib* (Chicago: The University of Chicago Press, 1924), p. 31.

25. See y. 'hrwny, "y'l 'št ḥbr hqyny wšmgr bn 'nt," kl 'rṣ nptly, h'wrk h.z. hyršbrg (hḥbrh lhqyrt 'rṣ yśr'l w'tyqwtyh, yrwšlym, tšk" ḥ, 1967), p. 56.

26. Pritchard, *ANET*, pp. 129 ff.

27. See P. C. Craigie, "A Reconsideration of Shamgar Ben Anath (Judg. 3:31 and 5:6)." *Journal of Biblical Literature*, 91 (1972), 239 f.

28. See 'hrwny, *op. cit.*, p. 57.

29. Cf. Jacob M. Myers, "The Book of Judges," *The Interpreter's Bible*, Vol. II, ed. by George Arthur Buttrick (Nashville, NY: Abingdon-Cokesbury Press, 1953), p. 727.

30. For an opposite conclusion, which assumes that Meroz was a treasonable entity which then earned a curse under the Mosaic covenant, see Boling, *op. cit.*, p. 114. If this were the case, why are the nonparticipating tribes not also cursed?

31. See Freedman, *op. cit.*, pp. 19 f.

32. This contradicts the opinion of Patrick D. Miller, Jr., *The Divine Warrior in Early Israel* (Cambridge, Mass.: Harvard University Press, 1973), p. 156.

33. Pritchard, *ANET*, p. 204.

34. Patrick Dwight Miller, Jr., "Holy and Cosmic War in Early Israel" (unpublished dissertation, Harvard University, Cambridge, Mass., 1963), pp. 77 ff.

35. Cf. Roland de Vaux, *Ancient Israel: Its Life and Institutions*, trans. by John McHugh (New York: McGraw-Hill Book Company, Inc., 1969), pp. 215 f. While he holds that the tribes as units were free to decide, he explains that Meroz, a town in Naphtali, was cursed because it did not follow the decision of its tribe. Though he does not agree with my suggestion above, he still recognizes the main point and tries to account for it.

36. Globe feels that there is every reason to believe that the song was composed shortly after the battle. Globe, *op. cit.*, p. 512. Craigie suggests that its initial setting was a victory celebration or at least that the initial composition was motivated by this particular victory. It sub-

sequently may have been used in the Covenant Renewal Festival. P. C. Craigie, "The Song of Deborah and the Epic of Tukulti-Ninurta," p. 254.

37. Judg. 5:4-5 suggests Yahweh's coming from Seir and Edom, i.e., the route of Sinai. See Freedman, *op. cit.*, pp. 19 f.

38. Eissfeldt regards chapter 4 as J material, Otto Eissfeldt, *The Old Testament*, trans. by Peter R. Ackroyd (Oxford: Basil Blackwell, 1965), pp. 254, 265. While J as a continuous source may not exist beyond the Book of Numbers, we may well have in this chapter a tenth-century writing, perhaps written by J himself. See the comment by Freedman in Boling, *op. cit.*, p. 97, note on v. 15. For a detailing of differences between the prose narrative and the song, see G. F. Moore in *A Critical and Exegetical Commentary on Judges* (Edinburgh: T. & T. Clark, 1949), pp. 107 ff.

39. The " *'lp*" (Judg. 4:6) is to be understood as a unit, perhaps of 10 men. Ten "*'lpym*" from each tribe would equal 200 men. See Boling, *op. cit.*, pp 54 f., note on Judg. 1:4, and p. 110, note on 5:8.

40. V. 15, following the translation of *The Jerusalem Bible* (Garden City, N.Y.: Doubleday & Company Inc., 1966).

41. See above, note 38. On holy war language see chap. II, note 58.

42. Deborah in Judg. 5:7, 12, 15; 4:4, 9, 10, 14. Barak in Judg. 5:12, 15; 4:6, 8, 9, 10, 14, 14, 15, 16, 22.

43. See the discussion of "Type A" Scholars—Schwally, Pederson, von Rad and Miller—in Chapter 1.

44. Freedman, personal note, Sept. 11, 1977.

45. See Boling, *op. cit.*, p. 5.

46. Martin Buber, *Moses: The Revelation and the Covenant* (New York: Harper & Brothers, Publishers, 1958), pp. 198 f.

47. See James S. Ackerman, "Prophecy and Warfare in Early Israel: A Study of the Deborah-Barak Story," *BASOR*, 220 (1975), 5-15.

48. See Ackerman, *ibid.*, who argues that the Deborah-Barak relationhsip was antecedent to the Samuel-Saul relationship which in turn was the most complete model for the 10-9th century prophet's self-understanding of his relationship to the North Israelite monarchy.

49. This is W. F. Albright's translation in *Samuel and the Beginnings of the Prophetic Movement* (Cincinnati: Hebrew Union College Press, 1961), p. 9. He suggests that Hosea may here be quoting material which was as early as the eleventh century BC. "The repetition of words in perfect balance . . . points to the eleventh century BC. . . ." *Ibid.*

50. For comments on the question of relationship of this battle to that of Deborah, see above, note 12.

51. See Noth, *Das Buch Josua*, p. 27; John Bright, "The Book of Joshua," *Interpreter's Bible* Vol. II, ed. by George Arthur Buttrick (New York, Nashville: Abingdon-Cokesbury Press, 1953), p. 553. Eissfeldt held that it was derived from E. Eissfeldt, *op. cit.*, p. 252. For a summary statement of the question of Pentateuchal sources and the Deuteronomic history, see David Noel Freedman, "Pentateuch," *The Interpreter's Dictionary of the Bible*, Vol. III, ed. by George Arthur Buttrick (New York, Nashville: Abingdon Press, 1962), pp. 712-717. Noth maintains that the Pentateuchal sources end with Numbers. Noth, *Das Buch Josua*, p. 16. Bright and Freedman (above references) accept the concept of the Deuteronomic history but hold that the Pentateuchal strands continued as source material for the Deuteronomic historian. See also chap. VIII of this book.

52. Eissfeldt feels that chapters 1-7 represent mainly L J E, while chaps. 8-12 are J E. Eissfeldt, *op. cit.*, p. 253. Bright sees J E as the basis of the history through chapters 1-12. Bright, "The Book of Joshua," p. 553. I delineate below the additions of D or DH.

53. See above, chap. III, A.1.e, and note 7.

54. See Jay A. Wilcoxen, "Narrative Structure and Cult Legend: A Study of Joshua 1—6," *Transitions in Biblical Scholarship*, ed. by J. Coert Rylaarsdam (Chicago and London: The University of Chicago Press, 1968), pp. 43-70.

55. Cf. J. Maxwell Miller and Gene M. Tucker, *The Book of Joshua* (Cambridge: Cambridge University Press, 1974), pp. 34 f, 53-55.

56. See Frank Moore Cross, *Canaanite Myth and Hebrew Epic* (Cambridge, Mass.: Harvard University Press, 1973), pp. 103-105.

57. For the borders of the Egyptian province of Canaan in the time of Rameses II, see Yohanan Aharoni and Michael Avi-Yonah, *The MacMillan Bible Atlas* (New York: The MacMillan Company, London: Collier-MacMillan Limited, 1968), No. 50., p. 41.

58. Cross, *op. cit.*, p. 104.

59. See Patrick Miller, *The Divine Warrior in Early Israel*, pp. 128 f.

60. Cross, *op. cit.*, p. 104. As will be apparent to the reader, I am indebted to Cross for the above analysis.

61. Israel's worship did not originate the event but perpetuated it, though worship may have focused its meaning. For historical possibilities of the Jordan crossing, see J. Alberto Soggin, *Joshua*, trans. by R. A. Wilson (Philadelphia: The Westminster Press, 1972), pp. 61 ff.

62. There is obviously a play on the name of Gilgal here in the verb *glwty*. Just what the reproach was which was rolled away (slavery?) is uncertain.

63. See James Luther Mays, *Amos* (Philadelphia: The Westminster Press, 1969), pp. 45, 46.

64. See Freedman, "Early Israelite History in the Light of Early Israelite Poetry," pp. 25 f, note 17.

65. See Dennis J. McCarthy, "The Theology of Leadership in Joshua 1—9," *Biblica*, 52 (1971), 165-175.

66. See above, chap. III. See also our exegesis of the Song of Deborah.

67. For the literary analysis here I follow Miller and Tucker, *op. cit.* DH adds 3:2-4, 6-10, 17b (p.34); Deuteronomistic editor adds 4:6-7, 21-24, 5:1 (p.42); 5:4-7 (p. 46).

68. The original meaning of this term probably referred to a unit. See above note 39.

69. Wilcoxen, *op. cit.* See above, note 54.

70. Soggin, *op. cit.*, pp. 83-87, esp. p. 87.

71. Miller and Tucker, *op. cit.*, pp. 53, 55.

72. For other spy stories in the Old Testament, see Num. 13 (cf. Deut. 1:22 ff), Num. 21:32; Josh. 7:22 ff.; Judg. 18:2 ff.

73. The tie between the chapters is thus made by the ancient recensions. Miller and Tucker (*op. cit.*, p. 54) hold that 6:27 is D. However, Noth (*Das Buch Josua*, pp. 9, 12) regards this verse as a part of the ancient recensions with vv. 25b-26 as younger supplements.

74. On searching out "the land," see 2:1, 2, 3, 9, 9, 14, 18, 24; 6:22. All these usages are from the usually designated ancient recensions, except the second case in v. 9 and v. 24: Both the older and younger recensions thus agree on this point. I follow Noth (*ibid.*, p. 24) on v. 9; on v. 24 I follow Miller and Tucker (*op. cit.*, p. 32), though Noth disagrees with them, *op. cit.*, p. 26.

75. See note 3 above, for background on the function of the spies.

76. Only holy war language, see chap. II, note 58. Both older (2:24a) and younger (2:24b) recensions agree on this point; the younger enlarges on the older. As Miller and Tucker are not specific here, I follow Noth, *op. cit.*, p. 24.

77. Miller and Tucker, *op. cit.*, p. 32.

78. Noth, *Das Bush Josua*, p. 20; the translation given here is my own.

79. See chap. III, A.1.c; on holy war language, see chap. II, note 58.

80. Both ancient and younger recensions include the ceremony. For a division of sources see Noth, *Das Buch Josua*, p. 36.

81. See above, Chap. III, A.1.d.

82. See Noth, *Das Buch Josua*, pp. 28, 30, 34.

83. See Josh. 24 and the discussion below.

84. For the remarks of Boling about the fact that Joshua appointed no successor see Boling, *op. cit.*, pp. 25, 63.

85. See Pritchard *ANET*, p. 320. Mesha was a 9th century Moabite king who rebelled against Israel (2 Kings 3).

86. See Weippert, above, chap. I,A.2.

87. See Pritchard, *ANET*, p. 320. See our discussion above on the Song of the Sea, chap. III, A.1.d.

88. For these see such commentaries as Miller and Tucker, *op. cit.*

89. For a discussion of the narrative of defeat see chapter VI.

90. Noth designates v. 2 as a younger source, and v. 27 as older. Noth, *Das Buch Josua*, pp. 44, 48.

91. Verses 1, 2, 7, 8, 10, 18, 26, 27. See note 58, chapter II.

92. Both the Exodus and the Joshua passages belong to the older rather than the younger recensions. See Noth, *ibid.*, p. 48.

93. "Yahweh": vv. 1, 7, 8, 18, 27; "Joshua": vv. 1, 3, 3, 9, 9, 10, 13, 15, 16, 18, 18, 21, 23, 26, 27, 28, 29.

94. See Noth, *Das Buch Josua*, p. 52.

95. Cf. Miller and Tucker, *op. cit.*, p. 78.

96. "Yahweh": vv. 8, 10, 11, 12, 12, 14, 14; "Joshua": vv. 1, 4, 6, 7, 8, 9, 12, 15.

97. The list is made up from a basic foundation itinerary, which was then supplemented by younger recensions. See Noth, *Das Buch Josua*, pp. 58, 60; Miller and Tucker, *op. cit.*, p. 88.

98. Noth, *Das Buch Josua*, p. 60.

99. For the possible relation of this event to the battle of Deborah against Sisera see above, note 12.

100. The LXX indicates that they surprised the camp in territory unfavorable to chariots.

101. See vv. 6, 8, 9, 11, 12, 14. All of these except vv. 11, 12 belong to the older recensions. Noth, *Das Buch Josua*, p. 62. For holy war language, see note 58, chap. II.

102. "Yahweh": vv. 6, 8, 9, 12, 15, 15; all of these are older recensions except vv. 12, 15. *Ibid.* "Joshua": vv. 6, 7, 9, 10, 12, 13, 15, 15; all are in older sources except for v. 15. *Ibid.*

103. We examine this passage in chap. V, B. 4.

104. See W. L. Moran, "Some Remarks on the Song of Moses," *Biblica*, 43 (1962), 323-327.

105. The prophetic books are outside the scope of this study. For comments on Isaiah in connection with DH, see chap. VIII, E.2.

106. See A. Glock, "Warfare in Mari and Early Israel" (PhD dissertation, University of Michigan, 1968, University Microfilms, Inc., Ann Arbor, Mich.), pp. 209-213.

107. Noth, *Das Buch Josua*, pp. 137 f.

108. Bright regards this as "a summary of the older stratum of the Pentateuch," uncertain as to how much is due to Deuteronomic editing. "The Book of Joshua" *The Interpreter's Bible*, vol. II, p. 544.

109. See Gerhard von Rad, *Studies in Deuteronomy*, trans. by David Stalker (London: SCM Press Ltd., 1963), pp. 14 f. Also, G. Ernest Wright, *Shechem* (New York: McGraw-Hill Book Company 1965), pp. 134 f., and James Muilenburg, "The Form and Structure of the Convenantal Formulations," *Vetus Testamentum*, IX (1959), 347-365, esp. 357 ff.

110. *Ibid.*: also Charles H. Giblin, "Structural Patterns in Josh. 24:1-25," *The Catholic Biblical Quarterly*, XXVI (1964), 50-69. Soggin *op. cit.*, p. 231. On the covenant form, see George E. Mendenhall, *Law and Covenant in Israel and the Ancient Near East* (Pittsburgh: The Biblical Colloquium, 1955), pp. 41 ff.; Dennis J. McCarthy, *Treaty and Covenant* (Rome: Pontifical Biblical Institute, 1963), pp. 145 ff; Klaus Baltzer, *The Covenant Formulary*, trans. by David E. Green (Oxford: Basil Blackwell, 1971), pp. 19 ff.

111. See Soggin's discussion, *op. cit.*, p. 230.

112. The Ten Words (Ex. 20:1-17), for example, devote only one sentence to Yahweh's action and emphasize commandments, while the Shechem covenant has only a sentence or so devoted to commandment (v. 14) and instead emphasizes Yahweh's action (vv.2-13).

113. This tradition of human fighting at Jericho corresponds to what we have found in the narrative sources. Soggin maintains that this is a different reporting from what is found in Josh. 6, but even he admits that it is not a contradiction and that Josh. 6 includes human fighting. Soggin, *op. cit.*, p. 234.

114. For the possible relation of the narratives to history, see John Bright, *op. cit.*, pp. 118 ff.

115. See chap. II, notes 67, 68, and chap. III, A.1.c.

116. The *"hornet"* is only a guess at an unknown term. *The New English Bible* makes a generalization: "I spread panic before you. . . ."

117. Noth, *Das Buch Josua*, p. 138.

118. This point is made by the oldest source. See Noth, *ibid.*, p. 136.

119. For a discussion of this new concept of political power, see chap. III, A.1.d, and B.3.

120. See the text at note 83 above, where I suggest that the emphasis on Joshua as warrior may have been a read-back from the period of the Kings.

Chapter Five

1. See M. Weinfeld, "The Period of the Conquest and of the Judges as Seen by the Earlier and the Later Sources," *Vetus Testamentum*, XVII (1967), 110 f.

2. See Walther Eichrodt, *Theology of the Old Testament I*, trans. by J. A. Baker (Philadelphia: The Westminster Press, 1961), pp. 306 ff.

3. See chap. III, A.1, and IV, A.

4. This framework is: Aram Naharayim, 3:7-9, 10b-11a; Moab, 11b-15, 30; Canaanite Coalition, 4:1-6, 23-24; 5:31b; Midian, 6:1-10; 8:28; Philistia and Ammon, 10:6-16; 12:7; Philistia, 13:1-5; 15:20; 16:31b. See Otto Eissfeldt, *The Old Testament*, trans. by Peter R. Ackroyd (Oxford: Basil Blackwell, 1965), p. 259.

5. The fact that this story, traditionally attributed to E, is found in the framework does not necessarily mean that it is not true to Israel in the time of the judges. See Robert G. Boling, *Judges* (Garden City, N.Y.: Doubleday & Company, Inc., 1975), p. 125.

6. The fact that 4 Q Judges omits vv. 7-10 may mean that the original textual tradition did not have this tradition here, but says nothing of its essential authenticity. On the early pre-kingship unity of the prophet with holy war see the article by James S. Ackerman, "Prophecy and Warfare in Early Israel: A Study of the Deborah-Barak Story," *BASOR*, 220 (1975), 5-15.

7. Here again we have language similar to that of E. See Eissfeldt, *op. cit.*, p. 262. For the actual use of the term *rîb*, see Micah 6:1 where the verb form is translated "plead your case." The prophets often borrowed this legal form to present their complaint against Israel.

8. See Walter Beyerlin, "Gattung und Herkunft des Rahmens im Richterbuch," *Tradition und Situation*, ed. by Ernst Würthwein and Otto Kaiser (Göttingen: Vandenhoeck & Ruprecht, 1963), pp. 1-29. We will discuss the *rîb* later in connection with Yahweh's war against his own people.

9. See Judg. 2:1 where in similar material the Egyptian deliverance is linked to the occupation in the *rîb* formulation.

10. See Boling, *op. cit.*, p. 126, and p. 30.

11. Traditionally, this narrative (Judg. 6;11-32) has been seen as two recensions 6:11-24 (J) and 6:25-32 (E). See George F. Moore, *Judges* (Edinburgh: T. and T. Clark, 1958), pp. 182 ff. Moore sees vv. 17b, 20 as secondary with corresponding changes in vv. 16 and 18, 19. This division is today disputed, and the whole is seen by some as a unified ancient narrative. See Boling, *op. cit.*, p. 130. Others cut the material up with a jigsaw puzzle effect. I provisionally hold to the unity of the material, but will follow Moore's more conventional approach, dividing between J and E. Moore, *op. cit.*, pp. 182 f., 190 f.

12. See Boling, *op. cit.*, p. 129.

13. Unlike all other direct calls, including that of Samuel, Gideon was a warrior rather than a prophetic figure. See chap. III, B.3, for a discussion of the call of Moses.

14. For discussion of Barak see chap. IV, B.2; I discuss 1 Sam. 9 briefly in this chapter.

15. For source classification here I rely upon Wolfgang Richter, *Die sogenannten vorprophetischen Berufungsberichte* (Göttingen: Vandenhoeck & Ruprecht, 1970), pp. 50, 97, 114.

16. See above discussion, A.1.

17. This might be translated "aristocrat." See Boling, *op. cit.*, p. 131.

18. Other than the call of Moses, the prophets were mainly bearers of the *rîb* against their own people, as for example Samuel (1 Sam. 3), Isaiah (Is. 6), etc. However Isaiah of Babylon (Is. 40) was closer to Moses in that he bore Yahweh's word of salvation from foreign domination.

19. I follow Boling here (*op. cit.*, p. 142 f) in seeing the end of this narrative with v. 22. Another military enlistment could hardly have been made in time to pursue the defeated enemy. The pursuit changes into a revenge for the death of Gideon's relatives, obviously a confusion of materials. See Boling, *ibid.*, p. 152. This ancient narrative is generally regarded as composed of J and E (see Eissfeldt, *op. cit.*, pp. 260, 264), though many commentators agree that the two strands can no longer be separated. See Jacob M. Myers, "The Book of Judges," *The Interpreter's Bible*, Vol. II, ed. by George Arthur Buttrick (New York, Nashville: Abingdon-Cokesbury Press, 1953), p. 729. Moore regards vv. 2-8 as seeming to be from E, "perhaps to a secondary stratum of that work," *op. cit.*, p. 199.

20. This text is perhaps a Deuteronomistic insertion. See Boling, *op. cit.*, p. 144, who notes that "this is a standing theme in Deuteronomic retrospect and prospect (Deut. 8:11-18; 9:4-5; cf. Is. 10:13-15)."

21. Cf. Deut. 20:8. This law is very ancient. See H. W. Hertzberg, *Die Bücher Josua, Richter, Ruth* (Göttingen: Vandenhoeck & Ruprecht, 1959), p. 195. See the Song of Deborah (Judg. 5:2, 9).

22. G. E. Mendenhall views this ancient folk tradition as resting upon a misunderstanding of a discontinued form of military organization based on the tribal unit, the '*elep*, and sees the 32,000 of the first army as identical with the 300 who defeated the Midianites. Mendenhall, "The Census Lists of Numbers 1 and 26," *Journal of Biblical Literature*, LXXVII (1958), 64, note 53. Yigael Yadin seems to regard the incident as an authentic "system of exemption employed by Gideon, who in fact exempted both the fainthearted and the inexperienced." Yigael Yadin, *The Scroll of the War of the Sons of Light Against the Sons of Darkness*, trans. by Batya and Chaim Rabin ([London]: Oxford University Press, 1962), p. 68; also note 4. Boling holds that Gideon's force was made up originally of 300 men, the full strength quota of the tribe of Manasseh which was reduced to "a relative handful of men, perhaps 50 or so." Boling, *op. cit.*, p. 144.

23. Boling, *op. cit.*, p. 148.

24. See for example Beyerlin, "Geschichte and heilsgeschichtliche Traditionsbildung im Alten Testament (Richter VI-VIII)," *Vetus Testamentum* 13 (1963), pp. 1-25. Beyerlin disagrees with Wellhausen and von Rad that Israel (the sacral league) began in the war camp, but that it began in Yahweh's deed of revelation which the exodus and Sinai tradition reported. *Ibid.*, p. 16 ff. Beyerlin is correct except that, as we have seen, Israel's poets and scribes regarded the exodus as Yahweh's war. Thus the people of Yahweh were indeed born in the experience of the war camp, but in the war camp as transformed by the action of Yahweh who alone was deliverer, the point of the Gideon narrative.

25. Gerhard von Rad, *Der Heilige Krieg im Alten Israel* (Göttingen: Vandenhoeck & Ruprecht, 1952), pp. 33 ff.

26. See "The Divine Nomination of Thut-Mose III," in Pritchard, *ANET*, pp. 446 f.

27. The noun form of *špt* is used only of Yahweh in the Book of Judges (11:27). See Boling, *op. cit.*, p. 5. See Boling's analysis, *ibid.*, p. 7.

28. See 1 Sam. 23:6 ff., where the use of the ephod refers to decision-making in a Yahwistic war.

29. Boling, *op. cit.*, pp. 7, 81. See also T. Ishida, "The Leaders of the Tribal Leagues 'Is-

rael' in the Pre-Monarchic Period," *Revue Biblique*, 80 (1973), 514-430. Ishida sees the judge as a person who arose spontaneously to organize tribal leagues called "Israel" in order to meet a military threat, after which the judge ruled over the league until his death. *Ibid.*, p. 529. This does not explain the leadership of Deborah nor Samuel who were primarily religious leaders, and who called upon the military person when confronted by a threat. See also Alan J. Hauser, "The 'Minor Judges'—a Reevaluation," *Journal of Biblical Literature*, 94 (1975), 190-200; Hanoch Reviv, "Two Types of Leadership in the Period of the Judges," *Beer-Sheva*, Vol. I (University of the Negev, Beer-Sheva, 1973, by Kiryat-Sepher, Ltd., Jerusalem), pp. 204-221 (Hebrew).

30. See the article by Judith Dishon, "Gideon and the Beginnings of Monarchy in Israel," *Tarbiz*, 41 (1971-72), 255-268 (Hebrew), who argues that Gideon did become king and the refutation by Samuel E. Loewenstamm, "The Lord Shall Rule Over You (Judges VIII:23)," *Tarbiz*, 41 (1971-72), 444 f. Judg. 8:22-23, where Gideon is offered and rejects kingship, is regarded as related to E by Eissfeldt, *op. cit.*, p. 262. Moore, *op. cit.*, p. 229, regards the verses as E.

31. See above, chap. III, A.1.d.

32. I discuss the question of the historicity of this dogma in connection with Samuel later in this chapter.

33. "ina pāna^{na} šar-rı-tu ina mātāti^{meš} ul ba-ši u be-lu-tu a-na ilāni^{meš} šar-ka-at", VAT, 8830, lines 7-8. From W. G. Lambert, *Babylonian Wisdom Literature* (Oxford: Clarendon Press, 1960), p. 162. See Loewenstamm, *op. cit.*, p. 445.

34. Boling, *op. cit.*, p. 183.

35. *Ibid.*

36. Martin Noth, *The History of Israel* (2nd ed., rev. Eng. trans.; New York: Harper & Brothers, 1960), p. 172, n. 2: "The Deuteronomistic historian supplemented the old tradition of Saul in accordance with his own ideas, by adding 1 Samuel vii, 2b-17; viii, 1-22; x,17, 27a; xii,1-25. Admittedly he made it easy for himself to reject the institution of monarchy by making Samuel win the decisive victory over the Philistines (1 Sam. vii, 10b-11), thereby fundamentally misrepresenting the real historical background to the emergence of the monarchy." Cf. also H. W. Hertzberg, *Die Samuelbücher* (Göttingen: Vandenhoech & Ruprecht, 1960), p. 49, who sees this passage as a theological reflection.

37. Eissfeldt regards chapters 7, 8, and 12 as having affinities with E, *op. cit.*, p. 271. Artur Weiser, disputing Noth's assumption, concludes that the material resembles E but that it is essentially older in its origins than E, going back to the difficulties with which the acceptance of kingship was burdened from the first. *Einleitung in das Alte Testament* (Göttingen: Vandenhoeck & Ruprecht, 1957), p. 133.

38. See Artur Weiser, *Samuel, Seine geschichtliche Aufgabe und religiöse Bedeutung* (Göttingen: Vandenhoeck & Ruprecht, 1962), p. 8.

39. For most of these arguments I am indebted to Weiser, *Samuel, Seine geschichtliche Aufgabe . . . , pp. 8 ff.*

40. Hans Jochen Boecker, in *Die Beurteilung der Anfänge des Königtums in den Deuteronomistischen Abschnitten des I. Samuelbuches* (Neukirchen-Vluyn: Neukirchener Verlag des Erziehungsvereins, 1969), pp. 9, 97 f argues against Weiser, holding that 1 Sam. 7; 8; 10:17-27; 12 are the free creation of the Deuteronomist. It seems evident to me, however, that his analysis is ruled unduly by his desire to uphold Noth's theory.

41. Cf. Weiser, *Samuel, Seine geschichtliche Aufgabe . . .*, p. 22 f.

42. W. F. Albright, *Samuel and the Beginnings of the Prophetic Movement* (Cincinnati: Hebrew Union College Press, 1961), pp. 10 ff.

43. *Ibid.*, p. 14.

44. See Hans Joachim Stoebe, *Das erste Buch Samuels* (Gütersloher Verlagshaus Gerd Mohn, 1973), pp. 167 f.

45. *Ibid.*, pp. 172.

46. See George E. Mendenhall, "The Incident at Beth Baal Peor" in *The Tenth Genera-*

tion (Baltimore and London: The Johns Hopkins University Press, 1973), pp. 106 f.

47. Eissfeldt, *op. cit.*, p. 279. It is interesting that the plagues are related to the wilderness period here.

48. See Stoebe, *op. cit.*, p. 150. There is a difference of scholarly opinion as to how much of this may have been a later forming out. See *ibid.*, note 1.

49. See Albright, *op. cit.*, p. 16.

50. See Boecker, *op. cit.*

51. Deut. 32:12, 21, 39. Here also the people have deserted Yahweh for other gods, thus breaking the first commandment. The poem is dated by Eissfeldt to the 11th century and by G. Ernest Wright to the 9th century or later, certainly pre-exilic. See Eissfeldt, *op. cit.*, pp. 226 f. See G. Ernest Wright, "The Lawsuit of God: A Form-Critical Study of Deuteronomy 32," ed. by Bernhard W. Anderson and Walter Harrelson, *Israel's Prophetic Heritage* (New York: Harper and Brothers, Publishers, 1962, pp. 66 f. For the prophetic oracles, see Hosea, Isaiah, and Micah.

52. See Stoebe, *op. cit.*, pp. 173 f.; see Weiser, *Samuel, Seine geschichtliche Aufgabe . . .*, *p. 20.*

53. For a discussion of the characteristics of law in the Old Testament, see Martin Noth, "The Law in the Pentateuch," *The Law in the Pentateuch and Other Studies* (Edinburgh & London: Oliver and Boyd, 1966), pp. 1-107.

54. Weiser sees no historical reality whatsoever in this report of victory. Weiser, *Samuel, Seine geschichtliche Aufgabe . . .*, pp. 8 f.

55. "Wie wenig das Ereignis unter sakralkriegerischen Aspekten gesehen wird, zeigt der folgende Abschnitt (10-14). Samuel ruft nicht in der Kraft des Geistes zu einem Kriegszug auf, er ist auch nicht mit göttlicher Unterstützung Führer zum Sieg. Im Grunde sehen die Israeliten tatenlos zu und greifen erst ein, als der Kampf entschieden ist. Dass hier die wunderbare Hilfe in einem Kriege Jahwes gemeint ist, steht ausser Zweifel, ebenso aber, dass die Stilisierung einen erheblichen Abstand zu diesem Theologumenon verrät. In dieser Hinsicht verrät die Darstellung Verwandtschaft mit dem Königsgesetz Dt. 17:14-20 und vermag vielleicht zu illustrieren, wie man sich das Funktionieren eines solchen Königtums ohne Macht gedacht hat." Stoebe, *op. cit.*, p. 174.

56. He regards chapter 7 as the work of the Deuteronomist, working without older material. *Ibid.*, p. 171.

57. In this, Stoebe agrees with von Rad, et al. See above, chap. I,A.1.

58. See chaps. III and IV.

59. See M. Tsevat, "The Biblical Narrative of the Foundation of Kingship in Israel," *Tarbiz*, 36 (1966-67), 101 (Hebrew).

60. Dennis J. McCarthy, "The Inauguration of Monarchy in Israel," *Interpretation*, XXVII (1973), 403.

61. See I. Mendelsohn, "Samuel's Denunciation of Kingship in the Light of the Akkadian Documents from Ugarit," *Bulletin of the American Oriental Society*, No. 143 (1956), 17-22.

62. See also 2 Kings 21; Jer. 22:13-17.

63. I discuss this further in an article, "The Concept of Political Power in Ancient Israel," *Annual of the Swedish Theological Institute*, VII (1970), pp. 12 f.

64. See above, chap. III, A.1.d.

65. See Artur Weiser, "Samuel und die Vorgeschichte des israelitischen Königtums, I Samuel 8" in *Samuel, Seine geschichtliche Aufgabe . . .*, pp. 25-45.

66. Moshe Weinfeld, *Deuteronomy and the Deuteronomic School* (Oxford: Clarendon Press, 1972), p. 169: "The anti-monarchic sentiments expressed in the traditions in 1 Sam. 8—12 are by no means deuteronomic, and the deuteronomic passages in the book of Kings, on the other hand, exhibit no anti-monarchic tendencies."

67. For examples in poetry, see Ex. 15:18; Num. 23:21; Deut. 33:5. Theophoric names (names referring to God) that have as one component *melek* (king) are found in Judg. 8:31 (Abimelech, "Father," i.e., God, "is king"); 1 Sam. 21:2 (Ahimelech, "Brother," i.e., God, "is

king"); 1 Sam. 14:49 (Malchishua, "King," i.e., God, "saves"). See Tsevat, *op. cit.*, p. 100.

68. Even Boecker, who holds that the anti-kingship material is the work of the Deuteronomic historian, regards this anti-kingship emphasis as a result both of Israel's experience with kingship and of the ancient tradition which was hostile to kingship. He regards this opposition to kingship on the basis of Yahweh's kingship as a historical reality from the beginning on. Boecker, *op. cit.*, pp 98 f. See my article mentioned above in note 63.

69. See our discussion on Ex. 15, chap. III, A.1.I.

70. Weiser argues for the historicity of the anti-kingship tradition, but regards the account of Israel's victory in the narrative of the battle with the Philistines in 1 Sam. 7 as a pious fiction. Weiser, "Samuels 'Philister-Sieg' " in *Samuel, Seine geschichtliche Aufgabe* . . ., pp. 22 f. A battle here or there might be regarded as fiction, of course, but if the one tradition is historical, the other can hardly be only theological reflection.

71. Roland de Vaux, *Ancient Israel: Its Life and Institutions*, trans. by John McHugh (New York, Toronto, London: McGraw-Hill Book Company, Inc., 1961), p. 99.

72. See Hans-Joachim Kraus, *Prophetie und Politik* ("Theologische Existenz Heute," Neue Folge Nr. 36; München: Chr. Kaiser Verlag, 1952), p. 30.

73. The king was to function as warrior only in relation to the command of the prophet and not vice versa. See the relationship of Joshua to Moses, Ex. 17, and Barak's relations to Deborah as discussed above, chap. IV, B.2. For a discussion of the titles "prince" and "king," see W. F. Albright, *Samuel and the Beginnings of the Prophetic Movement* (Cincinnati: Hebrew Union College Press, 1961).

74. Noth, *op. cit.*, p. 173; John Bright, *A History of Israel* (2nd ed.; Philadelphia: The Westminster Press, 1972), p. 184; Hertzberg, *Die Samuelbücher*, pp. 87 f.

75. See my discussion of the thesis of Manfred Weippert in chapter I, A.2.

76. See Edward F. Campbell, Jr., "Excavation at Shechem; 1960," *Biblical Archaeologist*, XXIII (1960), 107, who dates this incident "early in the Iron I period, probably in the first half of the twelfth century. . . ."

77. See Judg. 3:10, 28; 11:29-32; also 11:9, 27; 12:3. The narrative of Othniel against Cushan-rishathaim (Judg. 3:7-11) is written in the hand of the Deuteronomist or Deuteronomic historian, and is characterized throughout by the Deuteronomic theology. (For a discussion of this theology see chapter VIII.)

The interesting justification of warfare at 11:27 may have come from a later time. See Myers, *op. cit.*, pp. 766 ff on 11:12-28. However, wars were justified at an early period by Israel's near contemporaries. See Suppiluliuma's justification of his attack upon Tushratta of Mittani in Suppiluliuma's treaty with Mattiwaza in D. D. Luckenbill, "Hittite Treaties and Letters," *The American Journal of Semitic Languages and Literatures*, 37 (1921), p. 163. Text K Bo. I, No. 1.

78. Noth, *op. cit.*, p. 104 holds that this story "is certainly based on an old tradition and only appears to have undergone slight literary elaboration. . . ." See Hos. 9:9; 10:9.

79. Mizpah is probably to be identified with Tel en-Nasbeh, 8 miles north of Jerusalem, though some identify it with Nebi Samwil, 5 miles north of Jerusalem. See J. Muilenburg, "Mizpah," *The Interpreter's Dictionary of the Bible*, Vol. III, ed. by George Arthur Buttrick (New York, Nashville: Abingdon Press, 1962), p. 408 f.

80. The ark of God was at Bethel, suggesting that this was the present place of Yahweh's rule.

81. "People of Israel": 20:1, 3, 13, 14, 18, 19, 22, 27, 30; "people": 20:8; "tribes of Israel": 20:2, 12; "men of Israel": 20:20, 31-33, 35, 36, 38, 39, 41, 42, 48; "Israel": 20:29, 34, 35.

82. See 1 Sam. 14:38; Is. 19:13; Zech. 10:4 (Zeph. 3:6).

83. For a discussion of 1 Sam. 15 see Hans W. Hertzberg, *I & II Samuel* (Philadelphia: The Westminster Press, 1964), pp. 120-134.

84. See our discussion, above chap. IV, C. 2, also accompanying notes 85-87. Also "The Moabite Stone," *Ancient Near Eastern Texts*, ed. by James B. Pritchard (Princeton, N.J.: Princeton University Press, 1955), pp. 320 f.

85. For a discussion of the variant text of the LXX and problems in this story see Hertzberg, *I & II Samuel*, pp. 146 ff. While some would regard this statement as a late insertion (see Noth, *op. cit.*, p. 180, n. 1.), its fundamental idea is not late if compared with ancient Near Eastern literature of warfare. See Manfred Weippert, " 'Heiliger Krieg' in Israel und Assyrien: Kritische Anmerkungen zu Gerhard von Rads Konzept des 'Heiligen Krieges im alten Israel,' " *Zeitschrift für die altestamentliche Wissenschaft*, 84 (1972), and our discussion of his thesis in chap. I. It is also, of course, in harmony with our thesis about Israel's earliest literature. See chap. III and our discussion of the Song of the Sea.

86. Hertzberg, *I & II Samuel*, p. 153. For a discussion of a polemic against sophisticated weapons see above, chap. IV, C.4.e.

Chapter Six

1. This passage is regarded as J E. See George Buchanan Gray, *Numbers* (Edinburgh: T. & T. Clark, 1912), p. 164; also S. R. Driver, *An Introduction to the Literature of the Old Testament* (New York: Meridian Books, 1956), p. 62. See the parallel account in Deut. 1:41-45.

2. M. Noth sees this chapter as belonging mainly to ancient texts made up of two narratives, the Achan narrative (7:1, 5b-26) and the campaign against Ai (7:2-5a; 8:1-29). Martin Noth, *Das Buch Josua* (Tübingen: Verlag von J. C. B. Mohr [Paul Siebeck], 1953), pp. 38, 40; 43 ff. We will not discuss his concept of etiological origins here. John Bright also regards the text as ancient, consisting of J E. John Bright, "The Book of Joshua," *The Interpreter's Bible*, Vol. II, ed. by George Arthur Buttrick (New York, Nashville: Abingdon-Cokesbury Press, 1953), p. 583.

3. Noth regards this as a later supplement. Noth, *op. cit.*, p. 40.

4. This chapter is the beginning of the early source, probably written in the time of Solomon, which provides the structure of the Book of Samuel. See George B. Caird, "The First and Second Books of Samuel," *The Interpreter's Bible*, Vol. II, ed. by George Arthur Buttrick (New York, Nashville: Abingdon-Cokesbury Press, 1953), pp. 856 ff.

5. For a study of this reversal as stated in Deut. 2, see W. L. Moran, "The End of the Unholy War and the Anti-Exodus," *Biblica*, 44 (1963), 333-342.

6. Saul's battle with the Philistines at Gilboa was also a defeat (1 Sam. 31). This narrative is not treated here because it does not contain a theological interpretation. It is probable, however, that the writer interpreted the event as Yahweh's judgment upon Saul.

7. See Samuel N. Kramer, *From the Tablets of Sumer* (Indian Hills, Col.: The Falcon's Wing Press, 1965), pp. 267 ff. He dates the text, reconstructed from 22 tablets and fragments, to the first half of the second millennium BC—Pritchard, *ANET*, p. 455.

8. *Ibid.*, p. 269.

9. *Ibid.*

10. *Ibid.*, pp. 269 f.

11. *Ibid.*, p. 270.

12. *Ibid.* See also "The Moabite Stone" (9th c.), *Ancient Near Eastern Texts*, ed. by James B. Pritchard (Princeton, N.J.: Princeton University Press, 1955), pp. 320 f.

13. The former poem is regarded by Eissfeldt and Albright as an eleventh-century document. See Otto Eissfeldt, *Das Lied Moses Deuteronomium 32:1-43 und das Lehrgedicht Asaphs Psalm 78 samt einer Analyse der Umgebung des Moses-Liedes* (Berlin: Academie-Verlag, 1958), p. 24. For other early datings (U. Cassuto, M. Frank, Paul Winter, O. Skehan) see his discussion, *ibid.*, p. 21. For later dating (8th c.: Knob, Shrader, Dillm., Westphal, Oettlie, Ew., Kamp, and Reuss; 7th c.: S. R. Driver) see S. R. Driver, *Deuteronomy* (New York: Charles Scribner's Sons, 1895), p. 347. For W. F. Albright's view, see *Samuel and the Beginnings of the Prophetic Movement* (Cincinnati: Hebrew Union College Press, 1961), p. 21. Cf. also W. F. Albright, "Some Remarks on the Song of Moses in Deuteronomy XXXII," *Vetus Testamentum*, IX (1959), pp. 339-346.

For a ninth-century date, see G. Ernest Wright, "The Lawsuits of God" in *Israel's Prophetic Heritage*, ed. by B. W. Anderson and Walter Harrelson (New York: Harper & Brothers,

1962), pp. 26 f.

14. Cf. also Micah 6:1 ff. See Albright, *op. cit*, pp. 23 f.; also Herbert B. Huffman, "The Covenant Lawsuit in the Prophets," *Journal of Biblical Literature*, LXXVIII (1959), 285-295.

15. Translated by Albright, *op. cit*, p. 26.

16. In the Book of Deuteronomy, Yahweh's blessing is contingent upon Israel's response (1:19-46; 4:40; 6:1-3; 8:1 ff.; 13:18, etc.). The negative response forms a part of the cycle upon which the Book of Judges is built (Judg. 2:11-23), as well as the theological principle for the interpretation of the books of Samuel and Kings. See Gerhard von Rad, *Studies in Deuteronomy*, trans. by David Stalker (London: SCM Press Ltd., 1963), pp. 74 ff.

17. See Albright, *op. cit*, p. 24. In the Hittite annals there are statements of the gods attacking those who have broken covenant: (11) "Bevor aber der Winter zu Ende ging, (12)— weil die Leute von Kalašma aber mir vereidigt (13) gewesen waren und den Eid gebrochen hatten (14) und Krieg angefangen hatten, zeigten ihnen die Eidgötter (15) ihre göttliche Macht, und die Eidgötter (16) packten sie. Und der Bruder verriet den Bruder, (17) der Freund aber verriet den Freund, (18) und einer tötete den anderen" Annals of Mursilis, Rs. IV, ill-18, trans. by Albrecht Götze, *Die Annalen des Mursilis* (Leipzig: J. C. Hinricks'sche Buchhandlung, 1933), p. 193.

18. See George E. Mendenhall, *Law and Covenant in Israel and the Ancient Near East* (Pittsburgh: The Biblical Colloquium, 1955), p. 34; Klaus Baltzer, *The Covenant Formulary*, trans. by David E. Green (Oxford: Basil Blackwell, 1971), p. 33.

19. Albright, *op. cit*, pp. 25 f.

Chapter Seven

1. By pre-Deuteronomic sources, I mean those ancient sources that preceded and were used by redactors associated with the discovery of the original Book of Deuteronomy in the time of Josiah, about 622 BC.

2. For another summary of these conflicts see Roland de Vaux, *Ancient Israel: Its Life and Institutions*, trans. by John McHugh (New York, Toronto, London: McGraw-Hill Book Company, Inc., 1961), pp. 247-250.

3. 2 Sam. 5:17-25, 21:15-22, 23:9-17; 2 Sam. 5:6-10; 2 Sam. 8:3-8, 10-11; 2 Sam. 10—11, 12:26-31; 2 Sam. 8:2; 2 Sam. 8-13 ff.

4. 1 Kings 10:26 f.; 1 Kings 11:14 ff.; 1 Kings 11:26-40, 12:1-24.

5. 1 Kings 15:6,7; 1 Kings 15:16 ff., 32; 2 Kings 14:8-14; the Syro-Ephraimitic war, 2 Kings 16:5, 2 Chron. 28:5-8, Is. 7 ff.

6. 2 Chron, 21:16 f.; 2 Chron. 26:6 f.; 2 Chron 28:18; 2 Kings 18:8.

7. 1 Kings 15:27; 1 Kings 16:15.

8. 2 Kings 8:20-22; 2 Kings 14:7; 2 Kings 16:5 f., in which Aram (Syria) was really the party with whom Judah was in conflict.

9. 2 Kings 3:4-7. See also "The Moabite Stone," *Ancient Near Eastern Texts*, ed. by James B. Pritchard (Princeton, N.J.: Princeton University, 1955), pp. 320 f.

10. 1 Kings 15:20; 1 Kings 20:1-43, 1 Kings 22:1-38, in cooperation with Jehoshaphat of Judah; 2 Kings 6:8-7:20, probably Ahab; 2 Kings 8:28 f., in cooperation with Ahaziah of Judah; 2 Kings 10:32 f.; 2 Kings 13:3-5, 7, 22; 2 Kings 13:24 ff., 2 Kings 14:25.

11. 2 Kings 12:18; 2 Kings 16:5 f., Is. 7—8, the Syro-Ephraimitic war.

12. The Bible does not mention this. See Shalmanezer's inscriptions, Pritchard, *ANET*, pp. 277-279. For a discussion see John Bright, *A History of Israel* (2nd ed.; Philadelphia: the Westminster Press, 1972), pp. 239 f. The date was 853 BC.

13. See Pritchard, *ANET*, pp. 280 f. For a discussion see Bright, *op. cit.*, pp. 250 f.

14. 2 Kings 15:19 f.

15. 2 Kings 15:29.

16. 2 Kings 17:1-41. For a discussion see Bright, *op. cit.*, pp. 273 f.

17. 2 Kings 16:7-18.

18. 2 Kings 18:13-19:37; Is. 36-37. For a discussion of a possible second campaign see

Bright, *op. cit.*, pp. 284 ff. Cf. "The Oriental Institute Prism Inscription (H2)," Col. II, 73-83; Col. III, 37-49, *The Annals of Sennacherib* (Chicago: The University of Chicago Press, 1924), pp. 31,33 f.

19. 2 Kings 23:15-20.

20. I Kings 14:21-28.

21. 2 Kings 23:29 f; 2 Chron. 35:20-25. Necho was merely passing through to unite with Assur-uballit II at Haran in battle against Nebuchadnezzar. See Frank M. Cross, Jr., and David N. Freedman, "Josiah's Revolt Against Assyria," *Journal of Near Eastern Studies*, XII (1953), 56-58; William H. Hallo, "From Qarqar to Carchemish: Assyria and Israel in the Light of New Discoveries," *Biblical Archaeologist*, XXIII (1960), 34-61.

22. 2 Kings 24:1-4; cf. Jer. 46:2.

23. 2 Kings 24:2.

24. 2 Kings 24:10-17. For a discussion see Bright, *op. cit.*, pp. 325 ff.

25. 2 Kings 24:20-25:20. See Bright, *op. cit.*, pp. 327 ff.

26. 2 Sam. 15:18; 2 Sam. 20:1-22.

27. 1 Kings 15:27 ff.

28. 1 Kings 16: 8-10, 15-19.

29. 2 Kings 9-10, cf. 1 Kings 19:15-18; 2 Kings 15:10; 2 Kings 15:14 f.

30. 2 Kings 15:25; 2 Kings 15:30. These later changes of dynasties were related to state policy toward Assyria.

31. 2 Kings 11:1-16.

32. 2 Kings 12:20 f.

33. 2 Kings 14:19-21.

34. 2 Kings 21:23 f.

35. 2 Kings 25:25.

36. 1 Kings 18:40.

37. 2 Kings 1:9-12.

38. 2 Kings 10:18-28; 2 Kings 23:20.

39. See chapter V, especially sections B. 4 and G.

40. This narrative belongs to the pre-Deuteronomic source of the rise of David. See Martin Noth, *Überlieferungsgeschichtliche Studien* (Tübingen: Max Niemeyer Verlag, 1957), pp. 63 f. The narrative may be chronologically misplaced since the Philistine wars probably preceded it. See Bright, *op. cit.*, p. 194, n. 33; Noth *The History of Israel*, pp. 187 f, n. 1.

A discussion of the relationship between the troops and the militia will be found below, note 50.

41. These narratives also belonged to the pre-Deuteronomic source of David's rise. See Hans Wilhelm Hertzberg, *I & II Samuel* (Philadelphia: Westminster Press, 1964), pp. 295 f.

42. The seer with his omens as related to the army is reported by the Mari letters in connection with Hammurabi. See Pritchard, *ANET*, p. 482. 2 Sam. 5:24 may suggest the practice of simple magic. See also Shalmanezer III's "Thron-Inschrift" for a "trust (inspiring) oracle of Assur" in Pritchard, *ANET*, p. 277.

43. This probably belongs to the same pre-Deuteronomic source. See Hertzberg, *ibid.*

44. See above, chap. IV, in connection with note 85.

45. For source analysis, see note 41 above. See the presentation of Seti I (1318-1301 BC), Pritchard, *ANET*, p. 255.

46. See Noth, *Überlieferungsgeschichtliche Studien*, p. 65.

47. This pre-Deuteronomic source of the "Rise of David" includes all the narratives alluded to above, though Noth, departing from Alt, sees 8:1-14 as a separate pre-Deuteronomic source. Noth, *ibid.*, p. 65.

48. For the ancient history of Aram see Roger T. O'Callaghan, *Aram Naharaim* (Rome: Pontificium Institutum Biblicum, 1948). For relations with David see Benjamin Mazar, "The Aramean Empire and Its Relations with Israel," *Biblical Archeologist*, XXV (1962), 102 ff.; A. Malamat, "The Kingdom of David & Solomon in Its Contact with Egypt and Aram Naha-

raim," *Biblical Archeologist*, XXI (1958), 96-102. The "Succession Document" is generally regarded as consisting of 2 Sam. 9 to 1 Kings 2, less 2 Sam. 21—24, which are considered additions. A general treatment of this document is that of R. N. Whybray, *The Succession Narrative* (London: SCM Press Ltd., 1968). He follows the usual interpretation and fails rather completely to see any negative evaluation of kingship in the narrative.

49. It is obvious that this narrative is from a different source than that of the Ammonite war (11:1; 12:26-31). See Gerhard von Rad, *Der heilige Krieg im alten Israel* (Göttingen: Vandenhoeck & Ruprecht, 1952), pp. 35 f.

The sacral concept even of the standing professional army is suggested by Uriah's refusal to have relations with his wife, a refusal which was rooted in the law of sacral warfare.

50. In Egypt this difference existed already in the Old Kingdom. See R. O. Faulkner, "Egyptian Military Organization," *The Journal of Egyptian Archaeology*, 39 (1953), 35. In Mesopotamia in Hammurabi's time there was already a standing body guard. The law of Hammurabi shows that there was already a strong bureaucracy and independent cast of warriors. See A. von Pawlikowski-Cholewa, *Die Heere des Morganlandes* (Berlin: Verlag Walter de Gruyter and Co., 1940), p. 89.

In the earliest time the army of the state of Assur was made up of the militia, i.e., all freemen and property owners who possessed weapons at their own expense and who came when the king called. See Johannes Hunger, *Heerwesen und Kriegführung der Assyrer auf der Höhe ihrer Macht* (Leipzig: J. C. Hinrichs'sche Buchhandlung, 1911), p. 4. Already with Tukulti-Ninurta I (ca. 1234-1197 BC), however, the Assyrian force was made up of *kuradi* ("fighting men"), *ummanu* ("army" or "people", probably the main militia), and "the camp", the movable base with its tents and stores. The militia was not too dependable and might decide to go home if kept in the field too long. See the "Triumphal Hymn of Tukulti-Ninurta I," Col. III, 34 ff. as transliterated and discussed by R. Campbell Thompson and M. E. L. Mallowan in "The British Museum Excavations at Nineveh, 1931-32," *Annals of Archaeology and Anthropology*, XX (1933), esp. 117 and 223. After 720 BC the Assyrian Army was clearly composed of the standing army *(kissir šarûti)*, the militia of Assyria and provinces *(ummanate)*, and the auxiliaries of the vassal states. See Pawlikowski-Cholewa, *op. cit.*, p. 93.

Israel underwent a similar transition during and after the time of David. George E. Mendenhall writes, "The standing army of the United Monarchy was something radically different from the old folk militia of the Federation period. Though we are still very far from any adequate understanding of David's or Solomon's military organization (to say nothing of Saul's) yet the sources give a very strong impression that there was here also, as in most aspects of ancient Israelite culture, a radical break with older tradition. Army commanders are now *šārîm*, and it seems likely that the *šar 'elef* actually commanded a unit whose normal strength was a thousand men. The old tribal subdivisions disappear eventually under the impact of fiscal reorganization under David and Solomon, and the priestly historiographer(s) could not but assume that the 'elef of the Federation period was identical to the army unit familiar from the traditions of the much later period. Alternatively, it could be argued that the 'elef did survive as a social sub-unit (Mic. 5:1), but had so grown in size that its name corresponded much more closely to its size—no conclusion seems possible at present. What is new in the monarchy is the royal appointment of professional soldier officers, and the introduction of a military gradation in rank. See the traditions of the 'three' and the 'thirty' of David's army commanders (2 Sam. 23), the commanders of thousands and of hundreds (2 Sam. 18:1 f.), the 3,300 officers of Solomon's corvée (1 Kings 5:27-30) or the 550 commanders of 1 Kings 9:23. However the numbers be explained, whether historically or by literary criticism, it is clear that the officers are professionals; no longer are they folk leaders at the head of their fellow villagers or clansmen." George E. Mendenhall, "The Census Lists of Numbers 1 and 26," *Journal of Biblical Literature*, LXXVII (1958), 56-59, esp. 57 f.

51. See von Rad, *Der Heilige Krieg* . . . , p. 36.

52. Mendenhall, "The Census Lists of Numbers 1 and 26," pp. 58 f.

53. Some see these verses as the work of a redactor, but certainly they are pre-

Deuteronomic. See Henry Preserved Smith, *A Critical and Exegetical Commentary on the Books of Samuel* (New York: Charles Scribner's Sons, 1899), p. 324.

54. I deal extensively with the subject of warfare as judgment in chapter VI.

55. Solomon fought no wars, but the organization of his army moved even further along the lines of the Davidic development by the technological advance of chariotry and construction of a series of forts throughout the heart of his land (I Kings 9:15 ff.; 10:26 ff.). See Bright, *op. cit.*, pp. 208 f.

56. The royal psalms are: Ps. 2; 18; (2 Sam. 22); 20; 21; 45; 72; 89; 101; 110; 132; 144:1-11. See Brights's discussion, *op. cit.*, pp. 220 f.

57. Regarding Canaanite influences, as evidenced by the mythic references in vv. 7-15, see Frank Moore Cross and David Noel Freedman, "A Royal Song of Thanksgiving: II Samuel 22 = Psalm 18," *Journal of Biblical Literature*, LXXII (1953), 21. For the comparative victory hymns, see Pritchard, *ANET*, pp. 373 ff, and the translation by Campbell Thompson in *Annals of Archaeology and Anthropology*, 20 (1933), 118-126. See above chap. III, A.1.d.

58. See above, chaps. III, A.1, and IV, A.

59. See Luckenbill, op. cit., Col. V, 62-79, pp. 44 f.

60. While much of this statement is Deuteronomic in its present form, its original form is probably from the time of David. See Noth, "David and Israel in II Samuel VII," *The Laws in the Pentateuch* . . . , pp. 250-259.

61. See Noth, *Ibid.*, p. 255. The unity of the content of the chapter "lies in the fact that everything in the chapter is seen from the standpoint of the shrine of the Ark in Jerusalem." *Ibid.*

62. See 2 Sam. 12:1-15, where David is condemned for murder and for stealing another's wife, thus subject to the Mosaic law and punished for disobedience.

63. See my discussion on this battle in chapter V,F.

64. Freedman, personal note, Sept. 11, 1977.

65. See William McKane, *Prophets and Wise men* (Naperville, Ill.: Alec R. Allenson, Inc., 1965), pp. 13, 55-62.

66. *Ibid.*, pp. 65 ff. For the prophetic attack, see Is. 30:1-7; 31:1-3; Jer. 9:12, 23, 24.

67. *Ibid.*, p. 42. For further discussion on these changes, see Hayim Tadmor, " 'The People' and the Kingship in Ancient Israel: the Role of Political Institutions in the Biblical Period," *Journal of World History*, 11 (1968), 46-68.

68. See above, note 48.

69. See the article of Lienhard Delekat, "Tendenz und Theologie der David-Solomo-Erzählung," *Das Ferne und Nahe Wort, Festschrift, Leonard Rost* (Berlin: Verlag Alfred Töpelmann, 1967), pp. 26-36. One does not need to be as critical of the text as Delekat in order to see it as a negative evaluation. Cf. Hans Jochen Boecker, *Die Beurteilung der Anfänge des Königtums in der Deuteronomistichen Abschnitten des I. Samuelbuches* (Neukirchen-Vluyn: Neukirchener Verlag, 1969), p. 98, n. 2.

70. 1 Kings 2:13-46. See the article by Walter Brueggemann, "Life and Death in Tenth Century Israel," *Journal of the American Academy of Religion*, XL (1972), 96-109.

71. See our discussion of 12:1-3 in chap. II, A.

72. These chapters are generally considered to be composed of two literary recensions, J and P. See the conventional commentaries such as A. E. Speiser, *Genesis* (Garden City, N.Y.: Doubleday & Company, Inc., 1964), p. LIV. J is usually regarded as achieving its present form in the reign of Solomon, while P may be exilic. *Ibid.*, pp. XXV ff. For the history of these sources outside of Israel, see Claus Westermann, *Genesis*, BKAT (Neukirchen-Vluyn: Neukirchener Verlag des Erziehungsvereins, 1974), pp. 89 f.

73. Westermann, *op. cit.*, pp. 91 ff.

74. J, Gen. 4:17-22; 10:2-30; P, Gen. 5; 11:10-32.

75. Westermann, *op. cit.*, pp. 9 ff.

76. Pritchard, *ANET*, pp. 265 f.

77. See above, note 72.

78. For this "archaic" quality in Israel's self-understanding, see A. Glock, "Warfare in Ancient Israel," p. 213, and the discussion of this idea in chap. I, above, at the text accompanying note 32.

79. See Westermann, *op. cit.*, pp. 31-34.

80. Pritchard, *ANET*, pp. 60 ff., and pp. 4 ff.

81. See above, note 72, for the dating of Gen. 2 (J).

82. See Alexander Heidel, *The Babylonian Genesis* (2nd ed.; Chicago: The University of Chicago Press, 1951), pp. 10 f.

83. *Ibid.*

84. Pritchard, *ANET*, p. 4.

85. For a dating of the present redaction of Genesis 1, see note 72 above. This recension probably has a preliterary history at Jerusalem thoughout the period of kingship. See Gerhard von Rad, *Genesis*, revised edition (Philadelphia: The Westminster Press, 1972) pp. 63 f.

86. See von Rad, *ibid.*, pp 144 f.

87. See Hans Wildberger, "Das Abbild Gottes, Gen. 1:26-30. II," *Theologische Zeitschrift*, 21 (1965), 481-501.

88. Pritchard, *ANET*, pp. 101 ff., and pp. 72 ff.

89. See U. Cassuto, *A Commentary on the Book of Genesis*, Vol. I., trans. by Israel Abrahams (Jerusalem: The Magnes Press, the Hebrew University, 1961), pp. 74 ff.

90. See Herbert G. May, "The King in the Garden of Eden: A Study of Ezekiel 28:12-19," in Bernhard W. Anderson and Walter Harrelson (eds.), *Israel's Prophetic Heritage* (New York: Harper and Brothers, Publishers, 1962), pp. 168 f.

91. See Georg Fohrer, *Ezechiel, HAT* (Tübingen: Verlag J. C. B. Mohr [Paul Siebeck], 1955), p. 162.

92. Abraham Malamat, "Mari," *Biblical Archaeologist*, XXXIV (1971), 7.

93. See Bright, *op. cit.*, p. 49.

94. This should probably be translated "the slopes of Zaphon," Baal's mountain where he meets with the assembly of the gods. See Pritchard, *ANET*, p. 141, col. 2. The point is that in this kingship mythology the king is regarded as one of the gods who in the assembly decide the world's future.

95. See Gen. 11:1 ff. and Dan. 4:28 ff.

96. See above, chap. V, B.4. The radical character of such a view is apparent when it is recalled that other literature of the Near East regards kingship as the gift of the gods—"lowered from heaven." See Pritchard, *ANET*, p. 265.

97. See W. Malcolm Clark, "A Legal Background to the Yahwist's Use of 'Good and Evil' in Genesis 2—3," *Journal of Biblical Literature*, LXXXVIII (1969), 266-278. I am indebted to Clark's article for this idea. The translations which follow are my own.

98. See George Mendenhall, "Tribe and State in the Ancient World," *The Tenth Generation* (Baltimore and London: The Johns Hopkins University Press, 1973), pp. 184 f.

99. It is of interest that Paul makes of Jesus not the first but the second Adam who cannot be identified with but contrasted with the first Adam. See Rom. 5:12-21.

100. Pritchard, *ANET*, pp. 75,77. I am indebted here to the article by J. A. Bailey, "Initiation and the Primal Woman in Gilgamesh and Genesis 2—3," *Journal of Biblical Literature*, LXXXIX (1970), 137-150.

101. See above chap. III, B, on the prophetic vocation of Moses.

102. See B. Margulis, "A Ugaritic Psalm (RŠ 24, 252)," *Journal of Biblical Literature*, LXXXIX (1970), 292-304.

103. Compare 6:5 with 8:21.

104. This text is commonly regarded as P. See Mendenhall, *The Tenth Generation*, p. 47 f.

105. This is from the J source; J probably saw this curse as the reason for the displacement of the Canaanites.

106. See von Rad's analysis here, *op. cit.*, pp. 152 ff.

107. Pritchard, *ANET*, p. 164.

108. See H. and H. A. Frankfort, et. al., *Before Philosophy* (Baltimore: Penguin Books, 19?), p. 193.

109. See the discussion above, chap. V,B.4.

110. See Albrecht Alt, "The God of the Fathers," trans. by R. A. Wilson in *Essays on Old Testament History and Religion* (Oxford: Basil Blackwell, 1966), pp. 3-66.

111. This Biblical narrative of the confusion of tongues has its roots in Mesopotamian tradition. See Samuel Noah Kramer, "The 'Babel of Tongues': A Sumerian Version," *Journal of the American Oriental Society*, 88 (1968), 108-111. In this Sumerian version the confusion is caused by the god Enki, probably because of his jealousy of the god Enlil and his universal reign over mankind. The motif of man's pride and rebellion is introduced by the biblical traditionists. *Ibid.*, p. 111.

112. The first person singular verb occurs six times in Hebrew in the three verses.

113. The later Jewish literature reinterpreted the contrast in terms of idol worship. On the worship of other gods, see B. Gemser, "God in Genesis," Gemser, et al., *Studies on the Book of Genesis*, Oudtestamentische Studiën, Deel XII (Leiden: E. J. Brill, 1958), pp. 1-21.

114. See the Deuteronomic criticism found in I Kings 11.

115. See Thorkild Jacobsen, "Primitive Democracy in Ancient Mesopotamia," ed. by William L. Moran, *Toward the Image of Tammuz and Other Essays on Mesopotamian History and Culture* (Cambridge: Harvard University Press), 1970, pp. 157-170.

116. See Albrecht Alt, *op. cit.*

117. See John Tracy Luke, "Pastoralism and Politics in the Mari Period" (PhD Dissertation, University of Michigan, 1965, University Microfilms, Inc., Ann Arbor, Mich.).

118. See Kramer, "The 'Babel of Tongues,' " *Journal of the American Oriental Society*, 88 (1968), p. 111, note 15.

119. See Hans Walter Wolff, "The Kerygma of the Yahwist," *Interpretation*, 20 (1966), 138f.

120. The verb "to bless" is here in the archaic *niph'al* form which was originally reflexive as demonstrated by the fact that in a later period the grammar was "up dated" to the *hithpa'el* form. See Jer. 4:2.

121. See Noth, *Überlieferungsgeschichtliche Studien*, pp. 78-80. Noth holds that there were the Elijah, Elisha, and Isaiah cycles with perhaps an additional cycle whose narratives had in common the interference of prophets in the succession of Israelite kings and dynasties. He holds that to this cycle might have belonged 1 Kings 11; 12; 14; (20); 22; 2 Kings 9:10. *Ibid.*, p. 80.

122. For an excellent discussion of the themes of the DH in English see Frank M. Cross, "Kings and Prophets" in *Canaanite Myth and Hebrew Epic* (Cambridge, Mass.: Harvard University Press, 1973), pp. 219 ff. On this particular theme see *ibid.*, pp. 233 ff.

123. 2 Sam. 12:7-12. See Uriel Simon, "The Poor Man's Ewe-Lamb, An Example of a Juridical Parable," *Biblica*, 48 (1967), 207-242. For Ahijah's acclamation of Jeroboam and its fulfillment see John Gray, *I and II Kings, A Commentary* (2nd ed. rev.; Philadelphia: The Westminster Press, 1975), p. 11.

124. Hos. 1:4; Is. 1:2 ff.; Am. 1-2; Jer. 2. Most of the great prophetic books are made up of oracles of judgment. See Cross, *op. cit.*, pp. 228 f.

125. This presents something of a different picture from those who see king and prophet as dual heirs of the function of the judges as for example Cross, *ibid.*, p. 223. See our discussion above on Judg. 4, chap. IV, B.

126. See above, Section C (Nathan) and section B (Gad).

127. For Noth's judgment on this source see note 121. Gray holds that this incident was no doubt found by the Deuteronomist in an independent prophetic source, though the passage as it stands "is indisputably Deuteronomistic." Gray, *op. cit.*, p. 11. The fact that the prophet was from Shiloh and that he anointed Jeroboam, also from the North, makes his opposition all the more credible.

128. Shemaiah appears only here in Kings and in 2 Chron. 11:2; 12:5 ff. Gray holds that in

view of the known role of the prophet in the ancient Near East, "this may well be historical." Gray, *op. cit.*, p. 309.

129. The Greek text presents a "variant account in 12:24g-n (ed. Swete)," which omits the Deuteronomistic elaboration. It may be therefore an enlargement of a genuine local tradition. Gray, *op. cit.*, p. 335.

130. James A. Montgomery states that the stories of this chapter are told in graphic, nearly journalistic style, and "their data appear to be closely contemporaneous" with chap. 22— Montgomery, *A Critical and Exegetical Commentary on the Books of Kings*, ed. by Henry Snyder Gehman (Edinburgh: T. & T. Clark, 38 George St., 1951), pp. 318 f. Chapters 20 and 22 have to do with wars in the mid-ninth century between Israel and Aram. It is obvious that the events of chapter 22 happened after the battle of Qarqar of 853 BC, a battle not referred to in the Old Testament, in which Ahab had participated. The timing, however, presents a problem, and some therefore hold that the king could not have been Ahab. For a discussion see Gray, *op. cit.*, pp. 414 ff.

131. Gray, *op. cit.*, p. 358.

132. 1 Kings 22:8 ff. It is of interest that an otherwise unknown prophet is introduced here in a period when Elijah was so popular. This points toward the basic authenticity of the narrative. See Montgomery, *op. cit.*, p. 336.

133. I discuss this further in connection with the Elijah narrative. However, some would hold that the king could not have been Ahab. See note 130 above.

134. Gray, *op. cit.*, p. 449.

135. Walther Eichrodt, *Theology of the Old Testament*, Vol. I, trans. by J. A. Baker (Philadelphia: The Westminster Press, 1961), pp. 335 f. (underlining Eichrodt's).

136. Basically, these narratives found their present form by the end of the 9th century. See Odil Hannes Steck, *Überlieferung und Zeitgeschichte in den Elia-Erzählungen* (Neukerchen-Vluyn: Neukirchener Verlag des Erziehungsvereins, 1968), p. 134.

137. 1 Kings 17—19:18. These three, perhaps originally independent narratives, had an early pre-Deuteronomic unity. See Gray, *op. cit.*, pp. 372 f.

138. See Steck, *op. cit.*, p. 137.

139. "Während die Könige der Dynastie Omri tatsächlich die massgeblichen Gestalten ihrer Zeit in Israel waren, stellt die Ueberlieferung es so dar, als seien es die Propheten gewesen—Elia an der Spitze." Georg Fohrer, *Elia* (Zürich: Zwingli Verlag, 1957), p. 67.

140. For limitations of kingship in the North see Cross, *op. cit.*, pp. 219 ff.

141. I here agree with the analysis of Jepsen that Elijah considered Baal as a no-god. See A. Jepsen, "Elia und das Gottesurteil," in Hans Goedicke, ed., *Near Eastern Studies in Honor of William Foxwell Albright* (Baltimore and London: The Johns Hopkins Press, 1971), p. 306.

142. Presently at the Louvre, AO15775. See James B. Pritchard, *The Ancient Near East in Pictures* (Princeton, N.J.: Princeton University Press, 1954), no. 490.

143. 1 Kings 21:19. See 2 Kings 9:25 f where this was fulfilled in the Jehu revolution (cf. 1 Kings 21:20). See also 1 Kings 22:38; 2 Kings 9:36 f (cf. 1 Kings 21:23); 2 Kings 10:17. For a discussion of the problems involved in these sources see Gray, *op. cit.*, pp. 442 f., 455, 537 f.

144. See Stephen Herbert Bess, "Systems of Land Tenure in Ancient Israel" (PhD Dissertation, University of Michigan, 1963, University Microfilms, Inc., Ann Arbor, Mich.), pp. 83-116.

145. Freedman, personal note, Sept. 11, 1977.

146. Gray considers this narrative to be historical. Gray, *op. cit.*, p. 471. The event should be dated probably between 845 and 841. *Ibid.*, p. 528. See Pritchard, *ANET*, p. 280.

147. See above, chap. VI, on Yahweh's war against his people.

148. Montgomery holds that "any historical basis of this story is indiscernible," Montgomery, *op. cit.*, p. 381. Gray, on the other hand, sees a somewhat rationalized historical base. Gray, *op. cit.*, pp. 512 f. It should be remembered that even a man like Napoleon exercised charismatic powers over his troops which to many persons would appear miraculous.

149. See 1 Kings 20:35 ff. for the opposite attitude on the part of a prophet.

150. Montgomery, *op. cit.*, p. 384. Gray essentially agrees with this judgment, Gray *op. cit.*, pp. 468, 518.

151. Cf. Josh. 6:20 ff; Judg. 7:19 ff.; 1 Sam. 7:10, etc.

152. This probably took place in the first year of the reign of Jehoram the son of Ahab, when Jehoshaphat was co-regent with his son, Jehoram. See Yohanan Aharoni and Michael Avi-Yonah, *The MacMillan Bible Atlas* (New York: The MacMillan Company, 1968), p. 84. For another opinion see Karl-Heinz Bernhardt, "Der Feldzug der drei Könige" in *Schalom, Studien zu Glaube und Geschichte Israels* ed. by Karl-Heinz Bernhardt (Stuttgart: Calwer Verlag, 1971), pp. 11-22. For a treatment of historical problems, including that of the king of Edom, see Gray, *op. cit.*, pp. 468 f.

153. Gray, *op. cit.*, p. 489.

154. This narrative may be dislocated. See Gray, *op. cit.*, p. 597.

155. Montgomery, *op. cit.*, p. 434.

156. See the above discussion of Ps. 18, etc., section C of this chapter.

157. Gray questions the identification of the king in this chapter with Ahab and suggests Jehoash of the dynasty of Jehu. Gray, *op. cit.*, p. 418. But see Bright, *op. cit.*, p. 223, note 45.

158. See Pritchard, *ANET*, p. 482.

159. For a discussion of the historical situation see Gray, *op. cit.*, p. 615.

160. Gray holds that there are two parallel versions of the event, 2 Kings 18:17—19:9a, 36 f. and 19:9b-35. A few hold that this is a unity and that there were two different Assyrian delegations, *ibid.*, p. 659.

161. Noth holds that there was no miraculous deliverance, but that these narratives originated "from the fact that thereafter Jerusalem did not have to be conquered again by force. . . ." Noth, *The History of Israel*, p. 268, n. 3. Bright on the other hand, argues for a second compaign in about 688 BC, unrecorded by the Assyrian annals which are nonexistent in the last years of Sennacherib's reign. He argues that Hezekiah capitulated as suggested in 2 Kings 18:14-16, but that later Hezekiah revolted again and the event happened on Sennacherib's second campaign against this king. Bright, *op. cit.*, pp. 282-287. An argument for this reconstruction is the involvement of Tirhakah who would have been too young in 701 BC. The various sources beside 2 Kings are Is. 36—39, the parallel account in 2 Chron. 29—32, and the Annals of Sennacherib. Pritchard, *ANET*, pp. 287 f. Herodotus (ii, 141) repeated by Josephus, cites a parallel Egyptian legend of how Sennacherib was routed when an army of field mice swarmed over the Assyrian camp. For a discussion see Gray, *op. cit.*, pp. 660, 694.

162. Montgomery holds that these speeches have authentic color, their braggadocio comparing with the Assyrian monuments. Montgomery, *op. cit.*, pp. 487 f. Gray holds that the argument of the Assyrian officer is "likely enough in itself and probable in substance," though in its present form it may reflect the composition of the Deuteronomistic compiler. Gray, *op. cit.*, p. 665.

163. Gray concludes that the oracles of 19:21-34 were "probably genuinely Isaiah's, but not certainly so, and the oracles may not all have been declared at the same time." Gray, *op. cit.*, pp. 667 f.

164. Julius Wellhausen, *Prolegomena to the History of Ancient Israel* (New York: Meridian Books, 1957), p. 512.

165. *Ibid.*, p. 412.

166. *Ibid.*, p. 513.

167. *Ibid.*, p. 421.

168. *Ibid.*, p. 422.

169. *Ibid.*, p. 512.

170. Sigmund Mowinckel in his great work on the Psalms points up parallels between the Psalms and the enthronement literature of Babylon. See Sigmund Mowinckel, *Psalmenstudien* (Amsterdam: Verlag P. Schippers, 1961). Mowinckel drew back from the position that the king was the incarnation of Yahweh, holding that while Israelite kingship was strongly influenced by oriental practices, its main influence was Israel's historical rootage. See Sigmund Mowinkel,

He That Cometh, trans. by G. W. Anderson (New York, Nashville: Abingdon Press, [1954]), pp. 21-95. For more radical representations see Geo Widengren, *Sakrales Königtum im Alten Testament und im Judentum* (Stuttgart: Verlag W. Kohlhammer, 1955); S. H. Hooke, ed., *Myth, Ritual and Kingship* (Oxford: Clarendon Press, 1958). For criticism of this position see Noth, "God, King, and Nation in the Old Testament" in *The Laws in the Pentateuch* . . ., pp. 145-178, and de Vaux, *op. cit.*, p. 99.

171. Mowinckel, *He That Cometh*. For a more lengthy treatment of this, see my statement "The Concept of Political Power in Ancient Israel" in *Annual of the Swedish Theological Institute*, VII (1970), pp. 4-24.

172. Gray, *op. cit.*, p. 471.

173. Gray, *op. cit.*, p. 468.

174. Gray, *op. cit.*, p. 469.

Chapter Eight

1. Martin Noth, *Überlieferungsgeschichtliche Studien* (Tübingen: Max Niemeyer Verlag, 1957). For a concise English statement of Noth's view see David Noel Freedman, "Pentateuch," *The Interpreter's Dictionary of the Bible*, Vol. III, ed. by George Arthur Buttrick (New York, Nashville: Abingdon Press, 1962), pp. 716 f.

2. Noth, *op. cit.*, p. 12.

3. *Ibid.*, p. 110; p. 16.

4. *Ibid.*, p. 18.

5. *Ibid.*, pp. 18 ff.

6. *Ibid.*, pp. 95 f.; pp. 40 ff.; pp. 62 ff.; pp. 78 f.

7. *Ibid.*, pp. 73 f.

8. Freedman, personal note, Sept. 11, 1977.

9. Deut. 4:47; 5:31; 6:1, 10, 18, 21-23; 7:1 ff., 17 ff.; 8:1, 7 ff.; 9:1 ff., 10·11; 11:2 ff.; 12:1 ff.; etc.

10. Von Rad held that 7:16-26 and 9:1-6 are independent of the material which surrounds them and that they were war speeches used in a similar setting as the speech of the priest (20:2-4). Gerhard von Rad, *Der heilige Krieg im alten Israel* (Göttingen: Vandenhoeck & Ruprecht, 1952), pp. 72 ff. He finds the new political situation for the use of such speeches in the time of the Deuteronomist as due to the reorganized militia after the debacle of 701 BC, when the standing, mechanized army had collapsed. For criticism of this thesis see Y. Yadin, "The Reorganization of the Army of Judah under Josiah." *Bulletin of the Jewish Palestinian Exploration Society*, XV (1950), 86 ff.; English Summary, pp. iii, iv.

11. See Georges Minette de Tillesse, "Sections 'tu' et sections 'vous' dans le Deuteronome," *Vetus Testamentum*, XII (1962), 29-87.

12. The plural pronoun and/or verb is used once of Israel in 7:4, entirely in vv. 5, 7-8a, and 12a. Elsewhere the singular is used.

13. For a discussion on the *rp'ym* and a race of giants who were a warrior class in pre-Israelite Canaan of the 2nd millennium BC see B. Margulis, "A Ugaritic Psalm (RŠ 24.252)." *Journal of Biblical Literature*, LXXXIX (1970) 292-304, esp. 299 f.

14. See the above discussion and notes 11 and 12.

15. See Pritchard, "The Code of Hammurabi," *ANET*, 164 f.

16. The position of the Deuteronomist is that the promises were conditioned on obedience. Later writers (Job, Isaiah, etc.) saw the inadequacies of D's emphasis and gave other reasons for unfulfillment.

17. On the *ḥērem* as an ancient Near Eastern practice, see chap. IV, C. 2. For holy war terminology, see chap. II, note 58.

18. See the discussion above, chap. VII, D.4, and note 105.

19. See Suppiluliuma's justification of his attack upon Tushratta of Mittani in Suppiluliuma's treaty with Mattiwaza. D. D. Luckenbill, "Hittite Treaties and Letters," *The*

American Journal of Semitic Languages and Literatures, XXXVII (1921), p. 163, Text K. Bo. I, No. 1. In a sense, Psalm 78 is a theological justification of the transfer of leadership from Shilo to Jerusalem. Here again, the reason was Yahweh's judgment upon the rebellious North.

20. See above, chap. VI.

21. For a discussion of introductory matters and an exegesis of this passage see the article by Larry Miller, "An Exegetical Study of Deuteronomy 17:14-20" in the Library of the Associated Mennonite Biblical Seminaries, Elkhart, Ind., May 1974. For my remarks on this passage I am especially indebted to this article, an article which unfortunately has not yet been published.

In the section of this discussion relating to kingship, Israel is addressed in the second person singular verb and pronoun only in verses 14 and 15. The second person address is not repeated except in 16b where the plural pronoun and verb are used. In these latter verses (16-20), the king is spoken of in the third person, beginning with five negative statements which resemble apodictic commands (16-17). These are followed by a positive statement regarding the king's duties (18-19). The section ends with two negatives introduced with *lblty,* and with a promise (v. 20).

Verses 14 and 15 are universally accepted as a part of the original Deuteronomy. Verses 16 and 17 may be considered original with relative confidence, with the exception of 16b which is especially debated. The most problematic are verses 18 and 19, though even these may well be original.

22. See Gerhard von Rad, *Studies in Deuteronomy,* trans. by David Stalker (London: SCM Press Ltd., 1963), p. 22.

23. This question is related to the question of the origin of the Book of Deuteronomy. Answers to this have been the Levites (von Rad, *ibid.,* pp. 66 f), the royal court (Moshe Weinfeld, *Deuteronomy and the Deuteronomic School* [Oxford: Clarendon Press, 1972], pp. 184 ff.), and the prophets (E. W. Nicholson, *Deuteronomy and Tradition* [Philadelphia: Fortress Press, 1967], pp. 122 f.). These offices were not so isolated as some see them. Even Ahab knew the king's limitations (1 Kings 21). Prophets often arose from the priestly circles.

24. The prophet was also given because of the demand of the people, but in this the people were commended. See Deut. 18:16.

25. "Nations" *(gwym)* is used 23 times in Deuteronomy. The nations are strong and great, the ones driven out by Yahweh, who perish, who do wickedness, etc. When Israel forgets the covenant she will find herself "among the nations." For a full discussion see Larry Miller, *op. cit.,* pp. 11 f. See also our discussion on 1 Sam. 8, chap. V.

26. Some may say a permissive attitude toward it; however, this is liable to convey the idea of a permissive attitude toward apostasy, which is not at all the case, as we shall see.

27. See G. E. Mendenhall, "Election" in the *Interpreter's Dictionary of the Bible,* Vol. II, ed. by George Arthur Buttrick (New York, Nashville: Abingdon Press, 1962), p. 76.

28. See 1 Sam. 9:16; 15:17 ff.; 16:1 ff.

29. Larry Miller, *op. cit.,* p. 14: "In almost all cases it has something to do with loyalty to Yahweh, whether through obedience to him (e.g., 4:37; 7:6; 10:15, etc.) or through going to his place and offering (e.g., 12:5; 12:18; 14:24, etc.) or through ministering to his people (in the case of the Levites, 18:5 and 21:5)."

30. The infinitive absolute may hint at such a contrast: *śwm tśym.*

31. Larry Miller *op. cit.,* pp. 17 f.

32. What follows is my own translation designed to show the possibility that a series of apodictic commands directed against kingship may very well underlie this statement.

33. See above, chap. IV C. 4. e, and VII, B.

34. See Tablets 287,288. J. A. Knudtzon, *Die El-Amarna-Tafeln* (Leipzig: J. C. Hinrichs'sche Buchhandlung, 1915).

35. See Stephen Herbert Bess, "Systems of Land Tenure in Ancient Israel" (PhD Dissertation, University of Michigan, 1963, University Microfilms, Inc., Ann Arbor, Mich.), pp. 52 ff.

36. Translated by Larry Miller, *op. cit.*, pp. 27 f. from André Neher, *L'essence du prophétisme* (Paris, 1972), pp. 261 f.

37. Verses 18 and 19 are usually considered as secondary, from a Deuteronomist's hand. The argument for this is that the concept of *twrh* as a *spr* is relatively late. This argument is becoming more tenuous as our knowledge of the ancient Near East increases. The theology in any case corresponds with that of Deuteronomy. For a discussion of the issues see Larry Miller, *op. cit.*, pp. 6 f.

That this was to be a private rather than public reading is obvious by the stated purpose: that the king may learn to fear Yahweh by keeping his law. Also, the linguistic evidence points to a private reading. For an extended discussion see Larry Miller, *op. cit.*, pp. 24-26.

38. " . . . unto him ye shall hearken . . ." KJV (*'lyw tšm'wn*).

39. For a further discussion of introductory questions see Phil Rich, "The Law of the Prophet: An Exegetical Study of Deuteronomy 18:9-12" (Unpublished MS, Associated Mennonite Biblical Seminaries Library, May 20, 1975), pp. 1-5.

40. Saul's request was, "Seek . . . me a woman who is a medium" (*b'lt-'wb*), a term which occurs in the list in Deut. 18:11.

41. Gen. 41:8. The word "magician" does not occur in the list in Deuteronomy, but it is obvious that the same type of activity is involved here.

42. Here again, this list does not overlap with that of Deuteronomy, though it is the same type of magical activity. For references to these "wise men" throughout the chapter see 2:2, 10, 12, 13, 14, 18, 24, 27, 48.

43. See further Gerhard von Rad, *Wisdom in Israel* (Nashville and New York: Abingdon Press, 1972), p. 16.

44. See also vv. 9, 12.

45. See Weinfeld, *op. cit.*, pp. 268 f.

46. For a discussion of "brother" see above, A.2.a.(2).

47. This point is made in connection with the two statements of the Ten Words (Deut. 5:23-30; Ex. 20:18-20), and then is repeated here. The fact that this unmediated character enters into the eschatological thought of Jeremiah and others suggests its importance. See Jer. 31:33 f.

48. See Jer. 1:9 which is nearly a direct quote of Deut. 18:18b.

49. Quoted from Rich, *op. cit.*, p. 20.

50. See von Rad, *Studies in Deuteronomy*, p. 23.

51. The Hittite treaty stipulated that "the vassal must answer any call to arms sent him by the king." George E. Mendenhall, *Law and Covenant in Israel and the Ancient Near East* (Pittsburgh: The Biblical Colloquium, 1955), p. 33. For a discussion of Deuteronomy and the international treaty forms see Weinfeld, *op. cit.*, pp. 59 ff. See the discussion in chap. IV, A.4.

52. See above, A.1

53. See above, chap. IV, C.4.e.

54. See above, note 10.

55. See above, chap. V, especially section B. 4.

56. For another priestly address before battle see E. L. Sukenik, ed., "The War of the Sons of Light with the Sons of Darkness" in *The Dead Sea Scrolls of the Hebrew University* (Jerusalem: The Magnes Press, 1955), X, 2-5, a direct quote with minor changes. For a commentary see Yigael Yadin, *The Scroll of the War of the Sons of Light Against the Sons of Darkness*, trans. by Batya and Chaim Rabin ([London]: Oxford University Press, 1962), p. 211.

57. Cf. Judg. 7:2 f.

58. For volunteerism in Qumran's warfare see Yadin, *ibid.*, pp. 66-70. For examples in the time of the Judges see Judg. 5:2; 9:2 ff. There are some examples of exemptions outside of Israel, but not to such a degree.

59. Deuteronomy in its emphasis upon the curse compares with the Assyrian treaties. See Weinfeld, *op. cit.*, pp. 116 ff. Also Delbert R. Hillers, *Treaty-Curses and the Old Testament Prophets* (Rome: Pontifical Biblical Institute, 1964), pp. 30 ff. The latter author points out that

the emphasis on the curse was also characteristic of some of the earlier materials. *Ibid.*, p. 33.

60. For plural uses see vv. 14b, 62a, 63. Hillers shows parallels from international treaties where singular and plural are used interchangeably. This weakens the argument that plural forms in Deuteronomy denote a later edition. *Ibid.*, pp. 32 f.

61. The word covenant *(bryt)* occurs twenty-seven times in the present Book of Deuteronomy, spread throughout most of its sections though occuring only once in the legal section: 4:13, 23, 31; 5:2, 3; 7:2, 9, 12; 8:18; 9:9, 11, 15; 10:8; 17:2; 28:69, 69 (Eng. 29:1, 1); 29:8 (Eng. 9), 11 (Eng. 12), 13 (Eng. 14), 20 (Eng. 21), 24 (Eng. 25); 31:9, 16, 20, 25, 26; 33:9. For the covenant structure of Deuteronomy see Weinfeld, *op. cit.*, pp. 59 ff; Dennis J. Mc-Carthy, *Treaty and Covenant* (Rome: Pontifical Biblical Institute, 1963), pp. 109 ff.

62. For the argument that this introduces the DH see Noth, *op. cit.*, pp. 12 ff. I hold with Cross that the DH edited his work before the death of Josiah, 2 Kings 23:26 to the end of the book being a supplement by another editor or school. Part of this introduction in Deuteronomy may also be secondary, though I will not try to distinguish this. See Frank M. Cross, *Canaanite Myth and Hebrew Epic* (Cambridge, Mass.; Harvard University Press, 1973), pp. 287 ff.

63. See Otto Eissfeldt, *The Old Testament*, trans. by Peter B. Ackroyd (Oxford: Basil Blackwell, 1965), p. 176.

64. This verse is in a passage where Israel is addressed in the 2nd person singular pronoun and verb. Most of the address in chapters 1-4 is plural. See above. Hereafter all passages cited are in the plural unless we point out otherwise.

65. These two verses are mixed, partly plural and partly singular in their address.

66. For a discussion of DH's theology of election see Noth, *op. cit.*, p. 101.

67. This verse addresses Israel in the singular. See note 64. This statement presents difficulties in the light of the writer's emphasis on one God. See S. R. Driver, *A Critical and Exegetical Commentary on Deuteronomy* (New York: Charles Scribner's Sons, 1963), pp. 70 f., where he holds that Yahweh allots these as gods to be worshiped, citing Deut. 29:25. Rashi, on the other hand, regards the heavenly bodies not as gods but simply as natural phenomena allotted to the nations. In either case, DH sees Yahweh as related to the nations.

68. A small part of this material is in 2nd person singular address. See note 64.

69. Eissfeldt agrees with Noth that the main part of 1 Kings 8 is not to be credited to Solomon. Eissfeldt attributes it to the Deuteronomistic writer. Eissfeldt, *op. cit.*, p. 288.

70. See Freedman, "Pentateuch," *IDB*, III, pp. 716 f.

71. Israel is here addressed with singular pronoun and verb. See note 64.

72. The Deuteronomic passage addresses Israel in the singular, while the Kings passages' use of Israel is in the 3rd person plural. See note 64.

73. See the treaty between Mursilis and Duppi-Tessub of Amurru *Ancient Near Eastern Texts*, ed. by James B. Pritchard (Princeton, N.J.: Princeton University Press, 1955), p. 203 f. In the historical introduction the relations of Duppi-Tessub's grandfather, Aziras, are traced; Aziras fought with Suppiluliumas against the latter's enemies. But the command, "with my friend you shall be friend, and with my enemy you shall be enemy" which is followed by a statement of military obligations comes only after the historical introduction, in fact, after the primary stipulation of loyalty to Hatti alone. As before, the Mosaic covenant has no analogy to these military clauses.

74. Klaus Baltzer, *The Covenant Formulary*, trans. by David E. Green (Oxford: Basil Blackwell, 1971), pp. 31-34. See also Weinfeld, *op. cit.*, p. 66.

75. Noth, *op. cit.*, pp. 100 f.

76. DH follows a form of tradition known to us from various strata in Num. 13, 14. He has formulated the whole independently and has given the story special nuances. For example, in Num. 13:1, 2 the sending out of the spies was first commanded by Yahweh. Here it is the suggestion of the people. Cf. *ibid.*, p. 31.

77. Noth feels that it is questionable whether this passage is to be ascribed to DH or a later editor. But Baltzer shows how it is essentially unified to that which precedes it on the analogy of the covenant formula. See note 74.

78. There is no reason to regard this threat as exilic or postexilic. With the example of Israel to the North (722), most analysts must have seen the possibility of the end.

79. Noth holds that DH introduced a new period in Israel's history with Judg. 2:6 ff. which followed immediately upon Josh. 23. This period reached for DH to 1 Sam. 12 as is evident from the fact that the speech of Samuel (1 Sam. 12) clearly follows the same lines as the closing speech of Joshua (Josh. 23), terminating with a similar idea of judgment, which the speech of Moses had also emphasized in Deut. 1:6—4:28. But what Noth does not reckon with is the possibility that DH was dealing with traditional material in the speeches of Joshua and Samuel, and that the correspondences may be due to the type (Gattung) of literature which they represent, having come out of the same life situation. Cf. Baltzer, *op. cit.*, pp. 63-83. That DH ends both periods with traditional material does not at all invalidate the fact that this represents DH's thought. It only means that he is not as original as Noth had regarded him.

80. Eissfeldt assigns only 2:11-19 to the "Deuteronomistic survey," which compares to Noth's DH. See Eissfeldt, *op. cit.*, pp. 257 ff. Vv. 20 ff. may well be a later addition, written after the time of Josiah.

81. The fact that Israel's repentance is omitted in this introduction, in contrast to the introductions of the individual narratives, may be an indication that the introductions to the individual narratives preceded DH as a part of the older Book of Judges. See Walter Beyerlin, "Gattung and Herkunft des Rahmens im Richterbuch," in *Tradition und Situation*, ed. by Ernst Würthwein and Otto Kaiser (Göttingen: Vandenhoeck & Ruprecht, 1963), pp. 1-29.

82. See above, A.2.d.

83. Cf. William F. Albright, *Samuel and the Beginnings of the Prophetic Movement* (Cincinnati: Hebrew Union College Press, 1961), p. 26.

84. See Gerhard von Rad, *Genesis*, trans. by John H. Marks (rev. ed.; Philadelphia: The Westminster Press, 1974), pp. 23 f.

85. We have already noted that DH may have received this framework from an older work. See note 81 above.

86. Noth states that the basis for the tradition of the Othniel history (Judg. 3:6-11) is a riddle, but that on the whole it was formulated by DH. See Noth, *op. cit.*, p. 50.

87. Cf. Eissfeldt, *op. cit.*, pp. 258 ff. For Eissfeldt the editor is the Deuteronomist rather that the DH. His analysis is on the whole, however, in agreement with that of Noth, *op. cit.*, pp. 50 ff.

88. See Noth, *ibid.*, p. 51.

89. *Ibid.*, pp. 53 f.

90. *Ibid.*, p. 50.

91. For an example of other rejected confessions see Jer. 14 and 15.

92. My dependence on Noth's analysis throughout the period of the Judges is evident. The climactic character of the Jephthah introduction is apparent, even if the Samson narratives were included by DH, which Noth doubts. See Noth, *op. cit.*, p. 61. The Samson narratives are historical hero legends rather than narratives of holy war.

93. See Noth, *ibid.*, pp. 54 f. He holds with Wellhausen that 1 Sam. 7:2—8:22; 10:17-27a; 12:1-25 belong together on the ground of their language and content and are Deuteronomistic. Eissfeldt, however, holds that chapters 7, 8, and 12 represent an older tradition with a marked affinity to E. Eissfeldt, *op. cit.*, p. 271. For the opinion of Weiser, etc. see my discussion in chap. V, at note 37.

94. See Noth, *op. cit.*, pp. 91 f.

95. See above, chap, V,B.4 and G.

96. See Cross, *op. cit.*, pp. 274-289.

97. *Ibid.*, p. 284.

98. 1 Kings 15:26, 34; 16:19, 26; 2 Kings 3:3; 10:29; 13:2, 11; 14:24; 15:9, 18, 24, 28.

99. 1 Kings 15:11-15; 22:43-44; 2 Kings 12:2-3; 14:3-4; 15:3-4, 34-35; 18:3-8; 22:2; 23:25.

100. See Weinfeld, *op. cit.*, pp. 151-155.

101. 1 Kings 15:3-5; 2 Kings 8:18-19; 8:27; 16:2-4; 21:20-22; 23:32, 37; 24:9, 19-20.

102. Noth overlooked the positive element of this promise in DH's thought, a point corrected by von Rad. See von Rad, *Studies in Deuteronomy*, pp. 84 ff.

103. For discussion of this supplement see the statement on the Deuteronomic historian at the beginning of this chapter.

104. See above, B.2.a

105. Cf. Noth, *op cit.*, p. 54.

106. Note the use of "Israel" or "people of Israel" in 2 Kings 17:7, 9, 13, 18, 19, 20, 23; the plural pronoun and verb is used with the antecedent of Israel throughout.

107. Freedman, "Pentateuch," *IDB*, III, p. 716.

108. Noth sees this as the work of DH. Noth, *op. cit.*, p. 108. Eissfeldt assigns the main part of chapter 8 to the Deuteronomistic compiler. Eissfeldt, *op. cit.*, p. 288.

Chapter Nine

1. See John J. Collins, *The Apocalyptic Vision of the Book of Daniel* (Scholars Press for Harvard Semitic Museum, 1977), esp. pp. 191-218.

2. It should not be forgotten that Johanan ben Zakkai, again of the first century AD, also rejected the way of the Zealots to found the Jewish community around the study of the Torah, a community that has continued on that foundation for nearly 2000 years.

Index of Biblical References

Index of Names and Subjects

Millard Lind is professor of Old Testament at the Associated Mennonite Biblical Seminaries, Elkhart, Indiana. He received his doctoral degree in Old Testament studies from Pittsburgh Theological Seminary, Pittsburgh, Pennsylvania in 1964.

Lind has participated in the Summer Institute of Near Eastern Civilizations (Israel and Greece, 1965), was Research Associate of the American School of Oriental Research (Jerusalem, 1968-69), and was Scholar in Residence at the Ecumenical Institute for Advanced Theological Studies (Jerusalem, 1975-76). The manuscript for this book was written mainly while he was in residence at the Institute.

Millard Lind is a minister in the Mennonite Church and an active member of the College Mennonite congregation, Goshen, Indiana. He and Miriam Lind are the parents of six children and foster parents of a handicapped child.

The Christian Peace Shelf

The Christian Peace Shelf is a selection of Herald Press books and pamphlets devoted to the promotion of Christian peace principles and their applications. The editor (appointed by the Mennonite Central Committee Peace Section) and an editorial board from the Brethren in Christ Church, the General Conference Mennonite Church, the Mennonite Brethren Church, and the Mennonite Church, represent the historic concern for peace within these constituencies.

FOR SERIOUS STUDY

Durland, William R. *No King but Caesar?* (1975). A Catholic lawyer looks at Christian violence.

Enz, Jacob J. *The Christian and Warfare* (1972). The roots of pacifism in the Old Testament.

Hershberger, Guy F. *War, Peace, and Nonresistance* (Third Edition, 1969). A classic comprehensive work on nonresistance in faith and history.

Hornus, Jean-Michel. *It Is Not Lawful for Me to Fight* (1980). Early Christian attitudes toward war, violence, and the state.

Kaufman, Donald D. *What Belongs to Caesar?* (1969). Basic arguments against voluntary payment of war taxes.

Lasserre, Jean. *War and the Gospel* (1962). An analysis of Scriptures related to the ethical problem of war.

Lind, Millard C. *Yahweh Is a Warrior* (1980). The theology of warfare in ancient Israel.

Ramseyer, Robert L. *Mission and the Peace Witness* (1979). Implications of the biblical peace testimony for the evangelizing mission of the church.

Trocmé, André. *Jesus and the Nonviolent Revolution* (1975). The social and political relevance of Jesus.

Yoder, John H. *The Original Revolution* (1972). Essays on Christian pacifism.

———————————. *Nevertheless* (1971). The varieties and shortcomings of Christian pacifism.

FOR EASY READING
Beachey, Duane. *Faith in a Nuclear Age* (1983). A Christian response to war.

Drescher, John M. *Why I Am a Conscientious Objector* (1982). A personal summary of basic issues for every Christian facing military involvements.

Eller, Vernard. *War and Peace from Genesis to Revelation* (1981). Explores peace as a consistent theme developing throughout the Old and New Testaments.

Kaufman, Donald D. *The Tax Dilemma: Praying for Peace, Paying for War* (1978). Biblical, historical, and practical considerations on the war tax issue.

Kraybill, Donald B. *Facing Nuclear War* (1982). A plea for Christian witness.

———————. *The Upside-Down Kingdom* (1978). A study of the synoptic gospels on affluence, war-making, status-seeking, and religious exclusivism.

Miller, John W. *The Christian Way* (1969). A guide to the Christian life based on the Sermon on the Mount.

Miller, Melissa, and Phil M. Shenk. *The Path of Most Resistance* (1982). Stories of Mennonite conscientious objectors who did not cooperate with the Vietnam draft.

Sider, Ronald J. *Christ and Violence* (1979). A sweeping reappraisal of the church's teaching on violence.

Steiner, Susan Clemmer. *Joining the Army That Sheds No Blood* (1982). The case for biblical pacifism written for teens.

Wenger, J. C. *The Way of Peace* (1977). A brief treatment on Christ's teachings and the way of peace through the centuries.

FOR CHILDREN
Bauman, Elizabeth Hershberger. *Coals of Fire* (1954). Stories of people who returned good for evil.

Moore, Ruth Nulton. *Peace Treaty* (1977). A historical novel involving the efforts of Moravian missionary Christian Frederick Post to bring peace to the Ohio Valley in 1758.

Smucker, Barbara Claassen. *Henry's Red Sea* (1955). The dramatic escape of 1,000 Russian Mennonites from Berlin following World War II.